# THE
# ORIGINS
## OF
## CONSCIOUSNESS

### A STUDY OF THE
### TEN LUMINOUS EMANATIONS

By Rav Yehuda Ashlag
Commentary by Rav Michael Berg

VOLUME 1

For further information:
The Kabbalah Centre
155 E. 48th St., New York, NY 10017
1062 S. Robertson Blvd., Los Angeles, CA 90035

1.800.Kabbalah
www.kabbalah.com

Printed in USA, November 2024

ISBN: 978-1-952895-30-2
The Origins of Consciousness Volume 1

# תְּפִלָּה קוֹדֶם הַלִּימוּד מֵהָאֲרִ"י זיע"א

רִבּוֹן הָעוֹלָמִים וַאֲדוֹנֵי הָאֲדוֹנִים, אַב הָרַחֲמִים וְהַסְּלִיחוֹת, מוֹדִים
אֲנַחְנוּ לְפָנֶיךָ ה' אֱלֹהֵינוּ וֵאלֹהֵי אֲבוֹתֵינוּ, בְּקִדָּה וּבְהִשְׁתַּחֲוָיָה,
שֶׁקֵּרַבְתָּנוּ לְתוֹרָתֶךָ וְלַעֲבוֹדָתֶךָ עֲבוֹדַת הַקֹּדֶשׁ, וְנָתַתָּ לָנוּ חֵלֶק
בְּסוֹדוֹת תּוֹרָתֶךָ הַקְּדוֹשָׁה. מָה אָנוּ, וּמֶה חַיֵּינוּ אֲשֶׁר עָשִׂיתָ עִמָּנוּ
חֶסֶד גָּדוֹל כָּזֶה, עַל כֵּן אֲנַחְנוּ מַפִּילִים תַּחֲנוּנֵינוּ לְפָנֶיךָ שֶׁתִּמְחוֹל
וְתִסְלַח לְכָל חַטֹּאתֵינוּ וַעֲוֹנוֹתֵינוּ, וְאַל יִהְיוּ עֲוֹנוֹתֵינוּ מַבְדִּילִים בֵּינֵנוּ
לְבֵינֶךָ. וְכֵן יְהִי רָצוֹן מִלְּפָנֶיךָ ה' אֱלֹהֵינוּ וֵאלֹהֵי אֲבוֹתֵינוּ, שֶׁתָּכֵן
אֶת לְבָבֵנוּ לְיִרְאָתֶךָ וּלְאַהֲבָתֶךָ, וְתַקְשִׁיב אָזְנֶיךָ לִדְבָרֵינוּ אֵלֶּה,
וְתִפְתַּח לְבָבֵנוּ הֶעָרֵל בְּסוֹדוֹת תּוֹרָתֶךָ, וְיִהְיֶה לִמּוּדֵינוּ זֶה נַחַת רוּחַ
לִפְנֵי כִסֵּא כְבוֹדֶךָ כְּרֵיחַ נִיחוֹחַ, וְתַאֲצִיל עָלֵינוּ אוֹר מְקוֹר נִשְׁמָתֵנוּ
בְּכָל בְּחִינָתֵנוּ, וְשֶׁיִּתְנוֹצְצוּ נִיצוֹצוֹת עֲבָדֶיךָ הַקְּדוֹשִׁים אֲשֶׁר עַל
יָדָם גִּלִּיתָ דְּבָרֶיךָ אֵלֶּה בָּעוֹלָם, וּזְכוּתָם וּזְכוּת אֲבוֹתָם וּזְכוּת
תּוֹרָתָם וּתְמִימוּתָם וּקְדֻשָּׁתָם יַעֲמוֹד לָנוּ לְבַל נִכָּשֵׁל בַּדְּבָרִים
אֵלּוּ, וּבִזְכוּתָם תָּאִיר עֵינֵינוּ בְּמָה שֶׁאָנוּ לוֹמְדִים, כְּמַאֲמַר נָעִים
זְמִירוֹת יִשְׂרָאֵל גַּל עֵינַי וְאַבִּיטָה נִפְלָאוֹת מִתּוֹרָתֶךָ. כִּי ה' יִתֵּן
חָכְמָה מִפִּיו דַּעַת וּתְבוּנָה. יִהְיוּ לְרָצוֹן אִמְרֵי פִי וְהֶגְיוֹן לִבִּי לְפָנֶיךָ
ה' צוּרִי וְגֹאֲלִי.

### A Prayer from the Ari (Rav Isaac Luria)
to be recited before the study of the Zohar

Ruler of the universe, and Master of all masters. The Father of mercy and forgiveness, we thank You, our God and the God of our fathers, by bowing down and kneeling, that You brought us closer to your Torah and Your Holy Work, and you enable us to take part in the secrets of your Holy Torah. How worthy are we that You grant us with such big favor, which is the reason we plead before You that You will forgive and acquit all our sins, and that they should not bring separation between You and us. And may it be Your will before You, our God and the God of our fathers, that You will awaken and prepare our hearts to love and revere You, and may You listen to our utterances and open our closed hearts to the hidden studies of Your Torah, and may our study be pleasant before Your Place of Honor, as the aroma of sweet incense, and may You emanate to us Light from the source of our soul to all of our being. And may the sparks of Your Holy servants, through which You revealed Your wisdom to the world, shine. May their merit and the merit of their fathers and the merit of their Torah and holiness support us so we shall not stumble through our study. And by their merit enlighten our eyes in our learning as it is stated by King David, the Sweet Singer of Israel: "Open my eyes so that I will see wonders from Your Torah." (Psalms 119:18)"For the Lord gives wisdom; from his mouth come knowledge and understanding." (Proverbs 2:6) "May the utterances of my mouth and the thoughts of my heart find favor before You, God my Strength and my Redeemer." (Psalms 19:15)

The Study of the Ten Luminous Emanation (Talmud Eser Sefirot) by Rav Yehuda Leib haLevi Ashlag is a commentary on the principles of the Wisdom of Kabbalah from the Writings of the Ari (Kitvei ha'Ari) by Rav Isaac Luria (the Ari z"l): Tree of Life (Etz Chaim), Entrance to the Gates (Mavo She'arim), and the Eight Gates: Gate of Introductions (Sha'ar haHakdamot), Gate of Teachings of Rav Shimon bar Yochai (Sha'ar Ma'amrei Rashbi), Gate of Meditations (Sha'ar haKavanot), and so on. The Study of the Ten Luminous Emanations is divided into 16 volumes, in true order from easier to more difficult subjects, with two commentaries—Ohr Pnimi and Histaklut Pnimi— as well as a Table of Questions and Answers that help the beginner.

1. Ohr Pnimi (Inner Light) Commentary (inside the gray box) – A pinpointed commentary on the difficult and concealed words and concepts of the Ari that are brought up on every page with true clarity of the concepts in their spiritual character, divested of space, time, and corporeality. This commentary brings these concepts close to the mind of anyone who studies it.

2. Histaklut Pnimi (Inner Observation) Commentary (inside the gray box) – This is a general commentary that expounds upon each and every idea, guiding and bringing close these ideas to be understood in the mind of every average student who desires this wisdom. It is located in each volume following the words of the Ari and the Inner Light Commentary.

3. Table of Questions and Table of Answers – This is an explanation of the main words and concepts brought up in each and every volume of the Talmud Eser Sefirot. It is very good and necessary to review and remember the concepts. These tables follow the Inner Observation commentary.

4. Insights of Rav Michael Berg (outside the gray box) – Inspiring explanation on the teachings of both the Ari and Rav Ashlag that bring these concepts down to earth, focusing on how we can practically apply them in our daily life and what this means for our spiritual growth. These insights are adapted from Rav Michael Berg's Ten Luminous Emanations classes.

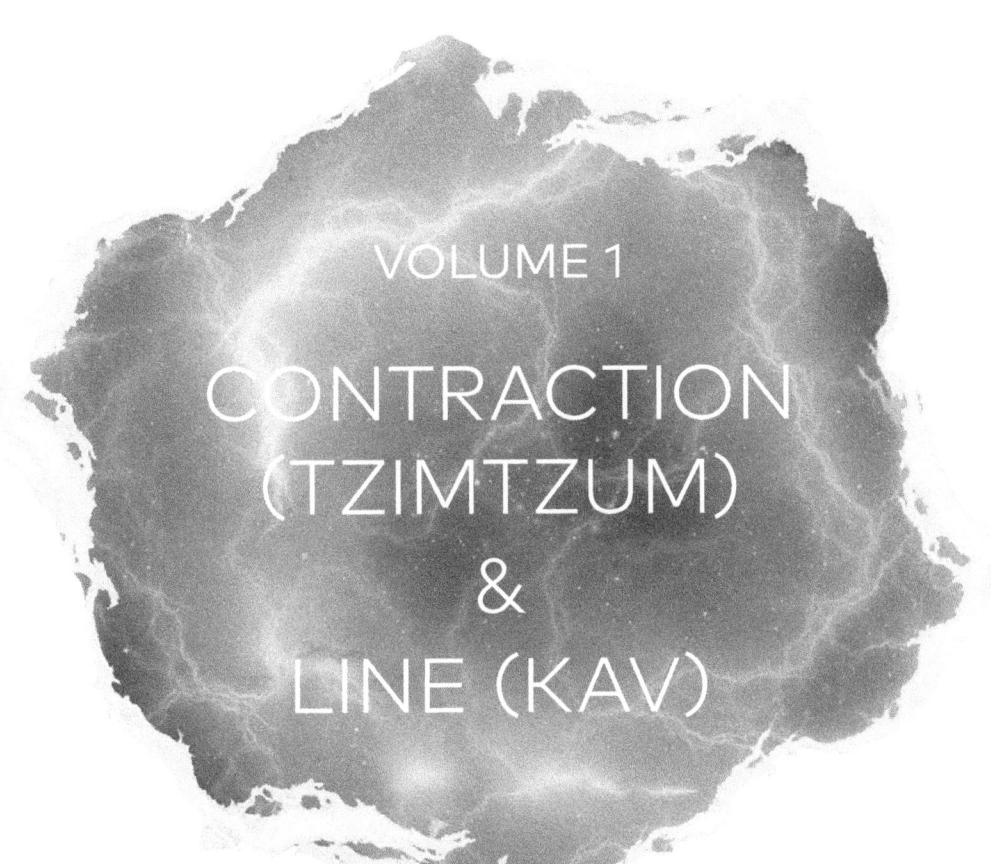

# VOLUME 1
# CONTRACTION (TZIMTZUM) & LINE (KAV)

# TABLE OF CONTENTS

# INTRODUCTION BY RAV MICHAEL BERG

It is important for us to be clear why we study from the Talmud Eser Sefirot ("Study of the Ten Luminous Emanations") written by Rav Ashlag. Rav Ashlag explains that every person needs to come to understand the Source of his soul and that the purpose of our lives is to achieve *dvekut* (cleaving and union) with the Light of the Creator. In the Article for the Completion of the Zohar, by Rav Ashlag, in his book The Wisdom of Truth, he says the following:

> The passage saying that every person is obligated to understand the root of his soul means that the Creator's desired and hoped-for purpose for His creations is the cleaving to Him, as it is written, "and to cleave to Him." (Deuteronomy 11:22) The sages explained this as meaning cleaving to the Creator's qualities; just as He is merciful, so we should be merciful etc. And the Creator's qualities are manifested by the holy Sefirot, as we know. This is the secret of the Acting Mind who leads His world and metes out with His creatures His beneficence and blissful goodness.

> But we must understand why this is called cleaving to the Creator, when it only seems to be an ordinary study. I will use an analogy to explain the concept that with every action in the world, the consciousness that created it cleaves to it and remains with it. Just as in a table, concealed within it is the consciousness of its carpenter and his craftsmanship, great or small, since, while he worked, he planned it in his mind. Once a person watching that action comprehends the mind concealed within the action, at that moment, he cleaves to the consciousness creating the action. That is, they totally unite.

> Because actually there is no distance or separation between spiritual things, even when they are clothed in divided physical forms. The consciousness within each one of them cannot be described in separate parts because there is no knife that can cut the spiritual so that it remains in separate parts. Rather, the main difference

between spiritual things is in their classification, that is, whether they are worthy of praise or condemnation, and also according to their compatibility components since a mind that thinks about the wisdom of the stars cannot cleave to the scientific mind. And even within a given wisdom there are many components since if one is wiser than another, even in one aspect of wisdom, this divides the two spiritually. But when two wise people contemplate of the same wisdom and their understanding of it is equal, then they are truly united, since nothing divides them. Read this carefully.

Therefore, when one person thinks about the actions of another and comprehends the wisdom behind his action, both have the same measure of power and thought and they are truly united.

When we examine something that was created by a person, and we make an effort to figure out, in the truest sense, what that person was feeling at the time as well as everything about them, we are actually unifying our mind with that person's mind. And this is also true about any physical creation. When we take the time to try to understand where the person who created this work of art was at, what they were thinking and feeling, then, as we go through that process and come to absorb it properly, we actually begin to think like that person, and as we do that, we unify our mind with their mind.

When two people are thinking about the same concept, in the same way, their minds are unified. But there are two important parts to this: One is to take the time to try to understand it, and two is to get it right. If we are looking at a table attempting to think about the creator of that table, and we think he was happy when he was making the table but, in fact, he was sad, or we think that he created it quickly yet it really took a long time, we are not unifying our mind with the person who created the table. Obviously we have done the first part, which is to try to unify our mind with their mind, with their being. But obviously we have failed. So, it is not enough simply to try to think about the creator, or the builder, and what he was doing, it is also important to be right in the way we understand it.

This is an important distinction. Rav Ashlag makes it clear that when we talk about learning Talmud Eser Sefirot, the purpose of the study is to unify our mind with the Creator's Mind. This means, if we misunderstand the Talmud Eser Sefirot we are not unifying our mind with the Creator's Mind. Although there are other reasons why it is good to study as it does reveal Light.

Therefore, when one person thinks about the actions of another and comprehends the wisdom behind his action, both have the same measure of power and thought, and they are truly united. This is like a person who meets a beloved friend in the marketplace and hugs and kisses him, and they cannot be separated due to the great unity between them. And thus, according to this rule, the consciousness of humans is the force that is the closest and most compatible to the Creator, and this is considered to be "the mean." This means that the Creator emanated one spark from that force and by that spark everything can return to Him. And it is written: "You made everything through Your wisdom," (Psalms 104:24) that is, the whole world was created through the Creator's wisdom and, therefore he who merits perceiving the ways in which the Creator created the world and its orders, cleaves to the Consciousness that created them, thus he cleaves to the Creator.

And therefore the mind of humans is so important because it is a gateway by which we can unify with the Creator. Through our minds, the Creator gave us the ability and a pathway—the Creator gave us a spark of His Light—through which we can come back to Him.

This physical world and more importantly the spiritual worlds that led to the creation of this physical world were obviously created through the Mind and through the Wisdom of God. Therefore when a person truly merits understanding the process by which the Creator created our world, he becomes unified with the Creator's Mind Who created this world. And therefore that person is unified with the Creator. So the purpose of the study of the Talmud Eser Sefirot is to achieve *dvekut*, union with the Creator through our mind, through our thought, because that is the gateway, the spark, that the Creator gave us to achieve it.

And this is the secret of the Torah, which is all the Names of the Creator that are applicable to His creations. And by them the created one achieves the consciousness of the Creator because the Creator referred to the Torah when He created the world as is known. And through the enlightenment that one attains through the Creation, by always cleaving to this Mind, one cleaves to the Creator. And through this, we understand why the Creator showed us His artisan's tool, for do we need to create worlds? From that, we learn that the Creator showed us His ways so that we know how to cleave to Him, which is by "cleaving to His qualities." (Yalkut Shimoni).

It is so important that we understand and have the consciousness that this is the only reason we are studying the Talmud Eser Sefirot because Talmud Eser Sefirot is the process the Creator went through, and therefore, by thinking through this process we unify with the Thought of the Creator, and we unify with the Creator.

It is a tremendous gift to be allowed to do this, and it is of utmost importance to remember throughout our study the singular purpose for which we are doing this. We are doing this to cleave to the Creator, to unify with the Creator. And we do that by understanding the Creator's process, by understanding His creation. How He did it. Why He did it.

When we study something in the Talmud Eser Sefirot and we understand it, that understanding is not the end of the story; it is the beginning. These thoughts should be percolating in our mind. The only reason we want to understand it is so we can think about it again and again and again. As we think about it again and again and again, we cleave, we unify with the Light of the Creator.

The way we can all achieve *dvekut* (cleaving) is, as we study a concept in Talmud Eser Sefirot, we do not just want to understand it, even if we do understand it perfectly. Take the time to think about the concept you have just learned before going on to the next thing—because what you are thinking about is the Creator; what you are thinking about are the Creator's Thoughts. And as Rav Ashlag makes very clear, this is one of the purest ways to connect to the Creator.

Rav Ashlag wrote an introduction to the Study of the Ten Luminous Emanations, which is now called, And You Shall Choose Life. This introduction has so many secrets that Rav Brandwein told the Rav you can only really understand it once you have studied the entire Ten Luminous Emanations. In verse 156 of his introduction he states:

> But there is a strict condition that while engaging in this Wisdom, one should not try to materialize things [the words in the books] through imaginary and material matters because this may constitute a violation, Heaven forbid, of [the Precept]: "You shall not make for yourself a graven image." (Exodus 20:3) In this case, one would actually receive harm instead of benefit (see verse 35). Therefore, our sages warned that one should not study this Wisdom except

after the age of forty, or [one can] study it from a Rav [Kabbalist], and so on. And all this caution is because of the said reason.

None of these concepts are physical. Rav Ashlag says that we have to be very careful that we do not have physical pictures of what is taught and learned in the Talmud Eser Sefirot. One of the things I hope to accomplish by going through this study slowly, and in being very particular and careful, is that we must be very clear that there should never be a picture in our mind of physical manifestations of Lines and Circles. Although we can use them as devices to grasp the concepts, we have to understand what is underlying them.

Therefore, with the Creator's help, I have prepared the commentaries *Panim Me'irot* and *Panim Masbirot*, which comment upon [the book] Etz Chayim ("Tree of Life") and, which I have prepared in order to save the learners from any materialization.

However, after the first four parts of these commentaries were printed and were disseminated among the learners, I realized that I had not finished my task of commentator as I had thought, and [that] all the great efforts that I had put into explaining and expounding so that things would be made clear with no difficulty were almost for nothing. This is because learners do not feel any great obligation to diligently study the meaning of each and every word before them and to repeat it numerous times in a way that would be sufficient for them to remember it well later on in the book every time this same word shows up again. And out of forgetting the meaning of a certain word, some things would become confusing. This is because these concepts are so subtle that not having the meaning of one word would be enough to confuse the entire issue.

This too is a lesson for us. When something we are trying to do is not going exactly the way we want, we can always draw inspiration from Rav Ashlag. He also tried and failed a few times.

Therefore, I have now taken a different route, according to the proverb "you got less you got it!" [less is more] and that is this book: The Study of the Ten Luminous Emanations (Sefirot) of the Ari [Rav Isaac Luria]. I have prepared a collection of essays from books written by the Ari, especially from his book Etz Chayim ("Tree of Life"). These are all the main essays that have to do with the explanation of the Ten Sefirot, and I have placed them at the upper part of each page.

Then I have proceeded to make one extended commentary called "Inner Light" and a second commentary called "Inner Observation," which explain each word and each concept mentioned in the words of the Ari [that appear] in the upper part of the page. I used simple and easy language to the extent that I could.

I have divided the book into sixteen volumes (lit. parts), each part being one lesson on a particular topic in the Study of the Ten Luminous Emanations (Sefirot), with the "Inner Light" explaining mainly the words of the Ari quoted in that lesson, and "Inner Observation" explaining the essence of the concept in general. In addition, I have arranged a Table of Questions and a Table of Answers covering all the words and concepts that are discussed in that part. After the learner has completed each volume (lit. part), he should test himself to answer every question contained in the Table of Questions properly.

And after he answers, he should look at the answer pertaining to that question in the Table of Answers, [same reference number for question and answer] to see if he answered it properly. And even if he knows the answers to all the questions from memory, he should repeat the questions many times over, until they will be as if contained in a box because then he will be able to remember the word whenever it is needed, or at least remember where it is located in order to find it. "And may it be the Creator's Will that he be successful." (Isaiah 53:10)

Whether we are learning from the original Hebrew writing or we are translating it to English, what we are actually doing is learning a brand new language. The word "Lines," in this context, can no longer mean *lines*. "Circles" can no longer mean *circles*. We have to completely transform our comprehension of words, and of language. When we use the word "Line," the word "Line" is a manifestation of a manifestation of a manifestation of the essence of the word "Line" that is in the Supernal Worlds.

To give a simple example, rain is obviously a physical manifestation—water that comes down from the Heavens. However, when the Torah uses the word "rain," it really means something completely different. It means a flowing of Light in the Supernal Worlds. We can only comprehend rain in the physical form, for the most part, because physicality is our frame of reference but the Torah never means rain. It means Light that falls from one spiritual level to the next. Thus what has to occur is that we have to retrain our mind to understand the true language of Kabbalah, which is completely different than the language that we know. This is why it is so important to study slowly, and do it correctly. The danger is that the language of Kabbalah uses words we know, and there is a relationship between these words. However, the words we know are much lower manifestations of that Light. Therefore our mind has to keep to the Source, not the manifestation.

Rav Ashlag tells us that it is very important to go over these words again and again and again—until this new language is something that we understand and remember forever. Now, for the rest of our lives, every time we come across the word in the context of Kabbalah, it will mean what it truly means and not what it physically means. When these words become part of our vocabulary, we will merit being able to remember them when we need them.

According to both Rav Ashlag and Rav Brandwein, it is impossible to really understand Talmud Eser Sefirot without the assistance of the Light of the Creator. One can comprehend calculus and physics with our mind, but the Wisdom of Kabbalah is the one wisdom that cannot be grasped without the assistance of the Light of the Creator. I hope that I have made clear the danger and the difficulty in truly understanding Talmud Eser Sefirot. Therefore, we need to be diligent in making sure we do not associate any of the words of Kabbalah with their physical meaning. We must take the time to truly know these words.

Rav Ashlag now continues to tell us how one should study the Talmud Eser Sefirot:

> First study the "Inner"—that is, the words of the Ari [that appear in this book in big bold letters]—to the end of the book. And even though you may not understand, repeat them a few times, according to the saying: "First finish, and then understand." After that, study the "Inner Light" commentary and put effort into it, to the point that you will be able to study and understand the "Inner" even without the help of the commentary. And after that, study the "Inner Observation" commentary until you understand it and remember it fully. After all this, test yourself with the Table of Questions, and after you have answered each question, check the answer that is marked with the same letter as the question; do this with each and every question.

You should study and memorize and repeat them a number of times until you remember them as well as if they were laid out in a box, because in each and every word of the third volume [part], you must remember the first two parts so that no meaning will be missing. And the worst thing would be that the learner would not even notice what he has forgotten; where things would either become confusing for him or he would arrive at an erroneous meaning for the matter because of his forgetfulness. And of course, one mistake is followed by ten other mistakes, until one comes to a complete misunderstanding and has to drop the study altogether.

# INNER LIGHT
# (OHR PNIMI)

## CHAPTER 1

This Chapter explains the subject of the first Contraction (Tzimtzum), in which the Endless Light (Ohr Ein Sof) contracted Itself in order to emanate the Emanations and create Creations. It includes five subjects:

1.  Before the Tzimtzum, the Endless (Ein Sof) filled the entire existence.

2.  The reason for the Creation was to reveal His Names and Appellations.

3.  The Contraction of the Light from around the Middle Point.

4.  After the Tzimtzum, the space that remained was circular.

5.  Since the Endless Light (Ohr Ein Sof) is equally even, the Contraction was also equally even. This is the secret of the Circle.

א) דַּע כִּי טֶרֶם שֶׁנֶּאֶצְלוּ הַנֶּאֱצָלִים וְנִבְרְאוּ הַנִּבְרָאִים, הָיָה אוֹר עֶלְיוֹן פָּשׁוּט מְמַלֵּא כָּל הַמְּצִיאוּת. וְלֹא הָיָה שׁוּם מָקוֹם פָּנוּי בִּבְחִינַת אֲוִיר רֵיקָנִי וְחָלָל, אֶלָּא הָיָה הַכֹּל מְמַלֵּא מִן אוֹר אֵין סוֹף פָּשׁוּט הַהוּא, וְלֹא הָיָה לוֹ לֹא בְּחִינַת רֹאשׁ וְלֹא בְּחִינַת סוֹף, אֶלָּא הַכֹּל הָיָה אוֹר א' פָּשׁוּט שָׁוֶה בְּהַשְׁוָאָה א', וְהוּא הַנִּקְרָא אוֹר אֵין סוֹף.

1. Know that before[1] the Emanations were emanated and creations were created, a simple Supernal Light[2] filled the entire existence.[3] There was no vacant place,[4] such as empty air[5] or space.[6] Rather, everything was filled[7] with that simple Endless Light, which had no aspect of beginning (lit. head) and no aspect of end.[8] Rather, everything[9] was one simple Light[10] that was equally even. And this is what is called the Endless Light (Ohr Ein Sof).[11]

ב) וְכַאֲשֶׁר עָלָה בִּרְצוֹנוֹ הַפָּשׁוּט, לִבְרֹא הָעוֹלָמוֹת וּלְהַאֲצִיל הַנֶּאֱצָלִים. לְהוֹצִיא לָאוֹר שְׁלֵמוּת פְּעֻלּוֹתָיו וְשֵׁמוֹתָיו וְכִנּוּיָו, אֲשֶׁר זֹאת הָיָה סִבַּת בְּרִיאַת הָעוֹלָמוֹת...

2. And when it rose up in His simple Desire,[12] to create the Worlds and emanate the Emanations, to bring into the Light the perfection of His actions and Names and Appellations, which was the reason for the creation of the Worlds...

ג) ...וְהִנֵּה אָז צִמְצֵם אֶת עַצְמוֹ אֵין סוֹף בַּנְּקֻדָּה הָאֶמְצָעִית, אֲשֶׁר בּוֹ בְּאֶמְצַע מַמָּשׁ, וְצִמְצֵם הָאוֹר הַהוּא, וְנִתְרַחֵק אֶל צִדְדֵי סְבִיבוֹת הַנְּקֻדָּה הָאֶמְצָעִית.

3. …then the Endless (Ein Sof) contracted Itself[13] within the Middle Point,[14] in the very middle of it. And that Light contracted and distanced Itself[15] to the sides around the Middle Point.[16]

ד) וְאָז נִשְׁאַר מָקוֹם פָּנוּי, וַאֲוִיר, וְחָלָל רֵיקָנִי, מִנְּקֻדָּה הָאֶמְצָעִית מַמָּשׁ. וְהִנֵּה הַצִּמְצוּם הַזֶּה, הָיָה בְּהַשְׁוָאָה א' בִּסְבִיבוֹת הַנְּקֻדָּה הָאֶמְצָעִית רֵיקָנִית הַהִיא, בְּאֹפֶן שֶׁמְּקוֹם הֶחָלָל הַהוּא, הָיָה עָגֹל מִכָּל סְבִיבוֹתָיו בְּהַשְׁוָאָה גְּמוּרָה, וְלֹא הָיָה בִּתְמוּנַת מְרֻבָּע בַּעַל זָוִית נִצֶּבֶת, לְפִי, שֶׁגַּם אֵין סוֹף צִמְצֵם עַצְמוֹ בִּבְחִינַת עָגֹל, בְּהַשְׁוָאָה א' מִכָּל הַצְּדָדִים.

4. Then what remained was a vacant place,[17] and air and empty space in the very Middle Point. So, this Contraction (Tzimtzum) was all equally even around that empty Middle Point,[18] in such a way that the place of that space was Circle-like all around[19]—completely equal and even. It had not the shape of a square with a right angle, since the Endless (Ein Sof) also contracted Itself in the likeness of a Circle, equally even all-around.

ה) וְהַסִּבָּה הָיְתָה, לְפִי שֶׁכֵּיוָן שֶׁאוֹר הָאֵין סוֹף שָׁוֶה בְּהַשְׁוָאָה גְּמוּרָה הֻכְרְחוּ גַּם כֵּן, שֶׁיִּצְטַמְצֵם עַצְמוֹ בְּהַשְׁוָאָה א' מִכָּל הַצְּדָדִים, וְלֹא שֶׁיִּצְטַמְצֵם עַצְמוֹ מִצַּד א' יוֹתֵר מִשְּׁאָר צְדָדִים. וְנוֹדַע בְּחָכְמַת הַשִּׁעוּר שֶׁאֵין תְּמוּנָה כָּל כָּךְ שָׁוֶה כְּמוֹ תְּמוּנַת הָעָגוֹל, מַה שֶּׁאֵין כֵּן, בִּתְמוּנַת מְרֻבָּע בַּעַל זָוִית נִצֶּבֶת בּוֹלֶטֶת, וְכֵן תְּמוּנַת הַמְשֻׁלָּשׁ וְכַיּוֹצֵא בִּשְׁאָר הַתְּמוּנוֹת. וְעַל כֵּן מֻכְרָח הוּא לִהְיוֹת צִמְצוּם הָאֵין סוֹף בִּבְחִינַת עָגוֹל.

5. The reason was that since the Endless Light (Ohr Ein Sof) was equal and completely even, it too had to contract Itself equally even on all sides, not contracting Itself more on one side than the other sides. We know through geometry that there is no shape as equally even[20] as the shape of the Circle. This is not the case with the shape of a square with projecting right angles,[21] or the shape of a triangle,[22] and similarly with other shapes. The Contraction (Tzimtzum) of the Endless (Ein Sof), therefore, had to be in the form of a Circle.

It is important to remember that the entire Wisdom of Kabbalah is based on spiritual matters that occupy neither space nor time. Neither lack nor change apply to them at all. All the changes discussed in this Wisdom do not imply that the First Phase is absent or assumes a different form. Rather, the change that is mentioned is merely an additional form, while the first form does not move from its place. After all, lack and change are part of the nature of physicality.

Herein lies the entire difficulty for beginners, since they grasp things according to their material manifestations, which are bound by time, space, change or substitution. The authors used them merely as symbols for their Divine roots. Therefore, I shall strive to explain each and every word according to its spiritual nature, stripped of time, space, and substitution. It behooves the readers to engrave well in their memory the explanation for these words because it is impossible to repeat them every time.

Everything we do at the Kabbalah Centres stems from the teachings of Rav Ashlag; and the strongest way to connect to Rav Ashlag is through the Study of the Ten Luminous Emanations (Talmud Eser Sefirot), especially the sections in the beginning. As Rav Ashlag says, the day Rav Isaac Luria (the Ari) revealed these secrets is just as important as the revelation at Mount Sinai because these secrets are beyond the level of prophecy. What the Ari, together with Rav Ashlag, reveal here is that we must greatly appreciate the merit we have to be permitted access to these words, which are beyond the level of prophecy.

One of the beautiful aspects of studying from Rav Ashlag is that we learn spiritual laws that we would not have understood otherwise. Rav Ashlag begins by teaching us two different rules: (1) there is no time or movement and (2) there is no addition or removal. No time and space is something that I think all of us can accept in a spiritual sense. When we are talking about spiritual forms, obviously they are beyond the realm of time and space because time and space only make sense within physical form. However, the idea that there is no lack and there is no change is not a given. The concept that there cannot be lack or change is a revelation of Rav Ashlag. What is more, he tells us the reason is because lack and change is a rule of physicality. There can be no lack or change in the spiritual essence.

This is an important lesson we can bring into our own lives. If we experience lack, if we experience big shifts and changes, it cannot come in any way from a connection to the Light of the Creator because, as Rav Ashlag tells us, there is no change, no lack, nor removal in a true spiritual essence. Lack and change is the way the physical world operates; it is the way the reality works in the physical world. This is the difficulty for those who begin this study.

Unfortunately, for most people who have studied Kabbalah throughout the ages, there has been a sense that time was involved, there has been a sense that there was space involved. There has been a sense that there was change and lack. When one reads from the Ari, it seems that this happened and that happened. This is why Rav Ashlag keeps stressing that these terminologies and words that are used by the kabbalists, and specifically here by the Ari, refer to terms that could be literally translated as time, space, change, and lack but are only signposts to their Supernal Sources.

Rav Ashlag mentions time and time again that it is important for all of us who study this wisdom to literally engrave in our minds this new language, and these new meanings within this new language. With this, what Rav Ashlag is telling us is that once he has given an explanation he will not repeat it. And if we forget this idea and continue to study, then we will never be able to truly understand.

1. Know that before[1] the Emanations were emanated and creations were created, a simple Supernal Light[2] filled the entire existence.[3] There was no vacant place,[4] such as empty air[5] or space.[6] Rather, everything was filled[7] with that simple Endless Light, which had no aspect of beginning (lit. head) and no aspect of end.[8] Rather, everything was one simple Light[9] that was equally even.[10] And this is what is called the Endless Light (Ohr Ein Sof).[11]

1. **Before:** The form of spiritual time will be well explained later on (see the end of Inner Observation, [Section 33-34] starting with the words: 'We still need…')

2. **A Supernal Light:** Namely the Light that extends from the Essence of the Creator. Know that all the Names and Appellations found in the Wisdom of Kabbalah are not, Heaven forbid, of the Essence of the Creator but merely apply to the Light extending from His Essence. As far as His Essence, we do not have any words and syllables at all. For this is the rule: Whatever we cannot comprehend, we do not know by name. Remember this and do not fail.

Those who study at the Centres know that when we refer to the word "Light" this never refers to actual physical light. Imagine how difficult it was for the people who studied from the Ari, before Rav Ashlag. I am certain that they concluded that Light was meant as some form of physical light. The knowledge that we take as a given was not available before Rav Ashlag.

Whether we are discussing Yud-Kei-Vav-Kei or any other Name, we understand now that none of these Names are God. They are manifestations of the Light of God and more specifically, they represent the way we react from those manifestations. One of Rav Ashlag's big revelations, which he will explain later, is that the Light of the Creator and our interaction with the Light that flows from the Creator is only understood by us to whatever degree we can understand. Therefore, when we talk about the Names and manifestations of God, we are talking about the terminology and understanding of the Vessel—coming from down, looking up. We never speak about the Essence of the Creator.

**"Whatever we cannot comprehend, we do not know by name."** This is another spiritual rule of Rav Ashlag to truly engrave in our mind. Whatever we do not comprehend or have an incomplete understanding of, we cannot describe using words. All of us throughout our lives, each day, talk about things we do not completely know nor completely comprehend. Now in taking this to an even higher level—as we begin to study—whether we talk about the World of the Light of the Creator from Ein Sof onward, even though we do not have a true comprehension of these concepts, we are still going to talk about them.

We all talk about things all the time that we do not truly understand. Therefore this rule of: "Whatever we do not comprehend, we cannot give it a name," is a rule in the spiritual world, it is not necessarily a rule that we follow. In fact, it is a rule that we definitely do not follow in our own lives, in our discussions, in how we talk and what we talk about.

There are two points to this. First is that the basis of understanding Kabbalah is being and seeking what is true. Without a connection to truth, a person cannot connect to the Light of Kabbalah. Thus when Rav Ashlag says, "Whatever we cannot or do not comprehend, we cannot give it a name," this is because it will not be true. Unfortunately, when we talk about things that we do not comprehend (which we all do), for the most part we are not really connected to the essence of truth. The kabbalists could not give names to things that they could not fully comprehend because that is not truth.

All of us discuss things, even teach things that we do not truly comprehend. Sometimes it is necessary, sometimes it is okay, but to whatever degree we are away from truth, we are separated from the Wisdom of Kabbalah. The Rav would always tell us that when Rav Ashlag was very young, he reached the point where he literally could not speak something that was untrue. This is why Rav Ashlag refers to the Wisdom of Kabbalah as the Wisdom of Truth (*Torat haEmet*).

The second important point Rav Ashlag explains is that although the kabbalists could not talk about that which they did not or could not fully comprehend, *we* can. Many of the concepts that we will discuss are things that we can connect to, to one degree or another, but not 100 percent. We are not on the level of "everything that we do not comprehend; we cannot give it a name." We will give names and speak of things that we do not fully comprehend. And it is okay that we do, within the framework of this wisdom.

As we continue with Rav Ashlag's Inner Light commentary, we truly need to appreciate these ideas, especially in these first few sections of the Talmud Eser Sefirot. There is a letter that Rav Brandwein had from Rav Ashlag (which unfortunately the Rav did not receive from Rav Brandwein), that describes a vision Rav Ashlag had where he asked the Creator to give him the levels of prophecy of the prophets, and he writes that the Creator told him: "The levels that you have achieved are higher than the levels of the prophets."

The Zohar explains that there are two levels of connection. There is the level of the prophets, which was considered a vision that is not clear, and then there is the level of Moses, which is a clear vision. All the kabbalists from the Ari's time until Rav Ashlag, probably saw on the level of the prophets. They could only understand on the simplest levels, in an unclear way. What Rav Ashlag revealed was a clear vision. Rav Ashlag, who received this from his teacher, received vision through Divine Inspiration. We have to have an appreciation for these words that are revealed. Unlike anything else that we study, which to one degree or another a *tzadik* (righteous soul) reveals through his own understanding, these concepts presented here are revealed only through Divine Inspiration, through Rav Ashlag who achieved a level of clear vision beyond the level of the prophets.

---

3. **Filled the entire existence:** This is seemingly very puzzling. After all, what is said here relates to before the creation of the Worlds. In such a case, what reality is here that the Supernal Light needs to fill? The idea is that all the Worlds and all the souls, both existing and those to be created in the future, along with whatever happens to them until the end of their correction, are already comprised within the Ein Sof (Endless), in all their glory and all their fullness. They are thus in such a way that we have to distinguish between two principles regarding the entire existence before us.

The First Principle is the aspect of how they exist and are set in the Ein Sof with all their perfection and glory. The second principle is the way they are arranged, evolve, and renew after the first Tzimtzum in the Five Worlds that are called: Adam Kadmon, Atzilut, Briyah, Yetzirah and Asiyah, as shall be explained (Inner Light, Part 2, Sections 8-9).

This is what the Rav [the Ari] meant that the Supernal Light that is drawn from His Essence "filled the entire existence," namely, the entire existence of the first principle, in the aspect of how they are laid out and exist in the Ein Sof before the Tzimtzum. He tells us that the Supernal Light filled them completely to the extent that there was no vacant place in them, in which to add to them any perfection or correction (read carefully in Inner Observation here).

---

Rav Ashlag says we have to understand two important aspects in everything that is in front of us in Creation: The First Reality is the way that our souls and the souls of all humanity—in their perfection, in their completion—already exist in the Endless World. The Second Reality is the way the Five Worlds—Adam Kadmon, Atzilut, Briyah, Yetzirah, and Asiyah—came into being after the First Contraction (Tzimtzum Alef). It is the way our souls came into being, the way our lives have gone in previous incarnations and this reincarnation. This Second Reality, is the one within which humanity is still working to achieve our correction. And these two Realities coexist at the same time.

The Ari says that the Supernal Light that flows from the Creator's Essence filled the entire Reality. This refers to the First Reality, which is the Reality of Perfection—the Endless World (Ein Sof) before the Contraction and removal of the Light. The Supernal Light filled them so that there was no empty space and no room for addition nor correction.

As an aside, Rav Ashlag does not go into this idea here because it is seemingly an idea without its conclusion. If you just read these words here, as Rav Ashlag writes them, it sounds as if the Endless World is perfect regardless of what occurs to humanity from the Tzimtzum on. Yet, Rav Ashlag explains in the book Thought of Creation that this is not the case. Rather, the Endless World is perfect because of the work that we, humanity, do and the perfection that we will achieve. And because the Endless World is not confined to the realm of time, therefore the perfection we will achieve is already a reality in the Endless World.

One of the things you find as you study from Rav Ashlag is that he does not always give the complete reason in each section. One of the gifts of Rav Ashlag was his ability to confine his thoughts and writings so he could at least take us to the next point. Rav Ashlag could have spent years on each word here of the Ari, literally writing thousands of pages. This is why Rav Isaac Luria could not contain his thoughts to writing. Rav Shimon bar Yochai also did not write. It takes a particular ability to simultaneously have the overflow of wisdom and still be able to confine it to writing.

Something interesting that we often see—certainly in the Talmud Eser Sefirot where Rav Ashlag speaks about a particular point—is that he gives a reason that may not have a complete rationale or he might talk about it in another place (article) with his complete rationale. He did this because this is the way he confined his thoughts in this area. This is a little bit of understanding of the reasoning and the process Rav Ashlag underwent in writing this commentary.

4. **Vacant place:** The explanation is that before the Worlds were created, when there was only Ein Sof alone, as said [Section 3], there was no "vacant place," namely, a place of lack that might be fit to receive corrections of any kind. This is because the Supernal Light filled that place, thus not leaving space for the Lower Beings to define themselves so as to add something to His perfection. But due to the Tzimtzum that took place, as shall be discussed, a new sense of lack came to be and a place was created that was available for correction. Yet, do not make the mistake [to think] that the book refers to a material place.

Forevermore, whenever we see the term "Empty Space" [vacant place], whether in the writing of the kabbalists or even in the Torah and the Books of the Prophets, we understand that it is referring to a lack or a place where there can be corrections. Rav Ashlag says that within the realm of the Endless (Ein Sof) there was no lack, and therefore, no place, no need for correction. The idea of lack, a place that was empty, a place that was made available for corrections only came about because of the removal of the Light of the Creator. But of course, Heaven forbid, do not think that Rav Isaac Luria (the Ari) is talking about physical space.

5. **Empty Air:** This does not refer to physical air, Heaven forbid, but to an aspect of spiritual Light that is so called. There are two aspects of Light in every complete Partzuf (Spiritual Structure), which are called Light of Chochmah and Light of Chasadim. The Light of Chochmah is the essence of the Partzuf, namely its vitality. The Light of Chasadim is just the Light clothing the Light of Chochmah in the Partzuf, since the Light of Chochmah cannot be manifested (lit. clothed) in a Partzuf unless it is first clothed with the Light of Chasadim. Yet at times, when the Partzufim (Spiritual Structures) are in a state of Katnut (Smallness), they have within them the Light of Chasadim alone.

> Know that this Light of Chasadim is called "air" or "wind," and when it is by itself, without the Light of Chochmah, it is called "empty air," namely, emptied from the Light of Chochmah; and therefore, it expects the Light of Chochmah to extend into it and fill it. The Rav [the Ari] teaches us that before the Worlds were created, that is, in the Ein Sof, this state of "empty air" did not exist at all because there is no lack over there whatsoever, as explained [Section 4].

When we read Rav Ashlag's explanation of the concept of Empty Air, and then ponder about other places in the Torah and the Books of the Prophets where air is discussed, we begin to understand what is being spoken about. Take the visions of Ezekiel, for instance—and there are many ideas there within the context of Rav Ashlag's explanations—they give us a sense that none of the visions of the prophets were referring to anything physical. These were all revelations of the wisdom of Kabbalah—the Talmud Eser Sefirot.

When discussing what was not in the Endless World (Ein Sof), Rav Isaac Luria chose only a few concepts. Soon we will see that there are a lot of components to the Correction (Tikkun) process. There are many different Lights. This list, seemingly, could itself be endless because if in the Endless World everything was perfect, one could probably come up with hundreds of words that refer to lack, that of course were not there. But the Ari is very specific in the terminology he used, in what concepts he would say were not there in the Endless World.

Rav Ashlag explains that in every complete revelation of Light, there are two types of Light: The Light of Wisdom (Ohr deChochmah), and the Light of Mercy or Giving (Ohr deChasadim). The Light of Wisdom is the essence and life of a being. The Light of Mercy, the Light of Giving and Sharing, is the Vessel—the concealer that surrounds the Light of Wisdom, as the Light of Wisdom cannot be revealed without the Light of Mercy, the Light of Sharing.

This is a lesson for each one of us. We may think that as long as we are in the process of sharing, in the Ohr deChasadim, we are involved in spiritual work and have a connection to the Light of the Creator, yet what the Ari is making very clear here is that the true giver of life and energy is the Ohr deChochmah—the Light of Wisdom. There has to be wisdom. There must be an understanding and deepening of wisdom to truly have vitality, to truly have spiritual life. Rav Brandwein tells the Rav very clearly in one of the letters: "One cannot have vitality, cannot have life, without a continual attainment of wisdom."

On one hand, there is no life-force, essence, or energy within a person unless there is wisdom and a deepening of the wisdom–Ohr deChochmah. On the other hand, wisdom without sharing, without Ohr deChasadim, cannot be revealed. And therefore, there has to be a very delicate balance between Ohr deChasadim and Ohr deChochmah. Actions of sharing (Ohr deChasadim) are the Vessel within which the Light of Wisdom (Ohr deChochmah) can enter; we cannot have only Ohr deChasadim. When Ohr deChasadim—the Light of Sharing—is without the Light of Wisdom, it is called Empty Air. It is devoid of the Light of Wisdom and it is waiting; the Ohr deChasadim (the Light of Sharing) is waiting for the Light of Wisdom to enter.

Therefore it is no coincidence that the Ari uses this one example of lack when he could have offered a whole list of different types of lack, because this revelation is important to the start of this study. The Ari is telling us right at the beginning of this study that all of us, to one degree or another, have done actions of sharing. We have done actions and continue to do actions of revelation. However, to the degree that we are lacking in Ohr deChochmah— and all of us are—to that same degree we are lacking in the deepening of our understanding of this wisdom; to this degree we are Empty Air.

All of our actions of sharing are in a state of waiting. Every action of sharing that we perform is dependent on how much we have deepened our wisdom. Then, and only then, can Ohr deChasadim, which is filled with Ohr deChochmah, reveal its true essence and power. This is a beautiful understanding as to why these words were chosen, though more importantly, the real understanding of the concepts of both Ohr deChochmah and Ohr deChasadim, as they relate to our own spiritual growth and need for deepening our spiritual understanding, specifically through the Study of the Ten Luminous Emanations (Talmud Eser Sefirot).

6. **Space:** To explain this word, one first needs to know the essence of a spiritual Vessel. It is this: When an emanated being receives abundance for its vitality from the Emanator, the emanated must have the desire and craving to receive its abundance from Him. Know also that this amount of desire and craving is the entirety of matter in the emanated being. Meaning that whatever is in the emanated being, besides this matter, is not related to its material aspect but to the aspect of its abundance that it receives from the Emanator.

Moreover, it is this matter that measures the greatness and stature of every emanated being, every Partzuf and every Sefirah. After all, the extension of the Supernal Light from the Emanator is certainly without limit or measure. Rather, it is the emanated being itself that limits the abundance, since it receives neither more nor less than the measure of its craving and Desire to Receive, which is the standard that applies to spirituality since no coercion applies to it, and everything depends on the Desire.

For this reason, we call this Desire to Receive the emanated being's ability (lit. Vessel) to receive, which is considered to be its matter, and because of [this Desire] it excluded itself from being part of the Emanator and assumed the name "emanated being," since it is bound by a kind of matter that is not found at all in the Emanator, Heaven forbid, since the Desire to Receive does not apply to the Emanator whatsoever, for whom shall He receive from? And understand this.

We need to truly appreciate these sections, especially this one, because this is what all teachings and the work of the Centre is based on. Moreover, we should truly appreciate that we have the merit that Rav Ashlag revealed this to our generation, and even more importantly, that permission was granted to him by the Creator to reveal it. No generation before us was able to have these words, these laws, this wisdom revealed to them. As we study, it is important to have gratitude for both the merit of Rav Ashlag's revelation and for our ability to receive it.

Here we learn three very important concepts:

1. What makes a Vessel is the Desire to Receive. Everything else within a Vessel is the Creator. There are only two parts to reality: there is the Desire to Receive and there is the Light.

2. The Light of the Creator constantly flows. It is only the Vessel (us) that restricts the flow of the Light of the Creator.

3. There is no coercion. Therefore the Light revealed must be to the extent that the Vessel desires it.

One of the ideas that we come to understand from this is the following: When we start our spiritual path, we begin to realize all kinds of negative traits and desires that exist within us. And there is a tendency—and this is really the ego—to want to beat ourselves up about it, thinking: *"I must be a bad person if I have these desires. I must be a disconnected person if I have these desires."* Yet what we learn from these words of Rav Ashlag is that not only is it not a problem that we have all kinds of desires, it is actually the true purpose of the creation and the essence of who we are. Although, as we delve deeper, we will see that because of the Tzimtzum there is a different process that we have to go through in order to receive. Nevertheless, the true essence of who we are and the true essence of why we were created is the Desire to Receive for the Self Alone.

It says about Moses that the Israelites spoke badly about him. There was not one negative action that the Israelites did not attribute to Moses. So much so that the Midrash says that as Moses walked into the Tabernacle, they looked after him and said that his thighs were big: "Moses is stealing all our money, eating and growing fat." And in another place in the Midrash it says that the Israelites were afraid that Moses was trying to steal their wives.

The students of the Baal Shem Tov discuss this in great detail. They ask the question, "While the Israelites were negative and complained often, what was it that permitted them to accuse Moses? In every lie there is at least a little bit of truth. That said, what was it about Moses that gave them that little bit of truth to believe all the things said about him?" And then explain that Moses was born with every negative trait. Of course he became a *tzadik* (righteous soul) and transformed each of them. And of course he did not do the things that people accused him of. Nevertheless there was a root there in Moses' soul. This is also true about all the great *tzadikim*. Rav Chaim Vital, the student of the Ari, was told by his teacher that because Rav Chaim Vital's soul is so great, his negativity, his darkness, will also be as great.

All of this helps us to realize about ourselves, that although we have all forms of desires and qualities that have been established in the world after the Tzimtzum, these are not the ways we ought to follow because we have to restrict the Desire to Receive for the Self Alone. As we will learn, after the Tzimtzum, there is a process of the Returning Light (Ohr Chozer), which has to do with restriction. Most importantly, what we learn from this understanding is that we should not beat ourselves up about it. As Rav Ashlag says this desire is all that we are; it is all that we were meant to be. There is nothing bad about it. Of course, we know that we are not meant to follow these desires; we have to restrict. However, we need to know that to have these desires, for them to be part of who we are, does not make us a bad person. It actually makes us who we are. It makes us the creation the Creator wanted us to be. And as we learn from Moses, and from Rav Chaim Vital, it can also shape us into the greatest tzadik. This is an important idea and understanding.

Later, we will explain that this matter has Four Levels: from the smallest to the greatest level of receiving. The Fourth Level is the greatness level of receiving, which is present in its entirety only in the Ein Sof, before the Worlds were created. And the secret of the Tzimtzum was performed only upon it alone. It shall be explained later that it was emptied of all the abundance it had from its relation to Ein Sof, and remained as an aspect of "vacant space." This is what the Rav [the Ari] meant when he said that in the Ein Sof, before the World was created, there was no aspect of "vacant space," as explained.

We think that this world is where people have desire—Desire to Receive for the Self Alone—however, Rav Ashlag says here that only in the Endless World was there a true, complete, and total Desire to Receive. This is such a paradox. In fact, everything in this world is only the lighter elements of that. The only place where the complete revealed Desire to Receive became manifest was in the Endless World. This brings us back to the point that obviously the Desire to Receive is not something negative. It is not only necessary but also the perfect and complete Desire to Receive can only be found in Ein Sof.

Rav Ashlag says that there are Four Stages of Desire. The Fourth and final Stage of desire, which of course is Malchut, is the only level upon which there was Tzimtzum, this restriction. This is what the Ari means when he tells us that before the Creation of the World—meaning in the Endless World—there was no void (chalal) because there was no Desire to Receive that was not fulfilled; the Desire to Receive in all its entirety, in its completion was filled in the Endless World.

---

7. **Everything was filled:** That is, there is nothing to add to it by the actions of the Lower Beings.

8. **No aspect of beginning (lit. head) and no aspect of end:** The concept of beginning (head) and end will be explained later [section 14].

9. **One simple Light:** This means that in It there are no levels, small or great, instead everything is equal, as will be explained.

10. **Equally even:** That is, there is no purity or coarseness in It, according to which the levels are arranged and categorized, since these distinctions came to be in the Worlds only with the advent of the Tzimtzum, as shall be explained.

---

Rav Ashlag says that what is unique about the Endless World is that it is a miracle; something that we cannot truly comprehend. If all the desires were filled—the greater desires and lesser desires within the Four Phases of Desire—that would seem to imply that even in the Endless World, since all desires and levels of the Vessel were filled, there would still be greater and lesser. Meaning, the First Phase of Desire is lower and it receives less than a greater desire. For example, if you have ten people and each one of them desires something different, in the Endless World, all their desires are filled, even though they still have different desires, different manifestations, and different degrees. However, what Rav Ashlag is saying, what the Ari is saying, is that **"it was all one simple Light."** Even though we cannot truly comprehend it, in the Endless World everything was the same—there was no greater or lesser. This is a concept that cannot make logical sense to us because it seems that there would be greater or lesser. Yet, as Rav Ashlag will tell us, this is one of the things that is beyond our understanding.

In the Endless World, there was no greater or lesser: **"It was all one simple Light."** The Ari says it was equal and explains that what makes a vessel darker is the Desire to Receive. Thus the less Desire to Receive the purer and cleaner a Vessel is. The more Desire to Receive, the darker it is.

In our world, when a person has a great Desire to Receive for the Self Alone—a coarse and dark Vessel—it disconnects him from the Light of the Creator. When a person has less Desire to Receive for the Self Alone—a purer Vessel— to that degree it does not disconnect him from the Light of the Creator. In the Endless World there was no realization of this.

In the Endless World, although there were lesser and greater Desires to Receive, these desires did not cause any separation or any Difference of Form between any of the Vessels, as states of purer or darker only came about after the Tzimtzum, after the constriction of the Light of the Creator. From the point of Tzimtzum and on, there was the beginning of differentiation between what is a purer Vessel or a darker Vessel. In the Endless World, it was all washed over by the Endless Light and there were no degrees, no separations. Even though in reality there might have been different levels, nevertheless they were all considered one.

There is an interesting elucidation that describes the time of the Final Correction, when Mashiach (Messiah) comes. It says: "They shall not hurt nor destroy in all My Holy mountain; for the earth shall be full of the knowledge of the Lord, as the waters cover the sea." (Isaiah 11:9) The knowledge of God and the connection and cleaving that we will all achieve will be so great; it will be like the water that covers the ocean. What does this mean? The ocean, as we know, has mountains and valleys within it. The bottom of the ocean is not a flat land. There are a great many ups and downs. Yet, when we look at the surface of the ocean, it is one equal line. And when the Light of the Creator is completely revealed—as it was in the Ein Sof, when the Light of Kabbalah is revealed in the world it will be so great. This does not mean there will not be differences as there were in Ein Sof but rather that the Light of the Creator will be so powerful and so overriding it will be like the ocean. Although there are many differences—highs and lows beneath the ocean—the Light of the Creator will be so overflowing and overpowering it will make everything unified, which is an interesting idea.

11. **Endless Light (Ohr Ein Sof):** Since we have no concept of the Ein Sof, we should question how we can know It by name because every name denotes conceiving; we conceive something according to the indication and meaning of the name, as is well known. We cannot explain it away by saying that the name Ein Sof merely indicates the negation of conception because then we should have used the name "inconceivable." But the idea is that this name indicates the entire difference between the Ein Sof and all the Worlds below It, which is that due to the Tzimtzum that occurred after Ein Sof, wherever this force is roused, it contracts the Light with which the illumination is concluded and reaches its end. Therefore, every end and conclusion in every illumination and in every Partzuf is drawn by means of the Tzimtzum alone.

Moreover, due to that 'conclusion' and 'end', all the realities and their fulfillment come out and materialize, along with all the changes that exist in the Worlds. And since the idea of Tzimtzum is not there, in the EinSof, no ending or conclusion applies there. Therefore, it is named Ein Sof (Endless) to indicate that there is no conclusion or end there at all. With this we understand that this Light is simple and equally even, for one depends on the other, as explained.

Rav Ashlag tells us that the Name Ein Sof (Endless) indicates the difference between that World and all the Worlds that come after the Constriction that took place. Everywhere that this power is awakened, it restricts the Light of the Creator there; therefore the Light flowing there has to be limited. Any ending, any restriction of revelation of complete Light is one of the reasons there are different Names of God. One Name is the Shin-Dalet-Yud (Shadai). The Midrash explains that the Name Shin-Dalet-Yud represents the Creator telling the world "enough" (she'amar le'olamo dai). The Creator stopping the world from being created represents the power of the Tzimtzum, of the restriction, of putting an end to a flow of Light.

One of the reasons Rav Shimon bar Yochai was not the one to write the Zohar, (it was Rav Aba who scribed the Zohar) and the Ari was not the one to write the Writings of the Ari—(it was Rav Chaim Vital who authored the Writings of the Ari) was because both Rav Shimon and the Ari were so completely connected to the Endless World that, they could not constrict their thoughts and put them down on paper. There is a certain quality that Rav Chaim Vital and Rav Aba had of being able to disconnect from the Endless World and only then could they write things down.

What Rav Ashlag is saying with this is that any time there is an end put on a revelation of Light, it comes from the power of Tzimtzum and restriction that was done. Before that, though, there was a flow of Light that does not stop. Moreover, all the differences that occurred in the Worlds and that continues to occur in the Worlds—all the different manifestations that occurred—were only caused by the Tzimtzum, by the stopping of the Light. The Tzimtzum, the constriction, the restriction of the Creator's Light, did not occur in the Endless World, so there cannot be an end in the Endless, which is why it is called the Endless World. Therefore, if there is one endless flow of Light, then it is obviously equal and simple because it has to be endless for it to be simple and equal.

To help us wrap our heads around this concept, Rav Ashlag tells us that calling it the Endless World does not tell us what it is, rather it is telling us *what it is not*. Meaning, in the Worlds that followed the Tzimtzum, after the restriction of the Creator's Light, there is an end to everything. To reflect on Rav Ashlag's question: "How can we give it a name if we do not have any comprehension of it?" the name Ein Sof (Endless) is not formed or given by an understanding of that Endless World because we do not have an understanding of that World, it is simply the indicator of the one essence, the one power, the one action that never occurs there but does occur in our world—the Tzimtzum, the putting a limit, the putting an end.

Let's follow the logical process: Rav Ashlag's question was: *"How can we give it a name? How can we give that world, the Endless World, a name if we don't comprehend it, if we don't connect to it?"* The answer is of course that we do not connect to that world, nevertheless, the name given to it was to give us an indication of the one thing that we know exists in our worlds after the Tzimtzum and does not exist in that world. What is the one thing that exists in our world that does not exist in that world? It is the concept of end. That world is the world with no end. Our world has an end because the Tzimtzum has end.

The idea of the Endless World is one of those concepts in which we should spend a week or two or three immersing our consciousness. Of course, we know that the Endless World exists, and that everything we see in our world is an illusion that covers up that World. The Endless World is in everything of our world. We have to aspire to push ourselves to begin revealing the Endless. This is true about many areas of life. The reality is that in every part of our lives there is a lot more Light, a lot more joy, a lot more fulfillment available, but we connect to the Tzimtzum reality of that revelation. Whether it is with our spouse or with our children, whether it is in our study or with our work, there is the totality of the Endless World within it. We however, to one degree or another, connect to the Tzimtzum Reality.

What we want to do is to strive and work toward connecting to the Ein Sof Reality of life, whether it is the Ein Sof Reality of our children, the Ein Sof Reality of our spouse, the Ein Sof Reality of the study, the Ein Sof Reality of the work because it is there. All too often we are looking for the next thing to give us more fulfillment, when in reality everything is here. I mean literally everything—take for instance flowers, the amount of Light and connection, joy, and fulfillment that we can get from connecting to the Ein Sof Reality of these flowers is greater than probably any of us have ever achieved in our lives. This is because what we do is connect to the Tzimtzum reality of everything in our lives.

It is important for us to take the time to really understand that the Creator is good. In Rav Brandwein letters to the Rav in the letters: "Taste and see that the Creator is good." (Psalms 34:9) Rav Ashlag also reminds us in his Introduction to the Study of the Ten Luminous Emananation (Talmud Eser Sefirot) to *"Taste and see that the Creator is good."* There are endless levels of tasting and sensing the Light of the Creator in everything with all of our being but we do not take the time. Each of us has aspects in every area of our lives where we are revealing Tzimtzum and not opening the door to the Ein Sof Reality of that situation. This is the work we need to do to really understand this and work on it, to reveal it, to think about it.

2. **And when It rose up in His simple Desire,**[12] **to create the Worlds and emanate the Emanations, to bring into light the perfection of His actions, Names and Appellations, which was the cause for the creation of the Worlds...**

When we read in Genesis that the Creator created our world, the reality is—as Rav Ashlag will explain the words of the Ari—that it is the Vessel that needed, wanted, and therefore caused the creation of our world. The Creator did not need Creation. The Creator only did us a favor and allowed us to do it, which is an amazing concept. We, the Vessel, wanted to elevate in our purifications and therefore needed, wanted, and asked for the creation of our world.

We wanted to reveal everything that comes forth so that we would have the ability to work on Bread of Shame, and earn a true *dvekut,* a true union with the Light of the Creator. This too, is one of those concepts that without Rav Ashlag we would not know what these words mean. Did the Creator have a desire to create the world? Rav Ashlag makes it very clear: it is the Vessel, we, that created this world. This is truly an amazing revelation.

It is important to realize that for thousands of years, whether people were studying from the Zohar or from the Writings of the Ari, before Rav Ashlag people did not have a concept of this whole idea of the Desire to Receive needing to take care of Bread of Shame, and therefore creating the worlds. Can you imagine how many great kabbalists, smart, great souls did not have the understanding we are going to receive, thanks to the work of Rav Ashlag? It is really an amazing gift that truly needs appreciation.

There is the idea that the Creator is called "…merciful and gracious…" (Exodus 34:6), and that the Creator's Names are simply a manifestations of the Creator's positive Light in our world. Everything that we experience in our world of a positive nature is a manifestation of the Light of the Creator. Rav Ashlag explains that although the Creator was fine with things as they were in the Endless World, the Vessel's desire to manifest differently still necessitated the creation of our world. This also brought about the realization of the Creator's Essence in our world. Meaning, the Creator's Essence of being merciful, the Creator's Essence of sharing, the Creator's Essence of all things that are good, became manifest in our world.

When the Ari says **"to bring into light the perfection of His actions, Names and Appellations,"** the Ari is referring to the phrase *"leheytiv lenivra'av"*—that the entire purpose of Creation was to give to the creations. When he discusses revealing the Creator's Names, it means the Creator's Essence: "…merciful and gracious…." (Exodus 34:6) How does the concept of *leheytiv lenivra'av* become manifest? How does the Creator give us good? He gives us good in all ways. The different Names of the Creator are just different manifestations, different ways that the Light of the Creator manifests in this world.

The notion that the Creator manifests according to the Vessel is a very important and fundamental concept that Rav Ashlag explains in depth in the Prologue of the Zohar. This section has many ramifications. What is different about Kabbalah, and specifically the way Rav Ashlag explains it, is that there is no absolute God in our world. Rather there is how we interact with the Light of the Creator, the Light of God in our world. The way we see God, the way we think about God, the way we feel the God and Light of the Creator in our world is the way the Creator manifests. This is a critical and basic understanding. In the Prologue to the Zohar verse 139A of the Sulam commentary, Rav Ashlag says:

> Know that this is the entire difference between this world before the Correction and the End of the Correction because before the End of the Correction, Malchut is called: Tree of Good and Evil, as mentioned before. The explanation is that Malchut is the secret of the Providence and Supervision of the Creator in this world, and as long as the recipients have not reached perfection so as to be able to fully receive His complete goodness that He conceived for us in the Thought of Creation, the Providence must in ways be of good and evil, reward and punishment. Because our Receiving Vessels are still filthy with selfish receiving this is much reduced in its capacity and it also separates us from the Creator. And the complete Goodness, in Its greatest extent that He conceived for us, is nothing but sharing, which is boundless pleasure without any restriction. This is not so with selfish receiving, which is very limited and restricted because satiation immediately extinguishes the pleasure.

> This is the secret of the verse: "The Lord has made everything for His own sake," (Proverbs 16:4) meaning that all the actions that occur in the world were created initially to only bestow to Him satisfaction. And so people are found attending to the dealings of the world in the exact opposite of what they were created for at first since the Holy One blessed Be He says, the whole world was created for My sake, namely, "The Lord has made everything for His own sake" (Proverbs 16:4) as well as, "all that is called by My Name; I have created for My glory." (Isaiah 43:7). And we say the exact opposite from one extreme to another because we say, the world was created just for us, and we wish to swallow all the goodness of the world for our stomach

for our pleasure and for our glory. No wonder, therefore, that we are still unworthy of receiving His complete goodness. And therefore His providence was fitted for us in the form of good and evil that is the form of reward and punishment since they are interdependent; reward and punishment are a consequence of good and evil. Since we use the receiving vessels for the opposite reason they were created for, we necessarily sense that the actions of Providence are bad for us for it is a law that the created being cannot receive evil from the Creator openly because it is a flaw, Heaven forbid, in His glory blessed be He, that the created being would conceive Him as a doer of evil; this is not appropriate to the Perfect Doer. Therefore, when a person senses bad, to the same extent the denial of the Creator's Providence is upon him, Heaven forbid, and the Supernal Doer, blessed be He, is hidden from him, which is the greatest punishment in the world.

The worst punishment in the world is when our certainty, our connection, our perception of the Creator becomes diminished. And what is the rule that precipitates this? To whatever degree we feel sad, to the degree that we feel bad, to the degree that we experience negativity, to that same degree is the Creator diminished in our mind, in our consciousness, in our life—and as Rav Ashlag say, it is in exact balance. To whatever degree we feel sadness, it is impossible to have that degree of the Light of the Creator in our life. There cannot be a revelation of the Creator and sadness together, at the same time.

To be clear: one can go through things in life that are not easy, one can experience difficulties and still have joy. There is a well-known story about Rav Zusha of Anopoli. He had a very difficult life. Once a student of the Maggid of Mezeritch, who was the teacher of Rav Zusha, asked the Maggid to teach him about the concept of blessing on difficulties, meaning to feel as blessed and joyful about things that seem to be bad as we are happy about good things that happen. The Maggid told the young man: "Go to my student, Zusha, and he will teach you about this." He did as his teacher instructed and when he arrived before Rav Zusha he said to him: "Our teacher, the Maggid, sent me to ask you how a person can feel blessed and be happy for things that are not positive in the same way that he is happy for things that are positive." Rav Zusha answered: "I don't understand. Our teacher should have sent you to someone who has had bad experiences in their life. I have never had anything bad in my life. How could I possibly teach you how to experience a bad thing in the same way as a positive thing?"

Rav Zusha got to the level where there was no bad. And because he got to the point where there was no bad experience, he was always completely connected to the Light of the Creator. Difficulties happen all the time and are part of our growth, nevertheless it is our choice how we react and respond to them. To the degree we experience sadness, to that degree we have to become disconnected from the Light of the Creator. This is the rule of the spiritual world. We cannot experience darkness while having a complete experience of the Light of the Creator.

Rav Ashlag continues:

> Thus sensing the good and evil in His Providence causes the sense of reward and punishment because he who strives not to separate from his certainty in the Creator, even when he tastes (senses) evil in Providence, is rewarded and, if Heaven forbid, he would not make an effort, he is punished as he is separated from the certainty in the Creator. And we find that even though He [the Creator] alone has done, does, and will do all actions in their entirety, nevertheless it remains hidden from those who sense good and evil because in a time of [sensing] evil, the Other Side is given power to conceal the Providence and faith [in the Creator]. Thus they [those who sense evil] have the great punishment of separation and become full of doubts and disbelief. And when they return with teshuvah (repentance), they receive a reward for that, and can again cleave to The Creator.

The idea here is that the Creator is only revealed based on our perception. If we, like Rav Zusha, have a perception of only good in our world, then we do not live in the World of Good and Evil, and therefore we can maintain a continuous and constant connection to the Light of the Creator. If we experience bad, it is only dependent on us. What happens in life is not necessarily dependent on us but how we experience it is dependent on us. If we experience it as a bad thing, as a negative thing, that precipitates and necessitates a disconnection from the Light of the Creator to whatever degree we are experiencing that bad, and then we are not revealing the complete revelation of the Names of the Creator—*Rachum veChanun* "…Merciful and Gracious…." (Exodus 34:6)

**There is no absolute perception of the Creator** is a very important concept revealed throughout the writings of Rav Ashlag. The Creator is revealed depending on how we experience our lives in this world, and we have the ability to either live within the Realm of the Tree of Knowledge Good and

Evil, where the Creator's Names are not completely revealed or we can begin living at least in the perfection of the Creator's Name, in the perfection of the Creator's revelation of "...merciful and gracious..." (Exodus 34:6), where the Creator is constantly sharing His abundance with us. This very important concept has many manifestations, and is what the Ari is discussing here.

---

12. **His simple desire:** We should not wonder how a desire is distinguishable in Ein Sof, which is lofty beyond any concept, so that it is said, "...it rose up in His simple desire, etc." This can be understood when coupled with what has been explained before, where by definition, every emanated being has in it the Desire to Receive its abundance from the Emanator—study this well. Except that in the Ein Sof it is "a simple desire," in the secret of "He and His Name are One," as said in Pirkei DeRabbi Eliezer, Chapter 1, and also in the words of the Rav [the Ari] later on, for the Light in Ein Sof is called "He" and the Desire to Receive in Ein Sof is called "His Name," and both are in the state of simple unity, without any separation whatsoever between them.

However, do not liken the separation and unity spoken of here to separation and unity in material terms, which are different by means of movement, with distance of space or closeness of space, since the spiritual essence holds no space at all, as is known. You should know though that separation among spiritual entities cannot take place in any other way but only through occurrences of Difference of Form. In such a way, if a spiritual entity acquires an additional form that is different from the form it already has, that spiritual being has departed from the state of "oneness" into two distinct aspects that distance themselves from each other in relation to the disparity of the two forms.

And just as material entities grow apart and join together by means of distance and closeness of space, so too, are spiritual entities separated or joined according to Difference of Form and Similarity of Form since Difference of Form differentiates between them while Similarity of Form attaches the one to the other. Remember this, since this is the first key to the Wisdom.

The basis and purpose of the creation of our world is to achieve Similarity of Form with the Creator, to be just like the Creator, and through this process we become completely unified with the Creator. Rav Ashlag, in his Introduction to the Zohar, speaks to this point. He says that different forms separate spiritual beings in two. When two people love each other, we can say that they are unified like in one body. The opposite can be said when they hate each other; they are completely separate, like the East from the West. This, of course, is not referring to physical space between them; this is dependent on Similarity of Form. When a person loves everything his friend loves and hates everything that his friend hates, we can say that they are unified.

This concept is something that hopefully most of us have often heard. However, we need more clarification because it is not simply about how we act; it is about how we think and it is about what we like and what we do not like. We should ask ourselves, "What about me is like the Creator's attributes?"

Many of us know that one has to give, one has to partake of actions of sharing. But we can take it a step further and really examine ourselves, *"How many of my thoughts are like the Creator's thoughts?"* Meaning, how many of my thoughts are based upon thinking about another person? It is a simple equation, the more I think about sharing with others—simply in the realm of thought, even if I do not do an action—the more my thoughts are connected to the Creator's thoughts and the more I am in a state of cleaving (*dvekut*), unified with the Creator in my mind.

The more I speak about other people in a positive way, in a way of sharing with them, the more my mouth is unified with the Creator. This is true throughout our lives. I hope many of us are asking ourselves how many of our actions are like the Creator. Meaning how much of our actions are of sharing and how much of them are of the Desire to Receive for the Self Alone. More importantly, and this is such a simple and straightforward question: "How much of my daily thought is of concern for other people?" The simple beauty of it is that every time we have a thought about another person, we have one more element of cleaving our mind to the Essence of the Creator. Every time we think only about ourselves, we bring upon us one more element of disassociation from the Light of the Creator. This simple, straightforward thought should permeate everything that we do.

Rav Ashlag says, "...he hates everything that His friend hates." What is the one thing we know the Creator does not like? He does not like the Desire to

Receive for the Self Alone. How much do we dislike the Desire to Receive for the Self Alone? Not how hard we are working on it to diminish it, but actually how much do we awaken a dislike for it. These thoughts, these feelings, these emotions also make us unified, in a state of *dvekut* or lack of *dvekut* with the Light of the Creator. These are the questions we have to constantly be asking ourselves. Our thoughts, our emotions and our feelings, both in what we like and what we dislike, as well as what we are thinking about and what we are not thinking about, are what establish the reality of whether we are more unified and have achieved more *dvekut* or less *dvekut* with the Light of the Creator.

Now you will understand the secret of: "He and His Name are One," mentioned before, and the simple unity in the Ein Sof that we are so particular about. This unity is one of the wonders of His omnipotence, for the distinction between the emanated being and the Emanator happened due to the form of the Desire to Receive that exists in the emanated but not in the Emanator, as has been explained earlier in the Inner Light commentary (Section 6). It is because of that Difference of Form that the emanated, which is distinct from the Emanator, acquires a name of its own and is called emanated rather than Emanator—study this carefully.

According to what has just been explained, we might make the mistake in thinking that the Light of Ein Sof that is called "He" does not completely cleave, Heaven forbid, to Ein Sof that is called "His Name," namely the Desire to Receive the abundance and the Light called "He." After all, the entire attribute of the Supernal Light flowing from His Essence called "He" is only to share; it has nothing whatsoever of the form of the Desire to Receive, as explained there. This is not so in the Ein Sof that is called "His Name," that has the Desire to Receive, for which reason it is different from the Supernal Light that has no Desire to Receive, Heaven forbid, as explained. And it is known that the Difference of Form creates separation, Heaven forbid.

This is what the Pirkei DeRabbi Eliezer teaches us, and the Ari later on, that this is not so, Heaven forbid, rather "He and His Name are One" in simple unity, with no distinction between them. And even though there is necessarily some Difference of Form between them, between "He" and "His Name," as explained, nevertheless this is not active there at all. And even though we do not understand this, it is so without any doubt. And concerning this the sages have said that the Ein Sof cannot be thought of or grasped at all, since this issue is beyond our mind.

As Rav Ashlag says, we have to be clear that although there were two essences in the Endless World: a Desire to Share and a Desire to Receive, nevertheless, there is a miracle—no separation was caused by this. Why? We cannot understand why. Logic would dictate that there *would* be a separation.

Whenever I read this, I am reminded of one of the known things about the Ohev Israel, the Apta Rebbe (Avraham Yehoshua Heshel of Apta, 1748 – 1825); he would never see the bad. Although the average person would see an obviously negative action as bad, no matter what someone would do, the Apte Rebbe could not see it as bad. He was connected to "He and His Name are One" (*Hu uShemo Echad*).

There is a well-known teaching of the Baal Shem Tov: **A person can only be judged if he judges someone else.** There are levels to this teaching and, many of us are trying to work on it. We see someone doing something negative, and we tell ourselves, "I cannot judge this person." Meaning, I obviously see what is bad here but I am not going to judge. This is in the Realm of what Rav Ashlag is saying here: we cannot comprehend it.

However, there are *tzadikim* (righteous souls) who get to the level where they are completely connected to the concept of the Ein Sof—where even the most negative actions cannot be seen as bad. For example, in the the Apte Rebbe's book Ohev Israel, he is always explaining things in a positive way, whether it is Noah or in an action that was done where even the Torah seems to be negative, the Apte Rebbe could not see it. We see negative things and try not to judge. He just did not see things that are negative because he was connected to this concept of *Hu uShemo Echad* of the Endless World.

On a higher level, it is important to know that every time we see something negative in someone else, we are connecting to separation. And every time we come to the point that we cannot see negative in another person, we are connecting to the secret of "He and His Name are One" (*Hu uShemo Echad*). It is said that when *Mashiach* (Messiah) comes we will be able to eat pork. There are many things that will happen because we have come closer to the concept of *Hu uShemo Echad*. There will be no separation even though things are right and wrong. We know that Nadav and Avihu, the two sons of Aaron, were the highest souls in their generation, yet they died because they seemingly disconnected. There are many explanations as to why Nadav and Avihu made all those mistakes. But it is mainly because they wanted to reveal the world of *Hu uShemo Echad* – where there is no right and wrong, where there is nothing that is wrong to do because when we go back to the World of *Hu uShemo Echad*, the Endless World, there are no negative actions. There have been many mistakes that were made in trying to come close to this concept. Nevertheless there is one thing we *can* do that is not a mistake and that is to diminish our perception of judgment. I am not referring to the level of simply seeing a person do something bad, and thinking, *This is bad but I am not going to judge this person*, rather it is to get to the point where one literally can no longer see the bad because in this way it connects us to the secret of *Hu uShemo Echad*—where even though things are opposite, one is light and one is dark, there is no difference.

Although we mentioned this concept earlier, there is a section in Rav Ashlag's Introduction to the Zohar, which is now the book The Thought of Creation, paragraph 14, which discusses the idea of the Endless World in a slightly different way and in greater detail. It is very important that we get this section clear in our mind. I would like to suggest that everyone read this at least twice.

> You find, out of necessity, that generally there are Three States to the souls. The First State is their existence in the Ein Sof, within the Thought of Creation, where they already have their future form that will appear at the End of the Correction (Tikkun). The Second State is their existence over the 6,000 years, where they were divided by the two above-mentioned Systems [of Impurity and Holiness] into body and soul, and were given the work with the Torah and the Precepts in order to transform the Desire to Receive in them into the Desire to Bestow Pleasure to their Maker and not at all for themselves.

> And during the period of this [Second] State, no correction comes to the bodies, only to the Nefesh (Lower Soul). This means that they

have to eradicate out of themselves any aspect of Receiving for Themselves, which is the aspect of the body, and remain only in the aspect of the Desire to Bestow, which is the form of the Desire of the soul. And even the souls of the *tzadikim* (righteous) will not be able to delight in paradise after death, only after their entire body has been decomposed in the earth.

The Third State is the End of the Correction of the souls after the Resurrection of the Dead when the complete correction will reach the bodies as well because then they will have transformed also the receiving itself, which is the form of the body, so that the form of pure bestowing will rest upon it, and they will be worthy of receiving for themselves all the goodness and delight and pleasure that exists in the Thought of Creation.

And when you look at these Three States, you will find that each one absolutely necessitates the existence of the other, to the extent that if it were possible for even a small part of any one of them to be cancelled, they would all be cancelled. For example, had the Third State, which is the transformation of the form of receiving to the form of bestowing not appeared, then the First State, of necessity, could not have appeared in the Ein Sof. After all, the perfection emerged [in the First State] in its entirety only because [this perfection] was destined to become manifest in the Third State, which already served in its eternity as if it were in the present. And all the perfection that was shaped in there, in that state, was as if it had been copied from the future into the present that is there. So, had it been possible for the future to be cancelled, there would not have been any reality in the present.

What Rav Ashlag is saying is that the perfection of the Endless World can only be because of the Third Reality, meaning, the perfection that humanity achieves. Rav Ashlag, in the Talmud Eser Sefirot, does not really talk about these Three Stages, but instead discusses the perfection that exists in the Endless World. It needs to be clear that the only reason there is perfection in the Endless World is because of the reality that humanity will achieve, the Final Correction (Gemar haTikkun), the complete transformation of the Desire to Receive to Desire to Share (which is where we are ultimately going) that exists in the Endless World. And because the Endless World is not dependent on time, therefore that reality—the Third Stage—exists in the

First Stage in the Endless World. This is a very important basic understanding which, as Rav Ashlag says, has to be clear in our mind.

Now we can return to the concept of "He and His Name are One" that exists in the Endless World, where "He"—the Light of the Endless World and "His Name"—the Vessel—are "One." Rav Ashlag says that this Reality is something beyond our comprehension because our mind cannot understand that two opposites can become one, completely unified with no differentiation. The law in the spiritual worlds is that unity can only be accomplished by a Similarity of Form. If one person is a giver and the other person is a giver, they are unified. If one person is a giver and one person is a receiver, they have to be opposites, they have to disconnect.

Yet in the Endless World there was "He and His Name are One," there was the sharing Light of the Creator and the Vessel, and they were unified as one. As Rav Ashlag says (Inner Light, Section 12): **"even though we cannot understand how that can be so, it is."** And this necessitates the question: If we understand what Rav Ashlag writes in The Thought of Creation, which is that the perfection that exists in the Endless World only exists there because it is partaking of the Final Correction, it is partaking of the transformation that humanity will achieve, then there is no question that there is unity in the Endless World between Light and Vessel because the Vessel in the Endless World is the Vessel that is already transformed, right?

Therefore, if at the end, the Vessel is already transformed and "He and His Name are One," the Light and the Vessel unified is easy to understand because when the Vessel wants to Receive for the Sake of Sharing and the Creator only wants to share then of course they can be unified. There is no separation between them because they are both givers. The Creator wants to give and the Vessel wants to Receive for the Sake of Sharing. So why does Rav Ashlag say that in the Endless World we cannot understand how the Light and the Vessel can be one?

The answer is that the Creator made it so that even without the Final Correction (Gemar haTikkun)—meaning even if the Vessel would have remained a complete Desire to Receive without the transformation to Desire to Receive for the Sake of Sharing—the reality in the Endless World would still be one of a complete union. Rav Ashlag says in The Thought of Creation that the Third Reality and the process that the Vessel goes through because of the need to remove Bread of Shame is a completely unnecessary step as far as the Creator is concerned. Rav Ashlag, in different essays—certainly when you read from the writings of some of Rav Ashlag's students—almost refers to the Vessel's need to remove Bread of Shame as a joke, which is difficult to comprehend.

The Creator in the Endless World had the Desire to Share and created a Vessel that had only a Desire to Receive. As far as the Creator is concerned there was complete union—which is the union that we cannot understand—and there was no need for any further steps. Then the Vessel decided by itself that it wanted to achieve an even higher level of perfection, if that can be possible, and it decided to go through the whole process that began with the Tzimtzum. But the Creator did not need any of that.

Thus, there are two steps: There is the Reality of the Endless World, which is the Creator's Desire to Share, and the Vessel's complete Desire to Receive—not transformed at all, in complete union (*Hu uShemo echad*). However within the Endless World there is a second reality, which is the Desire to Share (the Creator) and the Desire to Receive of the Vessel that is completely transformed because of the process of the 6,000 years, and that reality is able to exist in the Endless World because there is no time. This unity in the Endless World we can understand.

Therefore there are two levels of unity in the Endless World. There is the Creator's level of unity, which is a Desire to Share with a Vessel that only has a Desire to Receive, which is not what Rav Ashlag in the Thought of Creation calls the Third Stage, meaning that the Vessel is completely transformed and already exists in the Endless World. Since the Creator's Reality in the Endless World was a complete Desire to Share with the Vessel, there was a complete Desire to Receive and the Creator is fine, there is *Hu Ushmo Echad*, there is complete union.

The Second Reality in the Endless World is the Reality created by the Vessel where the Vessel completely transformed into the Desire to Receive for the Sake of Sharing, which is a union of Light and Vessel that is complete, however this perfection is only **perfection for the Vessel**.

Therefore there are two Realities in the Endless World. There is the Creator's Reality, which is a complete Desire to Share and a Vessel that has not transformed at all, the ultimate complete Desire to Receive had not transformed at all. Now, between these two, the sharer and receiver there was complete union. How can that be? That we cannot understand. We cannot comprehend where you have a complete sharer, which is the Creator and a complete receiver, which is the Vessel and still have "He and His name are one." The Creator's Reality we cannot understand, and that is the Reality that Rav Ashlag is speaking about in Talmud Eser Sefirot.

In The Thought of Creation, Rav Ashlag spoke about the Thought of Creation as already a second step, because the Creator does not need the Creation process. The Creator does not need the perfection of the Ein Sof, which has in it the perfect Third State already now since there is no time. That perfection in the Endless World is only in the reality of the Vessel and is only necessitated by the Vessel. The Creator created perfection. There was a sharing, there was receiving, and there was "He and His Name are One," there was complete union. How could that be? That is something, as Rav Ashlag says in the Talmud Eser Sefirot, we cannot understand. The Vessel began with a desire to remove Bread of Shame, and therefore started this process of the Three Realities: the Endless World, the 6,000 years, and the perfection of the Final Correction. Even in the process of the Vessel there is perfection because the Third Reality exists in the First Reality.

However, the perfection of the Endless World Rav Ashlag discusses in The Thought of Creation is a second perfection in the Endless World and is not part of the Creator's perfection. The Creator's perfection is even more perfect and simple. The Creator's perfection is not dependent on the Third Reality. The Creator's perfection in the Endless World is complete Desire to Share and a complete Desire to Receive not transformed, and there is "He and His Name are One." This is what Rav Ashlag is speaking about in the Talmud Eser Sefirot. In The Thought of Creation, Rav Ashlag is talking about the perfection that exists in the Endless World from the Vessel's perspective.

3. …then the Endless (Ein Sof) contracted itself [13] within the Middle Point, [14] in the very middle of it. And that Light contracted and distanced itself [15] to the sides around the Middle Point. [16]

13. **Contracted itself:** You already know the secret of, "He and His Name are One," which is that even though there is a Difference of Form in the aspect of the Desire to Receive included in the Ein Sof, this creates no distinction between it and the Supernal Light, rather they are in a simple unity. However, this mentioned form became the reason and cause for the creation of the Worlds and the manifestation of the perfection of His actions, Names and Appellations, as the Ari says here. Through the creation of the Worlds and their evolvement all the way down to this World, a possibility has been made and materialized for allocating a place for spiritual work by means of the Torah and the Precepts, not in order to receive but to give pleasure to the Creator.

It is then that souls are able to transform the form of the Desire to Receive that is in them—which separates them from the Emanator—into the form of the Desire to Share, namely to receive from the Emanator in order to give pleasure to Him, for He desires it so, as I wrote in Section 18, study there. This Similarity of Form with the Emanator is called Cleaving and Union, as said there, for then they are already divested of the form of the Desire to Receive and acquire the form of the Desire to Share, which is the form of the Emanator Himself. As you already know, it is the Similarity of Form that makes spiritual entities into one, and therefore, the Worlds return to their former state, as shall be discussed.

This is what the Rav [the Ari] meant: "And when it rose up in His simple desire to create…" "Rose up," meaning it rose up in terms of refinement and cleaving by reducing and contracting the amount of the Desire to Receive imprinted in it in order to match its form to the Supernal Light. And even though the Desire to Receive in Ein Sof, called Malchut of Ein Sof or "His Name," as mentioned earlier, had no deficiency in cleaving with the Supernal Light due to the Difference of Form in it, as said, nevertheless it adorned itself to match its form to the Supernal Light and withdraw from the magnitude of the Desire to Receive that is called its Fourth Phase so as to cleave more to the Supernal Light, since Closeness of Form creates cleaving, as said. This is what is meant by "rose up," that is, Malchut of Ein Sof, which is the state of "simple desire," elevated and cleaved to the Supernal Light, which means it reduced its Desire to Receive, as explained.

This is what the Rav [the Ari] meant in: "then Ein Sof contracted itself, etc [Section 3]," since it has already been explained (see Section 6) that the full extent of the abundance and Light and stature of the emanated being is measured by the amount of the Desire to Receive within It—study this well. And therefore, since the said Malchut of Ein Sof contracted itself and reduced the Desire to Receive within It, the Light and abundance were gone as a result, due to the diminishment of desire. This is the meaning of Tzimtzum—the elevation of the desire [of the Vessel] caused the Light and abundance to depart from there.

14. **Within the middle point:** This is seemingly puzzling. Since it has neither head (beginning) nor end, where does the middle come from? Moreover, are we dealing with something material that occupies space, Heaven forbid? But the idea is as we already explained that also in the Ein Sof Itself there is of necessity a distinct aspect of the Desire to Receive, though it is in a state of "simple desire," which means there is no differentiation between the levels, small or great, as said there. This is because the Desire to Receive that is there is not distinct so as to be an aspect of Difference of Form that creates some manner of separation, Heaven forbid; therefore, it is not any less in relation to the Supernal Light.

You need to know that the Supernal Light must extend through Four Phases until the Desire to Receive in the emanated is revealed up to its set and existent completion. The reason for stipulating the Four Phases is that the said Desire to Receive is comprised immediately with the extension of the Light from the root. After all, this is [what makes] the distinction: that the Light has departed from the Emanator and acquired a distinct Name, that is, the extension from the Emanator. As long as it does not include this Difference of Form of the Desire to Receive, surely it is still considered to be an Emanator rather than part of the extension that departs and is separated from the Emanator. For in spirituality, no distinction is imaginable, except through Difference of Form (as said in Section 6. Look there, and look at Inner Observation here).

It is important to keep reminding ourselves that these teachings of Rav Ashlag are truly a revelation of Ruach haKodesh (Divine Inspiration). And it is not simply the Ruach haKodesh of the prophets, which is a level where there is lack of clarity. Rav Ashlag's Ruach haKodesh was beyond the level of the prophets. Therefore when we read this—especially this section where Rav Ashlag explains the Four Phases—we know that we are literally witnessing a complete revelation of Ruach haKodesh. This is something to truly appreciate. It is crazy to think that thousands of kabbalists before the time of Rav Ashlag did not understand this. Without going into the details, Rav Ashlag in *Beit Sha'ar haKavanot* ("House of the Gate of Meditations") says a great deal about kabbalists—many of whom wrote books—yet did not really understand the concepts in a clear and concise way. And it was not their fault—the world was not ready for these revelations. Rav Ashlag's soul was chosen and he was able to reveal this Light—the revelation of the Four Phases, not only with Divine Inspiration but with clarity. We need to appreciate this gift of being privy to witness and connect to this level of Ruach haKodesh.

Rav Ashlag says that the Vessel cannot become solidified unless it goes through these Four Phases. It is important to understand the correlation here to our own spiritual work because Rav Ashlag explains that unless existence goes through these Four Phases it cannot be long-term. Therefore this is a very important understanding.

**The First Phase** is the Creator wanting to give, and because the Creator desired to give there was a creation of the Vessel. But this Vessel did not really want to receive all that the Creator wanted to give. For example: I walk into a room holding a bottle of purple liquid that the person next to me has never tasted and I say, "I want you to taste this." And this person, even though he may be thirsty for water, he is not thirsty for this purple liquid. He does not know what it is, whether it is good or if it is bad. Nevertheless, I really want him to taste it, to drink it. Finally he relents and accepts it. Does he have a Desire to Receive? Not really. He obviously has some level of desire if he says "Yes." However, it is not a real desire. It is simply that I want him to drink and he likes me and he does not want to offend me by saying no, so he says, "Yes."

The First Phase of the Four Phases is when the Vessel says "I will receive." It does not know what it is receiving, therefore it cannot really have a desire for it. But because the sharer [the Creator] wants to share, the Vessel says, "Okay, I'll take it." Obivously this is certainly not a strong, real desire.

What differentiates this new Vessel, this new reality from the Creator (the sharer) is that the Vessel now has a desire. The First Phase of desire says, "Yes, I will drink it. If you want me to, I will taste it." This becomes a new reality, and in the Vessel, this is the first inkling that there is a difference now between the Creator and the Vessel. As Rav Ashlag will explain, and the Ari discusses later (in Talmud Eser Sefirot, Volume 3), there has to always be a middle ground between any two stages, between any two Realities. The First Phase is really the middle ground between Light and Vessel because this Vessel has very little real difference between it and the Creator. It is almost like the perfected Vessel in the Final Correction but not quite, because a perfected Vessel has to have a real desire and then restrict upon it, nevertheless the First Phase is very close to the Creator's Reality, which is a Desire to Share.

As Rav Ashlag will explain, the First Phase is called Chochmah since this Desire is only a desire because, *"You are the Creator, You want to give me, so I will receive it. I do not even know what it is; I do not know if I will like it. I want to share with You; I want to do You a favor and receive it."* This desire is a little bit like the Creator but it is the First Phase that is becoming a Vessel because it is saying, "Yes, I want to receive." The reason for its receiving is not perfect, it is not the ultimate strong desire, yet it is already different from the Creator because the Creator never says, "I want to receive anything," even for the sake of sharing. The Creator only shares. Thus as long as the desire is not an ultimate strong desire and is only a way to say yes to the giver, then there is no way that that Vessel is going to be a strong Vessel.

However, as long as this desire is not made apparent by the emanated being itself [the Vessel], it is not fixed in the emanated. In other words, the emanated needs to yearn to receive the abundance. This is when it is considered that the Desire to Receive is revealed by the emanated itself. This yearning can only exist when it no [longer] contains that abundance because only then is it possible for [the emanated] to yearn for that abundance, so that the Desire to Receive will be manifest in it of its own accord. Then the Vessels of Receiving are complete and set.

This teaches us about our own spiritual work, as well as helps us understand other people's processes. Athough a person has to go through the First Phase where they receive Chochmah (wisdom, understanding) they have to lose it. They have to come to a place where they lose it and then desire it for themselves again. If a person has not gone through or does not go through this process, then as the saying goes "if you don't work hard for it, and you think you found it, don't believe it's going to last." (Tractate Megillah 6b) This is what Rav Ashlag is saying here.

Rav Brandwein, in one of the letters he wrote to the Rav, says that in the Study of the Ten Luminous Emanations you will find everything that has occurred in our world from the time of Creation until now, and onward, yet sometimes when we study this wisdom, we do not see everything that exists in our world. Thus part of the work is in finding how this manifests in our world and how the Study of the Ten Luminous Emanations is the explanation of the reality that occurs all around us.

Thus what Rav Ashlag is saying here certainly applies to our own spiritual work. Very often there are people who become involved in activities at the Kabbalah Centres because they are excited by what they have learned, they have connected to the Ohr deChochmah (Light of Wisdom), the First Phase; they come to understand things in an incredible way, and it is so great. But Rav Ashlag says that it will not last; it cannot last. There cannot be a lasting or sustaining of this Light; there has to be a complete loss of it, and then a true awakening to receive it anew. This is the only way this Light can be sustained. This is a very important lesson both in understanding how the Vessels were created as well as growing our awareness of our own spiritual development and the process that every student must go through.

> Another thing you need to know is that every extension of Light from the Emanator, just as it includes the aspect of the Desire to Receive, as said, it also of necessity includes the Desire to Share. For otherwise, the Emanator and the Emanated would be in a state of Opposition of Form, which is complete separation, Heaven forbid, since the Opposition of Form would have made them as far apart from each other as east is from west. Therefore, each Light that extends from the Emanator must include the aspect of the Desire to Share, so that there will be closeness of form between the Emanator and the Emanated Being.

To create a perfect Vessel, the Creator has to create two opposite Desires within the Vessel. The Creator knows that if He created only a Desire to Receive within this Vessel, it would not be able to sustain itself. The Vessel must also have a Desire to Share. But it is a joke because what does the Creator want? The Creator wants the Vessel to receive. Does the Creator care whether the Vessel will share or not? No. But for the Vessel to be able to receive the Light it has to have this little "joke" in the back of its mind: *"Yes, I also want to share, and therefore I can receive the Light of the Creator."* If the Vessel had no inkling of a Desire to Share, it could not receive the Light of the Creator, because the Light of the Creator is only sharing, and if the two desires are completely opposite they cannot be attached. Therefore, the Creator had to create a trick within this Vessel. He created a Vessel with the Desire to Receive that also contained a trick within of a Desire to Share.

How many times in life do we fall for this trick, thinking we have a true Desire to Share? Rav Ashlag says this Desire to Share that we are born with is a joke and it is not a reality. It is a trick that the Creator had to inject within the Vessel, within us, to allow us to receive the Creator's Light, because if we did not have a Desire to Share, the Vessel, we, would be completely disconnected. We see it very often, both in ourselves and in others. We find people who have an innate Desire to Share, which we now know is a joke. It is a trick. It is what the Creator needed to supply the Vessel for it to continue receiving and receiving and receiving, by telling itself, *"I'm also doing the sharing, and therefore I'm allowed and it's all right for me to continue receiving."* What we have to do when going through this process is completely disassociate ourselves from that Desire to Share because it is not a real Desire to Share, and then we can awaken a true Desire to Share.

Any natural in built Desire to Share that we have, that others have is not a real Desire to Share. It is a fail-safe Desire to Share that the Creator had to instill within the Vessel so that it would be able to receive. We find this when a person with the largest ego, the most Desire to Receive for the Self Alone still has a Desire to Share. Where does that come from? That is a trick the Creator had to put into that Vessel. It is not something that is real, that will be sustained. The only Desire to Share that is sustained is the Desire to Share that is removed and is then brought back. This is a very important idea.

---

When this Desire to Share is revealed in the emanated being, a great Light is drawn from the Emanator, correlating to the awakening of this desire. This Light is universally called Light of Chasadim. However, the First Extension from the Emanator, in which the Desire to Receive is included, as explained above, is universally called the Light of Chochmah or Light of the Essence. Remember well these two kinds of Light.

Know that the second Light, the Light of Chasadim, is much more inferior to the first Light, the Light of Chochmah because the former is drawn with the strengthening and the awakening of the emanated from its own accord due to its desire to make its form similar to the Emanator, which is why it strengthened and awakened to become an aspect of the Desire to Share, as explained. This is not so with the First Extension, which is the Light of Chochmah. It flows directly from the Emanator, and the emanated has no part in its flow. It is, therefore, incomparably superior. Thus, the Light of Chochmah is considered the essence and vitality of the emanated, while the Light of Chasadim is considered merely a Light of correction to complete the emanated being.

Now you can understand the Four Phases and levels stipulated in every emanated being, as said. At first, the Light extends and departs from the Emanator, as said, as Light of Chochmah, in which the Desire to Receive alone is included. This is the First Phase. Then the aspect of the Desire to Share grows stronger in this Light and causes the Light of Chasadim to flow, as said. This awakening is considered the Second Phase. This Light of Chasadim then extends a big extension, which will be explained later. This is the Third Phase.

This process is one that is certainly true of the first Vessel that ever came into being, the first Vessel of the Light of Ein Sof. However, it is also true of any true process, even the spiritual process that humanity goes through, that each and every one of us go through.

The **First Phase** is when the Creator wants to share, and the Vessel that is created does not really have a desire, nevertheless it knows its purpose: *"I was created to receive, so I'll receive."* For example: If I visit a person at their home and although I am not at all thirsty, the host offers me a drink that I do not want and probably do not even like, yet I know he has a strong Desire to Share so I say, "Okay" and I take it. There is clearly no real desire there. This stage is called the First Phase, it is Chochmah.

Because of the innate Desire to Share—the trick—that was instilled into the Vessel by the Creator—my Desire to Share becomes awakened; there is a little taste of Bread of Shame. Even though I received without desiring to receive, nonetheless I still got something from the person. Now I have a Desire to Share, and this Desire to Share is called Binah. And that awakening from the Vessel is called the **Second Phase**.

To summarize: I visit a person's house, he gives me something. I accept it, not because I have any desire for it but because he wants to share it with me. However now I feel a little bit uncomfortable because he has given me something even though I did not really want it. Now I want to share. I want to do something in return so I will not feel so bad, and I do an action of sharing. This process represents the first **Three Phases**.

> After the Three Phases have emerged and are revealed to completion, the Desire to Receive, which is included in the first extension, awakens again and draws the Light of Chochmah again. This is the utmost perfection of the permanence of the Desire to Receive in the Partzuf, since it is revealed in the sense of yearning, that is, when there is no Light of Chochmah in the Partzuf but only Light of Chasadim, namely, after the said Third Phase. For then the emanated was in a position to yearn to receive the Light of Chochmah, a yearning that makes the Desire to Receive established in the Emanated and completes its Vessel of Receiving. This is not the case with the First Extension (as said [at the beginning of Section 14] in the paragraph starting with the words: "The reason for stipulating…").

After the Vessel has an awakened Desire to Share it becomes all about sharing and it shares a huge amount of Light of Mercy (Ohr deChasadim), a tremendous amount of Light that does not have any connection to that first Light because now the Vessel has become all involved in sharing, involved in awakening from its own strength, its own desire. The Vessel no longer has a connection to the Light of the Creator and now it wants that back because it once tasted what that Light could be. It once tasted that Light and now it has also tasted what it is like to be only sharing. The Vessel decides: *"You know what? I really liked that first feeling more, I really liked the Light of Wisdom (Ohr deChochmah) better."*

Here is an example. I come to someone's home and he puts a steak in front of me but I have never seen a steak before in my life. He tells me to eat it. I do not really have a desire for it but he very much wants me to eat it, so I do him a favor and I eat the steak. Then to some degree or another, I enjoy it. Now, however, I feel bad that I have done nothing in return for the steak, so I go and help him wash the dishes. A while later, I feel hungry because I am now aware of what the next steak will taste like. I do not want to help him wash the dishes. I do not want to help him clean the house. I only want that steak again. Now I can have a true desire for steak because I have had it and I have experienced the time when I did not have it due to my desire to share. Now I really want that steak back, now I really want the Light of the Creator back—this is the time when the Vessel becomes complete.

---

Therefore, the Vessels of Receiving are only completed with the Fourth Phase, which is also called the Second Awakening. After the completion of the Fourth Phase in the Ein Sof, a Tzimtzum took place in it, which means the departure of the Desire to Receive from that Fourth Phase. This caused the departure of the Light of the Ein Sof from there (as said in [the end of] Section 13, starting with: "This is what the Rav [the Ari] meant…"—study this carefully).

---

The Ari talks about the Endless World (Ein Sof) as a simple place where not very much happens. Obviously, a lot did take place in the Endless World, and what Rav Ashlag is saying here is that the Vessel becoming a Vessel occurred in the Endless World—the Four Phases actually occurred in the Endless World. The Vessel went through receiving for the sake of receiving—meaning the Creator wanted to give the Vessel Light; then there was an awakening of a Desire to Share; then the Creator gave the Vessel the ability to share and receive the joy that sharing is; and then there was a real awakening of the Desire to Receive, which is the Fourth Phase, Malchut. All this occurred within the Endless World.

After the Vessel says, "I really want that Light," and the Light fills it up, which is the Fourth Phase, the Vessel realizes that it will never be happy unless it goes through a process of transformation to remove the Bread of Shame, this is where the Tzimtzum occurred.

This elucidates the Four Phases stipulated in every emanated being. The First Phase is called the First Extension or Chochmah; the Second Phase is called the First Awakening or Binah; the Third Phase is called the Second Extension or Zeir Anpin; the Fourth Phase is called the Second Awakening or Malchut.

| Light of Chochmah | Masculine | Chochmah | First Phase | First Extension |
|---|---|---|---|---|
| Desire to Share | Feminine | Binah | Second Phase | First Awakening |
| Light of Chasadim | Masculine | Zeir Anpin | Third Phase | Second Extension |
| Desire to Receive | Feminine | Malchut | Fourth Phase | Second Awakening |

The two Extensions are considered masculine as they are the aspect of abundance flowing from the Emanator, since the First Extension is the abundance of the Light of Chochmah and the Second Extension is the abundance of the Light of Chasadim.

When the Vessel decides to awaken itself, when it decides to do something of its own accord, it obviously diminishes the amount of Light that can be revealed. This is an important concept that applies to everyone, but specifically those of us who dedicate our lives to helping others. To the degree that we take ourselves out of the picture, meaning where we do not consider our actions as our own, to that degree the Ohr deChochmah—the real Light of the Creator—can come into it. Conversely to the degree that we believe that we are doing, to the degree that our ego becomes involved, to the degree that we think we are manifesting, to that degree we will only manifest the Ohr deChasadim.

Light that is awakened by the Vessel can only be of a low Light, which is the Light of Mercy (Ohr deChasadim). Rav Ashlag has already made it very clear that this level of Light is terribly insignificant as compared to the real Light of the Creator, which is the Light of Wisdom (Ohr deChochmah). Ohr deChasadim is the Light of the Creator that is clothed and concealed by the desire of the Vessel. Thus obviously there is a much greater limit to what this type of Light can do.

Therefore to the degree we remove ourselves from the process, to that degree we allow the Light of the Creator, the Ohr deChochmah, to flow. When we think that we are doing, when we inject ourselves into that revelation, we cause only Ohr deChasadim to be revealed. So even with the greatest acheivement that we can accomplish, as long as we are involved in it, it can only be Ohr deChasadim, which is a tremendously lower level than the real Light of the Creator, than the Ohr deChochmah.

The two Awakenings are both feminine since they are the aspect of the awakening of the Emanated and the strengthening of desire on its own accord. The first strengthening is the awakening within the emanated following the Desire to Share, which becomes the root for the Light of Chasadim, as said. The second strengthening is the awakening within the Emanated following the Desire to Receive, which becomes the aspect of a Vessel of Receiving for the Partzuf in all its desired completion, and it is universally called the Fourth Phase.

Before I discuss Rav Ashlag's explanation as to how this fits into the words of the Ari, I want to repeat that this is a stage every person goes through in their spiritual work. In the First Phase one receives wisdom. For example, one comes to the Kabbalah Centres or one comes to an understanding and that understanding awakens something within the individual. What does it awaken? It hopefully awakens, a Desire to Share. People get stuck in different stages. Some get stuck in a Desire to Share—I want to give. They give and give and give nonetheless, they are still only revealing the Ohr deChasadim, which is a very low level of Light. When this is the case, a person has to go through the Fourth Phase, they have to go through a stage where the Light that they had is taken away from them. Then they work on it, awakening a real desire for it, and get it back. If a person, in their spiritual work, never gets to the point where they lose the Light and then awakens within themselves a true desire to get it back, it will never be sustained, as Rav Ashlag says.

The Talmud says: "A man does not fully understand the words of the Torah until he has come to stumble over them." (Tractate Gittin 43a) To whatever degree a person has fallen and then re-gains it back, to that degree those words are his. If a person goes through a process and gains wisdom and then awakens a Desire to Share, and shares and shares, this will not be sustained unless that person falls and loses it all and then awakens a true desire to receive it back.

The Baal Shem Tov teaches that when a person begins his spiritual process, the Creator gives him gifts to ease him into the path. But at some point, when the person has to earn it for himself, all is taken away from him. Only the person who goes through the process of having it all taken away from him and then awakens his Desire to Receive, and does the work he needs to do—gets to keep it. But if a person does not fail—meaning the person does not lose it, but rather stays either in the level of Chochmah or in the level of Binah and Zeir Anpin, which is an awakening of a Desire to Share—it is not sustainable. It is only when a person goes through the Fourth Phase that it can be sustained, meaning he has gone through the process of the removal of Light, a Tzimtzum, and then he has awakened the Desire to Receive for the Self Alone.

Let us reflect on these Four Phases and how they apply to us. I think everyone goes through Chochmah; everyone gets to the point where they receive wisdom—some they may want, some they may not want. Then, hopefully, they awaken a Desire to Share, they awaken Binah, and they awaken some manifestation of that in Zeir Anpin. Yet how many people go through the process of Tzimtzum, meaning that they lose both their desire and the Light, and then they awaken a true desire for that Light? Only a person who has gone through these Four Phases will actually have a sustainable connection that lasts.

This is what happens even on the most basic level—people become spiritual, and they start forgetting about their Desire to Receive. However, the Vessel cannot sustain itself without a Desire to Receive. There has to be a reawakening of that Desire to Receive—and then work from there. Only with a true disconnect from the Light of the Creator can a person truly earn and maintain a lasting connection with the Light of the Creator.

This Fourth Phase is called the Middle point in the Ein Sof, which is what the Rav [the Ari] meant when he said (here, Etz Chayim [Tree of Life], 1:3): "And then the Ein Sof contracted Itself within the Middle Point, in the very middle of it." It is so called since it is the Vessel of Receiving for the Light of Ein Sof, [a Vessel] that is entirely measureless and limitless. Therefore, its existence is likened to a point in the inside and in the middle of that Light; and the Light circles it and is attached to it, round and round immeasurably.

It is in this manner alone that it is possible for it to contain Supernal Light without measure or limit at all. This is not the case with other Vessels of receiving after the Tzimtzum and below, namely in the Lower emanated Beings. In them, the Vessels of receiving are considered to be containing their Light within and inside them; namely it is the walls of the Vessels—which relate to their Four Phases—that impose a limit and measure upon the Light within them. This is due to the coarseness of the Vessels, as shall be discussed later. It is not so in the Ein Sof, where the Light and Vessel are in simple unity, in a state of "He and His name are One" (as said in Section 12, starting with: "According to..."). Thus, the Vessel does not limit the Light it contains at all, and therefore, the Light in it is considered Endless.

Thus, the secret of the Middle Point in the Ein Sof was well elucidated. It does not refer to material, tangible space or area, Heaven forbid; rather it is the Fourth Phase that is included in Ein Sof that is so named after its simple unity with the Supernal Light, as explained. The subject of the Tzimtzum that takes place within the Middle Point has already been explained in Section 13, starting with [the words]: "This is what the Rav [the Ari] meant: And when it rose up..."—study there carefully.

This is a necessary and amazing understanding. There is a Desire to Receive in the Endless World and there is a Desire to Receive after the Endless World. What the Ari and Rav Ashlag reveal here is that although the desire is the same, the *way* it receives becomes different. When we think about the Desire to Receive, we may imagine that all Desires to Receive are the same but they are not. There is the Desire to Receive of the Endless World and there is Desire to Receive that occurred after the Tzimtzum. These two Desires to Receive are completely different.

How do we naturally receive? We receive internally: *I am happy; I feel good; I feel connected; I feel the Light of the Creator.* But the Desire to Receive in the Endless World was a Vessel that was capable of partaking in enjoyment even when it was not receiving. It was a very high level of receiving because imagine how could one possibly receive endlessly? If there is a Desire to Receive, that receiving has a limit. There is an important distinction here to understand. Not only do we have to purify our Desire to Receive and go through a process of transforming it into a Desire to Share but the actual process by which we receive also has to become different.

One of the concepts Rav Ashlag speaks about in the Introductions is that we have to come to the point where we enjoy someone else's joy as much as we enjoy our own joy; to feel someone else's pain as much as we feel our own pain. As a matter of fact, it says if a person is not capable of feeling the pain of those around him, in the community around him, he will not merit seeing the coming of Mashiach (Messiah). This is such an important concept.

If a person does not feel the pain of others they will not merit seeing the Redemption (Ge'ulah). Therefore we have to awaken this desire and ability to feel someone else's pain as our own. I often think, that if someone tells us that they have a stomach ache, and we have just recently experienced one, we would know what it feels like. Yet, there is no way that we can awaken within ourselves that same feeling of pain for that person as we did for ourselves. This inability to feel the pain or the joy of others, to whatever degree limits our connection to the Light of the Creator, and more dangerous than that, Heaven forbid, it limits our ability to experience the Redemption. This is something that we have to work on.

Rav Ashlag says here that the Desire to Receive in the Endless World was an amazingly beautiful Desire to Receive, meaning the Vessel of the Endless was even able to feel the Light that it was not receiving directly. To use an example from our experience it is as though someone else is feeling joy and it feels to me like my own joy. This feeling is a taste of the Endless Vessel; the Vessel in the Endless World. Whereas all the Vessels that followed the Tzimtzum, are Vessels that can only internally experience the joy that comes to us; even with physical things. And with spiritual matters, how much joy do we feel in our connection to the Light of the Creator in comparison to the joy we feel when someone else is having a connection to the Light of the Creator? To begin tasting of the Desire to Receive of the Endless World requires our work.

Rav Ashlag says it is very important to understand that the Desire to Receive for the Self Alone becomes transformed through the process of Tzimtzum— now there is darkness within the Desire to Receive for the Self Alone—where now the only way, the base way, the low way that we feel joy is for ourselves internally. This is why, when discussing the Endless World, the Ari uses the term the Central Point, indicating that the Light surrounds it and is around it, meaning *I do not have to receive inside to feel the Light of the Creator.* The Light of the Creator can be out there and I feel it. It can be in another person, it can be happening out there. That ability to start feeling that the Light of the Creator is everywhere even if I am not receiving it right now, nonetheless I feel the joy of it—this is a taste of the Vessel in the Endless World.

Therefore, when Rav Ashlag says that the Vessels after the Tzimtzum have the Light within them, meaning they limit the amount of Light that comes into them: *"I can only enjoy what happens to me (whether physical or spiritual),"* this is not true. Even though the term Desire to Receive or the Vessel is the same term used with regard to both the Endless World and after the Tzimtzum (Restriction), the two are different Vessels. Before the Tzimzum, the Vessel does not limit the amount of Light and therefore, the Light that it receives is endless. One of the lessons we learn from this is that we have to grow our connection to the Vessel of the Endless World. What is the Vessel of the Endless World? It is being able to partake of the joy of someone else as if it is our own; it is being able to truly feel the Light of the Creator even if the connection is not happening to me but it is happening to someone else.

---

15. **Distanced itself:** Spiritual distance has already been clarified in Section 12, starting with [the words], "Do not liken…,"—look there. It has also been explained that in the Ein Sof there was no distance, Heaven forbid, between the Middle Point, which is the secret of the Vessel, and the Light; see there. But after the Light contracted from within the Middle Point, its Difference of Form from the Light became apparent since the Supernal Light has nothing of the aspect of the Desire to Receive, and the point is in the category of Desire to Receive, which is different from the Light, as said. And since the form of the one became different from the other, they are as far away from each other to the extent of the level of this difference, as said. This is what the Rav [the Ari] meant in: "…and distanced itself, etc."

---

When the Ari says that the Light became distanced, this is the same thing that occurs to us. The question we have to ask ourselves is, "How distant are we from the Light of the Creator?" which only means one thing: How different are we—in our nature, in how we act, in who we are— from the Light of the Creator? This difference indicates distance. And it says that when we get closer to the month of Elul (Virgo), the Creator is open, the Creator is closer to us than in any other time. What is special about Elul is that the universe, the framework, the Light of the Creator is more around to push us towards the change in our essence, in our nature, that we need to make to get close to this Light.

Therefore the question we have to ask ourselves is, "How far are we?" How much distance have we created? Do we create more or less distance, day after day, or week after week through our actions, our thoughts, our words? Are they more of a Desire to Share or are they more of a Desire to Receive?

---

16. **To the sides around the Middle Point:** The mentioned Four Phases are also called Four Sides. The Rav [the Ari] is implying here that even though the Tzimtzum occurred only in the Middle Point, which is the Fourth Phase, as mentioned, the Light nevertheless departed from all Four Phases since the concept of "a little bit" does not apply to spiritual essences. Therefore, it was gone from the other Three Phases as well.

---

What Rav Ashlag is saying here is that if something happens in the spiritual sense, it happens completely; if something does not happen in the spiritual sense, it does not happen completely. This explains why the Light had to leave Chochmah, Binah, and Zeir Anpin (the first Three Phases). Although the purpose of the Tzimtzum was only concerning the Fourth Phase of the Vessel, nevertheless the Light had to leave the first three Phases because if it leaves a Vessel, it leaves it completely. If it comes to a Vessel, it comes completely. "A little bit" does not occur in the spiritual world. And this is an important concept that has a lot of ramifications.

There is a famous quote in the Midrash, which is referred to in the Zohar, where the Creator says, "Open to me an opening no greater than the eye of a needle and I will open to you Supernal Gates." The Kotzker Rebbe (Rav Menachem Mendel of Kotzk, 1787 – 1859) asks, "Why does the Midrash and the Zohar use the example of the eye of a needle when talking about something small? One could say 'small as a grain of sand.' There are many examples one can give for small things. Why did the Zohar and the Midrash specifically cite the eye of a needle?"

The Kotzker Rebbe answers that although the opening can be small—the opening that we have to make through our work has to be complete. And the "eye of a needle" indicates a small opening that is open complete from side to side. If the example of a grain of sand were used, it would only indicate the size is small. The Zohar specifically used "the eye of a needle" to reveal to us that though the opening that we create can be small in size, it nonetheless has to be complete because an incomplete opening does not work. This has ramifications to our spiritual work.

There is another lesson from the Kotzker Rebbe where he discusses the *mikveh* (spiritual immersion). When one goes into the *mikveh*, one needs to completely immerse themselves in the water of the *mikveh*. If even one hair remains out of the water and the person is not completely immersed, the person does not become pure. Why is this? It is the same idea—the amount of the work we do is not as important as the completeness of it. If our work is not complete, it is not connected to the Light of the Creator because there is no "little" or "lot" in the spiritual work, there is only "complete" or "incomplete." This has no relationship to the quanity of our work because what is important is the completeness of the work that we are doing.

There is a story from the period of Eliyahu HaNavi (Elijah the Prophet) that explains this well: The people were both serving the Creator and also worshipping idols. Eliyahu HaNavi asked them: "How long will you keep hopping between two opinions?" (I Kings 18:21) He told them they have to make a choice. One can either engage in idol worship or commit completely to the Creator. There is no middle ground. This begs the question, did he really mean that they should make a choice to go either completely to the negative, or completely to the positive? Is it not better to be in some sort of middle ground, which is probably where most of us are—sometimes we are really bad, sometimes we are really good, which when all is summed up it puts us somewhere in the middle? The answer is it is not better. As Eliyahu HaNavi said, we have to make a choice. And the choice is not about quantity. It is not about how much work one does, it is about how complete is the work.

In the work that we do in our spiritual growth, there are things that excite us and things that do not excite us. We may even have a vision that the work we are doing is grand and being great excites us. However, when it seems that the work is somehow diminished, not as exciting nor as revealing, not manifesting in the ways—both physically and spiritually—that we had hoped, our appreciation of the work we are doing is diminished.

One of the things that Rav Ashlag tells us we can learn from this law is that although we are blessed to do the work that we do, it is almost not important. Let me be clear it is not that this work is unimportant because it is. However, the idea is that it is less important *what* a person does; what is important is that whatever a person does be complete. When what we do is complete then we are connected to the Light of the Creator. If what a person does is incomplete, then that person is disconnecting from the Light of the Creator. There is no middle ground. You are either connecting to the Light of the Creator or you are connecting to darkness.

This means *not* to ask ourselves "Is what I have accomplished great or is it small?" The question to ask is: "In the work that I am doing, am I completely 100 percent in it?" And if I am completely in it, then I am completely connected to the Light of the Creator regardless of how important it is, or how unimportant it is, how great its manifestation is or how limited the manifestation. The singular most important question we have to ask ourselves is: *"How complete am I in it?"* If I am holding back, if I am incomplete in investing myself wholly in the work that I am doing, I am not connected to the Light of the Creator. If I am completely invested in the work that I am doing then I am completely connected to the Light of the Creator regardless of what the manifestation is, regardless of what I am doing because there is no "a little bit." This is a very important lesson and understanding.

These words and concept from Rav Ashlag, are something we can think about for a whole week or more and I hope that we take the time to internalize it, to digest these words. I very much enjoy reading the Haftarahs from Jeremiah and Isaiah, who are two of my favorite prophets. The words of these Haftarahs are truly amazing, both in their phrasing and the way their prophecies were revealed. These words from Rav Ashlag are no less in prophecy, no less in Divine Inspiration (*Ruach haKodesh*) than the words of the prophets. I truly believe that a phrase like this, which came through *Ruach haKodesh* to Rav Ashlag, is one of those concepts that we can think about for a long time and find a tremendous depth and a tremendous taste of the profundity of that phrase "…the Light nevertheless departed from all Four Phases since the concept of "a little bit" does not apply to spiritual essences…" and of this wisdom. We can come to the level of: "Taste and see that the Creator is good." (Psalms 34:9)

4. Then what remained was a vacant place,[17] and air and empty space in the very Middle Point. So, this Contraction (Tzimtzum) was all equally even around that empty Middle Point,[18] in such a way that the place of that space was Circle-like all around[19]—completely equal and even. It had not the shape of a square with a right angle, since the Endless (Ein Sof) also contracted Itself in the likeness of a Circle, equally even all-around.

17. **What remained was a vacant place:** This has been explained above in Sections 4 and 5—look there.

18. **This Contraction (Tzimtzum) was all equally even around that empty Middle point:** That is, without differentiating between the levels, being small and big. You might argue that since a Difference of Form inside the Middle point has already been made apparent by the departure of the Light from it, by necessity the smaller dimensions have become defined—one lesser than the other—through the Difference of Form within the previous Three Phases. In such a case, the Third Phase for example, would be purer than the Middle Point (the Fourth Phase), since the amount of Desire to Receive in it is lesser than in the Fourth Phase. Similarly, the Second Phase would be purer than the Third Phase, since the amount of the desire in it was lesser than in the Third Phase. The First Phase would be the purest of them all, since it has the least amount of Desire to Receive, and therefore its Difference of Form is not as recognizable as theirs. But this would have meant that there is a distinction between small and big levels. How then, does the Rav [the Ari] say that "the Tzimtzum was equally even around the empty Middle Point"?

The answer is that the Tzimtzum did not turn the Middle Point into an aspect of "finite." In other words, if the reason for the Light departing from the Point was because of its Difference of Form, surely it would have become an aspect of "finite," namely the least level, without any lesser than it. Then we would have differentiated between the previous Three Phases as more important than the Middle Point in a way of one above the other. But this was not the case, since the Tzimtzum did not occur due to the Difference of Form in the Point, as that would be impossible since we are still dealing with Malchut of Ein Sof, where there is no Difference of Form between It (Malchut) and the Light, as both are in [a state of] simple unity in the secret of "He and His name are One," as said.

Rav Ashlag asks, "How can the Ari say that the Tzimtzum occurred equally? How can the Ari say that after the Tzimtzum and during the Tzimtzum there was no difference between the Light leaving the first Three Phases and the Light leaving Malchut?" Rav Ashlag answers that the Tzimtzum did not make Malchut, the greatest Desire to Receive for the Self Alone, an end. If the reason the Light left the Vessel was because of the Difference of Form of the Vessel, then certainly the Light leaving would have made it so that the Fourth Phase (the greatest Desire to Receive for the Self Alone) would be an end and completely different from the first Three Phases, completely separate from the Light of the Creator. That would mean that the Fourth Phase would be viewed to be the lowest of the Four. And that said, it could be interpreted that the first Three are more important than the Fourth—that the First is purer than the Second, and the Second is purer than the Third and the Third is purer than the Fourth. If the reason for the Tzimtzum was the Difference of Form, then the Tzimtzum would not have occurred equally. The reason things occur indicates the residue of what occurs, and the desire or the awakening that we have to do any action is what manifests. What the Ari and Rav Ashlag are saying here is an amazing concept.

If you look objectively at the reality after the Tzimtzum, the Malchut is worse than the first Three. This is the objective reality. If we take a snapshot of the reality after the Tzimtzum, the greatest Desire to Receive is at a state of greater separation from the Light of the Creator than the first Three, therefore it worse than the first Three. But there is no objective reality. What influences and creates reality is the *reason* why things occur.

As the Ari and Rav Ashlag make clear, the reason the Tzimtzum occurred was not because of a problem; it was not because of a Difference of Form between the Light and Vessel. And because the reason for the Tzimtzum was not negative, the manifestation cannot be negative. The Tzimtzum had to occur equally becaue if one looks at it objectively, the Fourth Phase seems worse than the other Three, however one cannot look at something in its state right now, one has to look at the reason behind it coming to this state. If the reason of it coming to this state is a positive reason, then the reality now has to be positive, and if the reason behind it coming to this state right now is negative, then the reality now is also negative.

The important lesson is: **The thought and reason behind what we do is more important than what we do.** If we manifest great things but the reason and thought behind it was not great, was not perfect, was not pure, then it does not make a difference what the objective reality of the manifestation is. What makes a difference is the reason, the cause, and if the cause is perfect, even if the manifestation is objectively imperfect, objectively negative, objectively bad, as far as the Light of the Creator is concerned (which is the only true reality), it is positive. If the cause is negative, then it does not make any difference what the objective manifestation is—it is negative.

This is such an important lesson because with everything we do, we are so often fooled by manifestation. We tend to see a manifestation as either positive or negative and that influences everything. We think if the manifestation is positive, then everything is good; if the manifestation is negative, then everything is bad. But what the Ari is revealing to us and what Rav Ashlag is clarifying is that there is no objective manifestation. There is no such thing as objective reality.

The cause of the Tzimtzum is more important than the effect because the cause of the Tzimtzum was not something negative. It was not that the Vessel felt different from the Creator. The cause was an ethereal, almost impossible-to-understand desire of the Vessel to elevate itself, although it was perfect. The cause of the Tzimtzum was positive, therefore the effect, in reality, was positive.

If we are blind to the cause, which all of us often are, we just look at what happens, and what do we have when we look at what happens? We have a Fourth Phase, which is the greatest Desire to Receive, which is the greatest separation from the Light of the Creator, which is a negative reality here. But there is no negative reality if the cause was positive. For us the lesson is that the cause, the reason, the thought behind what we do is so much more important than what the manifestation is, what the effect is. Very often when we are trying to be spiritual, we think, *"If my consciousness, if my cause, if my thought beforehand is not pure, then the manifestation will not be that good."* This is not true. In fact, the thought could be good and the objective physical manifestation may not be good or conversely the thought could be bad and yet the objective physical manifestation could be good. It makes no difference, the only thing we have to be looking at is what the spiritual manifestation is. And we cannot see that with our physical eyes, but we can know it. Rav Ashlag and the Ari make very clear here that because the cause of the Tzimtzum was positive, even though the effect would seem to be objectively dark and negative and different, it is not.

We need to really take the time to work through these two concepts in our mind: one, that there is no difference between the Light leaving the Fourth Phase and the rest of the Phases, which is such a powerful and amazing revelation. And two, the concept of the cause being the effect, being the manifestation, regardless of what it looks like objectively, physically, which makes no difference. This is an enormous concept.

I would like to give an example here because this point needs to be clarified. There are four people, the first is a *tzadik*, a tremendously righteous person, and the fourth is a *rasha* (a selfish person). The two in between are on the continuum, not a great *tzadik*, not a *rasha*. If we create a world where being a *tzadik* or a *rasha*—positive or negative—makes no difference, and within that world everything is unified as it was in the Ein Sof, where there was *Hu uShemo Echad* "He and His Name are One" (which we cannot comprehend), even though the Vessel, the Desire to Receive for the Self Alone, is objectively different from the Light, with a complete Difference of Form, there will be complete unity. In that made up world, the fourth person, the *rasha*, is not considered a *rasha* because there is no differentiation.

It says when the *Mashiach* comes there will be no difference between good and bad, which is why, for instance, we will be eating pig. The word *chazir* (pig in Hebrew) as a matter of fact comes from the idea that when the *Mashiach* comes it will return to be an animal that is eaten. Another example is the mistake that Nadav and Avihu made was that they thought that everything was permitted now because *Mashiach* had come. Similarly with Korach, where there is a point at which everything becomes sort of nullified, everything becomes equal.

So again, if you have these four people who are living in that perfect world— where being positive or being negative does not make a difference, and everything is the same, and the *rasha* says, "You know what, even though I am not separate from the Light of the Creator in this world, I want to become better. Let's create a new world within which I can work." Objectively, within this new world where the *tzadik* is a *tzadik* and the *rasha* is a *rasha*, there should be a difference, meaning one would know to identify the evil person and say he is evil and one would recognize the righteous person and say he is righteous. This is the secret Rav Ashlag reveals: because the desire and the cause that made the *rasha* experience a desire to change was not as a result of his separateness from the Light of the Creator, since in that world there is no positive and negative, therefore the Light leaving and objectively revealing a difference between the four people, does not occur. If the cause was positive, the effect cannot be negative.

Rather, the Tzimtzum took place only in the secret of: "…it rose up in His simple desire to create the Worlds…" (See the commentary in Section 13, starting with: "Explanation…"—study there.) This means that He wished for that Similarity of Form that will be manifested through the creation of the Worlds, namely, the Form of Receiving for the Sake of "Giving pleasure to the Creator," which has a very great advantage to it. On the one hand, it is complete sharing because the desire is entirely to give pleasure to the Creator and nothing for one's self. Therefore, its form is entirely similar to the Supernal Light of the Emanator, and it is thus cleaved to Him to the utmost degree. On the other hand, it is possible for it to deepen and enlarge its Vessel of Receiving to no end or limit, since now the form of receiving creates no Difference of Form because it is derived from the Desire to Share.

The Vessel had a desire to change; it was not a desire to remove a blockage, nor was it a desire to correct something that was wrong. The vessel wanted to elevate itself in perfection. I read an article about a person who had an ability to take a good idea and make it great. Taking a good idea and making it great is obviously very different from taking a problem and solving it. This is the difference Rav Ashlag makes clear here. There was no problem that Malchut, the Vessel, wanted to solve. This is a very important distinction for us to be clear about. The Tzimtzum did not occur because there was a problem and a need for a solution. The Tzimtzum occurred because there was a good situation that the Vessel wanted to make great; the Vessel wanted to elevate itself in perfection. Rav Ashlag says the Vessel wanted to come to the place where it is in complete likeness to the Light of the Creator.

Rav Ashlag, in his Inner Observation in this Volume, asks the following: "How much work do we have to do to remove the Bread of Shame?" It almost seems impossible. How does one earn endless fulfillment? The only way to earn endless fulfillment, meaning to give work in return for endless fulfillment, is to work endlessly and obviously that is impossible. That said, how do we take care of Bread of Shame, meaning how can we work for what we want to receive if we cannot work endlessly, and if we are going to receive endlessly, how do we pay for that in endless work?

The answer that Rav Ashlag gives here is that it is not about earning what we will receive, rather it is about changing the paradigm, changing who we are, transforming our Desire to Receive to a Desire to Share, and by doing so we can tell the Creator, "Give me endlessly. The reason I want to receive endlessly is because I want to share with You. I want to give You the joy of giving me." In this way we can receive endlessly because we keep saying, "Give me more, give me more. And the reason why I receive this 'more,' the reason I want You, the Creator, to share with me is because I want to give You the joy of giving." This is not a joke or a game. It is the real essence, consciousness, we will attain. If it gives the Creator pleasure to share with us, then we can receive (not earn) endlessly because the receiving will no longer create a Difference of Form between us and the Creator. And when we achieve this consciousness, the only reason that we receive is if it gives pleasure to the person giving it to us. This is the seed of the logic of the world that we live in; it is the seed of the process that we are part of.

To return to the Rav Ashlag's question concerning removing Bread of Shame, it would seem logical that to remove Bread of Shame we need to earn what we receive. However, as Rav Ashlag tells us, it is impossible for any of us to earn the lasting and ultimate fulfillment that the Creator will give us. Thus it is not about working for the Light that we receive, rather it is about transforming ourselves completely so that we can Receive endlessly For the Sake of Sharing, for the sake of giving the Creator the joy in giving to us. There is no amount of work that we can do to earn endless fulfillment. What has to occur is the transformation between the Desire to Receive to a complete Desire to Share, so that we can tell the Creator, "Give me endlessly so that I can share with You, so that I can give you the joy of sharing."

Rav Ashlag explains that when an individual and humanity as a whole achieves this transformation, that is a beautiful and superior reality. To come to the point where we want to receive *only* because it will give the Creator pleasure. When we achieve this point, this reality, this level of transformation, then there is no aspect in us that separates us from the Creator. In the same way the Creator's single desire is a Desire to Share, our single desire is a Desire to Share. How do we fulfill our Desire to Share? We fulfill it by receiving.

The Creator reveals and fulfills His Desire to Share by sharing, and we ultimately will reveal our Desire to Share by receiving. Once we transform ourselves into a complete Desire to Share and we receive only because we want to give joy to the person or the Creator who is sharing with us, then we are completely unified and bonded with the Creator. The added bonus of this situation is that when we completely transform our Desire to Receive to a Desire to Share and all of our receiving is only for the purpose of giving joy to the person sharing with me, then we can truly awaken more and more Desire to Receive.

When a child is a toddler, and his or her parent has a Desire to Share with their child, the child receives by being held and being played with. This is what the toddler wants and enjoys. When the child grows older, eight or nine years old, then the parent can study with the child, and can give them even more. The child's vessel to receive expands over time thereby giving the parents more opportunities to share with the child. Obviously this example of a child is within the realm of the Desire to Receive.

What Rav Ashlag is saying is something really beautiful: after the Final Correction (Gemar HaTikkun) we will be sitting around thinking, how else can I help the Creator share with me? What other desires can I awaken to allow the Creator to share with me endlessly? Can you imagine if after we achieved our transformation, we have to start awakening different desires that we allow the Creator to fulfill. It is really such a beautiful concept.

Once we have completely transformed, and the only reason we want the Creator to share with us is because we know the joy that it gives Him, then firstly we are in complete *dvekut* (cleaving) and completely unified with the Light of the Creator. And secondly, we can now expand our Desire to Receive. We can find new ways in which we can give the Creator the opportunity to share with us. At this point the receiving does not create any Difference of Form, does not differentiate us at all from the Creator because it comes from a Desire to Share. What is so beautiful is that at this point we actually have to find newer and better ways to expand our Desire to Receive because paradoxically, the more we expand our Desire to Receive the more we are expanding our Desire to Share.

It is written: "He fulfills the desire of those who fear Him" (Psalms 145:19). In the No'am Elimelech, Rabbi Elimelech of Lizensk explains that the Creator awakens desire within those who are close to Him. It is not good for a righteous person not to desire, as he limits what the Creator can give him. Once a person achieves this *dvekut*, this union with the Light of the Creator, then the Creator asks him, *"Please desire more, please create more needs,"* and the Creator actually creates the desire for the righteous person.

This is in accordance with the words of the sages (Tractate Kidushin, 7a) regarding an important man, where the **bride** supplies the money for the wedding [ring] and **he** says, "Behold you are married to me," the marriage is valid. And even though the Torah said: "and put it in her hand" (Deuteronomy 24:1), and stipulates that the groom is beholden to supply the money for the wedding [ring], nevertheless in the case of an important man, she receives pleasure in him receiving, and thus [his receiving] is actually considered as an act of giving—study there carefully. Thus, Receiving for the Sake of Sharing is giving rather than receiving. For an important man who receives money from his bride is regarded as if he gives her money, and it is as written in the Torah: "and put it in her hand," (Ibid.) because he receives only for the sake of giving pleasure to his wife, who will be honored by his receiving.

The Torah says that when a man gets married, the groom has to give the bride something. Today, he gives her a ring. Nevertheless, the Talmud in Kiddushin brings an example where the bride can give the groom something, and it be considered as if the groom really gave to the bride. This is when the groom is a respected and important person, meaning a person who by giving to him gives you pleasure. As it is for us when we serve the Rav, in serving the Rav we are not giving to the Rav but are receiving. The Rav allows us to share with him, so that we receive the joy from the giving. An important person is one who we desire to share with. Why do we desire to share with him? Because we enjoy the fact that he permits us to share. The reason we enjoy giving is selfish because the person is important, and it gives us a good feeling to share with a person who is more important than we are. What happens in this kind of situation is that giving becomes receiving, right? When I give to an important person, I am then receiving. I am receiving the pleasure of the giving.

Therefore, the concept we are meant to get to is not that we remove Bread of Shame by working; rather the reason we are in this world is to transform our Desire to Receive to the Desire to Share completely. Once we have completely become a person who only Desires to Share, then we can begin receiving—receiving for the sake of giving the other person pleasure. And now we can ask the Creator to give us endlessly so that we can give the Creator pleasure in giving. And with this we are completely unified with the Creator because the Creator gets to give us everything, and we get what we want, which is to receive everything. However this receiving does not separate us from the Light of the Creator because in such a reality when we receive it is an action of giving. Once we have transformed our receiving, it is an action of giving. This is the basis of the purpose of our work and the logic behind it.

---

According to this explanation we find out that the main reason for the Tzimtzum was solely because of the yearning for the new form of Receiving for the Sake of Sharing, which is destined to be made manifest through the creation of Worlds (as said in Section 13, starting with [the word] "Explanation"). It was not at all due to any coarseness it perceived in the Middle Point because there was no coarseness or difference, Heaven forbid, as said. Hence the Middle Point did not become an aspect of "end" due to the Tzimtzum. Thus it is impossible to discern matters such as small and great. This is why the Rav [the Ari] said that the Tzimtzum was completely equal and even.

19. **The place of that space was Circle-like all around:** Of necessity, some image had been made due to the Tzimtzum. And even though the Tzimtzum was equally even (as made clear in the last paragraph), and not due to Difference of Form, nevertheless after the Tzimtzum and the departure of the Light from that Middle Point, it was revealed that it is not fit for the Supernal Light to attach to it because of the magnitude of the Form of Receiving that was in it. Once this became apparent, it fell from the level it held while in Ein Sof.

And so it is already considered as an "end," which denotes such coarseness that there is none lower than it. For this reason, only this Middle Point remained as vacant space—no longer worthy of being clothed by the Light (as said in Section 6, starting with [the words]: "In order to explain…")—but the Three Phases that precede in height and purity are still worthy to have the Light be clothed in them after the Tzimtzum as well. Nevertheless, we explained earlier (in the last paragraph) that it does not assume the aspect of "end" for the reason given—study there.

This is why the Rav [the Ari] is particular when he says: "The place of that space was Circle-like all around," meaning, not an actual end, but like the end in a round image, which its end is in its center. This way, you can imagine those Four Phases as four Circles within each other like onion layers. The central Circle is the Fourth Phase, surrounded by the Third Phase, which in turn is surrounded by the Second Phase, which is surrounded by the First. In this way, there is no discerning up or down, right or left, among them. For the first phase, for example, encircles all of them with its first half from above, while with the second, it encircles them all from below. It is thus with the other phases, and therefore, there is no up and down, right and left, in such a way that among them there is none greater above the other, but they are all the same, as one [entity] equally even. The reason, as has already been explained (in the previous paragraph), was that the cause for the Tzimtzum was not a Difference of Form—study there well. This is why the Rav [the Ari] specifies it in his words: **"Circle-like all around, completely equal and even."** Understand this well.

The picture of the Circles indicates the beginning of the change; it indicates the beginning of a consciousness and an understanding that there is a difference here. Let's examine this idea in relation to our spiritual development. Unfortunately, many people do not have the realization that the Desire to Receive for the Self Alone is bad and that it disconnects us from the Light of the Creator. Usually the understanding that the Fourth Phase—the greatest Desire to Receive for the Self Alone—is different and worse than the other three lesser desires comes slowly. Each one of us in our realization of our filthy Desire to Receive for the Self Alone goes through the same process. First there is awareness that *the great Desire to Receive for the Self Alone I have is just a little bit different than everything else about me*. And then there comes a point where it occurs to us, as it occurs in the process of the creation of our world, where there is the complete realization of darkness. As Rav Ashlag and the Zohar speak about in the Prologue (*Hakdama*), Malchut now is *Man'ula* (a Lock)—it locks and closes everything up, as it is written: "Her feet go down to death...." (Proverbs 5:5) This realization that it is a place of darkness, it is a place where death is, occurs slowly.

First there is a kind of ambiguity as Rav Ashlag goes through the Phases between section 18 and section 19—first there is a difference; then there is no difference; then again there is a difference but it is a small difference. This back and forth is the First Phase, and then eventually we come to the realization of how great the difference is between who we are—based on our Desire to Receive for the Self Alone—and the Light of the Creator.

This is the same process that occurs now after the Tzimtzum, for different reasons of course. Nonetheless, the realization that the great Desire to Receive for the Self Alone may be different from the Light of the Creator is beginning to become clear. The reason the Ari uses the example of Circles within Circles is to Indicate that although they are different from each other, they are not completely higher and lower than each other because this process of differentiation—where the Desire to Receive for the Self Alone is completely in Difference of Form from the Light of the Creator—occurs slowly.

I know that I keep repeating myself in every lesson, but to have the ability to read these words and to whatever degree understand them is a tremendous merit. In reading the words of the Ari, it sounds like the Ari is saying that there is only one Circle here, and that the Tzimtzum created one Circle. However Rav Ashlag says that when the Ari says: "The place of that space was circle-like all around," we should picture four circles. Yet the Ari does not explicitly say four Circles; he seems to be talking about one Circle. So what does this mean?

It is important to appreciate that gift of clarity our generation merits to have through these revelations of Rav Ashlag. Of course, we know that the Ari did not write this; Rav Chaim Vital heard it from the Ari, and Rav Shmuel Vital, Rav Chaim's son, wrote it down. Why did the Ari not write it down? He did not write it down because he could not limit his thoughts to words and certainly not to writing. The Kabbalists say that everything that the Ari revealed to Rav

Chaim Vital was like a drop in the ocean compared to what the Ari knew. And what Rav Chaim Vital gave to his son Shmuel Vital was a drop of his ocean compared to what Chaim Vital knew, and what Rav Shmuel Vital wrote down was a drop of his ocean in comparison to what he knew. One can imagine how diluted, to one degree or another, what we receive is from the Writings of the Ari. On the other hand, when one has an atomic bomb, even a small part of the bomb is very, very big. This understanding is not to diminish the power of the Writings of the Ari but instead is to elevate our appreciation of the revelation of Rav Ashlag.

Although in reading the words of the Ari it seems to be discussing one Circle, Rav Ashlag makes it clear that the way to understand this is in the picture of the four Circles—knowing of course that it is not the picture that is important but rather the understanding that it gives us because Rav Ashlag merited a clear vision. To really appreciate the clarification, is not in thinking that the Ari says one thing and Rav Ashlag says another but rather that the Ari's revelation came in a way that was not completely clarified. The greatness of the revelation of Rav Ashlag is that he was able to remove any ambiguity; he was able remove any of the shells that cover the revelation of the Ari (Rav Isaac Luria). We need to appreciate the amazing revelation and work of Rav Ashlag, and the merit we have to study from his writings.

5. The reason was that since the Endless Light (Ohr Ein Sof) was equal and completely even, it too had to contract Itself equally even on all sides, not contracting Itself more on one side than the other sides. We know through geometry that there is no shape as equally even[20] as the shape of the Circle. This is not the case with the shape of a square with projecting right angles,[21] or the shape of a triangle,[22] and similarly with other shapes. The Contraction (Tzimtzum) of the Endless (Ein Sof), therefore, had to be in the form of a Circle.

20. **Equally even:** This has already been clarified in the previous paragraph.

21. **A square with projecting right angles:** This means that if there was a distinction between up and down, right and left, this would have been described by the image of the square, since it has those four sides, which is what we call the mentioned Four Phases. But this was not so. Rather, it bore the image of a Circle, which does not have such distinctions, as said in previous paragraphs.

22. **The shape of a triangle:** This indicates a level of only Three Phases, where the Fourth Phase is missing. These three sides are up, right and left, and the lower side is missing. This is called the image of a triangle.

When Rav Ashlag went to London for a few years, he wrote the Panim Meirot uMasbirot ("Shining and Enlightening Face"), which is a commentary on the Etz Chayim section of the Ari's Writings. He did not publish all of it at once. He would send parts of it to his students, and when they would receive it they would make a meal connection. Obviously this was a time of joy. They were happy both for the revelation of Rav Ashlag and also because they were able to partake of that revelation. Thus every time we complete a section in this revelation from the Ari and from Rav Ashlag, it is an important milestone.

So we will end with this. What we have to understand is that this is the spiritual source of the square. This is the spiritual source of the triangle. The fact that we have triangles and squares and circles in our world is not a coincidence. Now that we learnt and understood this, every circle we look at has an inkling, an aspect of this perfect Tzimtzum. Every square that is in our world has an aspect of the Four Phases, being upper and lower from the other. Every triangle in our world represents an even further delineation, meaning with Chochmah, Binah, and Zeir Anpin without Malchut included.

The Ari and Rav Ashlag are not simply using these terms because they are good terms to indicate or describe the spiritual reality. These are truly the essences of these realities. Besides learning about how our world came to be, we are also getting an opening into an understanding of our physical reality. What a circle really is. What a square really is. What a triangle really is.

We are beginning to understand that when a kabbalist looks at a circle, at a square, at a triangle, they do not see circles, squares, and triangles; they see these revelations, because that is the truth. The physical manifestations in our world are all of these realities, lessons, and understandings. It is a really beautiful and important concept.

# INNER LIGHT
# (OHR PNIMI)

## CHAPTER 2

Chapter 2 explains that from the Endless Light (Ohr Ein Sof), a Line of Light was drawn into the Worlds that were emanated and created within the contracted space. It contains five subjects:

1. Out of the Endless (Ein Sof), a Line of Light was drawn into the space.
2. The head (beginning) of the Line touches the Endless (Ein Sof) but its end does not.
3. Through the Line, the Endless Light (Ohr Ein Sof) extends to the Worlds.
4. All the Worlds are in that place of the contracted space.
5. Before the Tzimtzum, it was "He and His name are One," and there is no mind that can conceive this [concept].

# WRITINGS OF THE ARI, ETZ CHAYIM, GATE 1 BRANCH 2

א) וְהִנֵּה אַחַר הַצִּמְצוּם הַנַּ"ל, אֲשֶׁר אָז נִשְׁאַר מְקוֹם הֶחָלָל
וַאֲוִיר פָּנוּי וְרֵיקָנִי בְּאֶמְצַע אוֹר הָאֵין סוֹף מַמָּשׁ כַּנַּ"ל, הִנֵּה
כְּבָר הָיָה מְקוֹם שֶׁיּוּכְלוּ לִהְיוֹת שָׁם הַנֶּאֱצָלִים וְהַנִּבְרָאִים
וְהַיְצוּרִים וְהַנַּעֲשִׂים. וְאָז הִמְשִׁיךְ מִן הָאוֹר אֵין סוֹף, קַו א'
יָשָׁר מִן הָאוֹר הָעָגֹל שֶׁלּוֹ מִלְמַעְלָה לְמַטָּה, וּמִשְׁתַּלְשֵׁל, וְיוֹרֵד
תּוֹךְ הֶחָלָל הַהוּא.

1. After the said Tzimtzum,[1] when a space and empty, vacant air remained in the very center of the Endless Light (Ohr Ein Sof), as mentioned earlier, there was already a place for the emanated, created, formed, and made beings to be in. Then[2] He drew down from the Endless Light (Ohr Ein Sof) a single straight Line, from its Circular Light,[3] from Above Downward,[4] evolving and descending into that space.

ב) וְרֹאשׁ הָעֶלְיוֹן שֶׁל הַקַּו, נִמְשָׁךְ מִן הָאֵין סוֹף עַצְמוֹ וְנוֹגֵעַ
בּוֹ, אָמְנָם סִיּוּם הַקַּו הַזֶּה לְמַטָּה בְּסוֹפוֹ אֵינוֹ נוֹגֵעַ בְּאוֹר אֵין
סוֹף.

2. The Upper Head of the Line[5] is drawn from the Endless (Ein Sof) Itself and touches It.[6] But the conclusion of this Line, down at its end,[7] does not touch the Endless Light (Ohr Ein Sof).

ג) וְדֶרֶךְ הַקַּו הַזֶּה נִמְשָׁךְ וְנִתְפַּשֵּׁט אוֹר אֵין סוֹף לְמַטָּה.

3. The Endless Light (Ohr Ein Sof) is drawn and extends downward through this Line.

ד) וּבַמָּקוֹם הֶחָלָל הַהוּא, הֶאֱצִיל וּבָרָא, וְיָצַר וְעָשָׂה כָּל הָעוֹלָמוֹת כֻּלָּם.

4. In the place of that space, He emanated, created, formed and made[8] all Worlds.

# WRITINGS OF THE ARI, SHA'AR MA'AMREI RAZAL, TRACTATE SHABBAT

ה) קֹדֶם הַד' עוֹלָמוֹת אֵלּוּ, הָיָה הָאֵין סוֹף, הוּא אֶחָד וּשְׁמוֹ אֶחָד בְּאַחְדוּת נִפְלָא וְנֶעֱלָם יִת', שֶׁאֵין כֹּחַ אֲפִלּוּ בַּמַּלְאָכִים הַקְּרוּבִים אֵלָיו וְאֵין לָהֶם הַשָּׂגָה בָּאֵין סוֹף יִת', כִּי אֵין שׁוּם שֵׂכֶל נִבְרָא שֶׁיּוּכַל לְהַשִּׂיגוֹ, לִהְיוֹת, כִּי אֵין לוֹ מָקוֹם וְלֹא גְבוּל וְלֹא שֵׁם.

5. Before these Four Worlds,[9] the Endless (Ein Sof) was "He is one and His name is One,"[10] in such wonderful and concealed unity. Not even His closest angels[11] have such ability, and they have no conception of the Endless (Ein Sof), since no mind of any created being can comprehend Him, since He has no place, no boundary, and no name.[12]

1. After the said Tzimtzum,[1] when a space and empty, vacant air remained in the very center of the Endless Light (Ohr Ein Sof), as mentioned earlier, there was already a place for the emanated, created, formed, and made beings to be in. Then[2] He drew down from the Endless Light (Ohr Ein Sof) a single straight Line, from Its Circular Light,[3] from Above downward,[4] evolving and descending into that space.

1. **After the said Tzimtzum:** Do not mistakenly think that because of the Contraction of the Light from the Middle Point there was some kind of change in Ein Sof, Heaven forbid, for there is no disappearance or change in spirituality, needless to say in such a lofty place (as said in the beginning of the Inner Light Commentary). Rather, this whole Contraction (Tzimtzum) became a new reality, additional to the Ein Sof, in such a way that the Ein Sof remained in all its simple unity as it was before the Contraction in a state of, "He and His Name are One." And the Contraction that was done to the Middle Point is understood to be the manifestation of a new World from which the Light departed and where a place of space and emptiness remained, according to previous explanation. Within that space, all the Worlds were emanated as shall be discussed presently.

We mentioned earlier that when Rav Ashlag was in London he worked on the Panim Meirot uMasbirot, which was his first try and attempt at explaining the Ari's writings of the Etz Chayim. But after his students started studying from it, he said "I feel that I didn't do the job properly." Therefore, he revealed Talmud Eser Sefirot. In comparing the way Rav Ashlag explains concepts in the Panim Meirot uMasbirot and here in the Inner Light (Or Pnimi), it is clear that although in the Inner Light Rav Ashlag explains things in more detail, it is obviously impossible to explain everything.

Rav Ashlag says of his commentary on the Zohar that it is a ladder that you ascend, and then on our own discover the rest of the treasures that can be found there. The same is true of the Talmud Eser Sefirot. This is why it is so important to envelop our minds as much as we can in these concepts because we have to achieve an altered state—a state that thinks like Rav Ashlag—to truly understand the Talmud Eser Sefirot. That is why Rav Ashlag does not explain every word but instead gives us enough of a boost, enough of a ladder, so that we can then have clarity on everything else.

I was trying to find a parable, something that could sort of signify what Rav Ashlag did. Imagine watching a 3D movie that is being shown on a screen. Without 3D glasses we would see one reality, yet with 3D glasses on we see a completely different reality that is obviously deeper and richer. Rav Ashlag in his explanation of Talmud Eser Sefirot gives us 3D glasses. Although the glasses are not what creates the reality, they allow us to see what is happening. The same is true of Rav Ashlag's revelations. If we think about them and understand them enough, they give us a new way of looking at and comprehending the Ari, and with this we can understand everything. It is not as if Rav Ashlag explains every word and then our understanding comes from that but rather the understanding comes by enveloping our mind in Rav Ashlag's explanation and through that we can truly comprehend what the Ari is revealing.

Rav Ashlag says: **"There is no disappearance or change in spirituality."** So when we talk about the world after Tzimtzum, when we talk about the world of the *Kav*—the Line of Light that emerges afterward—we are talking about a new reality that is separate and parallel to the reality of the Endless World. Nevertheless the Tzimtzum did not occur in the Endless World and the *Kav* (Line) did not occur in the Endless World. The Endless World existed, and will exist forever. When we discuss the Tzimtzum and the Kav, we are speaking specifically about a new reality that comes into being, one that does not at all affect the reality of the Endless World. The first concept we have to be clear about is that the Tzimtzum and onward does not affect anything to do with the Endless World. The Endless World exists, and will exist as it existed in the beginning. The Tzimtzum, the *Kav*, and everything that follows only occurs in a new reality and does not affect the Endless World at all. This is something we need to keep in mind in every word of the Talmud Eser Sefirot.

In a different section, Rav Ashlag tells a parable of a person who is in a room that has all the treasures in the world. It has diamonds and gold. It has the best foods; it has everything. However the room is so dark that the person sitting in the room thinks he has nothing. Now, if someone enters and gives him a flashlight, which he turns on, he will be able to see there is a diamond on the floor. He will realize that although he thought he had nothing, now he can see that there is a diamond worth $500,000 lying on the floor. And as he looks around the room, he notices $50,000,000 worth of gold. He goes about the room and starts seeing everything that he has, until eventually he sees he has everything.

This same is true of the Ein Sof and these new realities that are being created. These new realities are illusions of darkness within the one reality of the Endless World, and these illusions of darkness do not change the Endless World. Just like the man sitting in the darkened room, once he received the flashlight, the only thing that changed was his realization, his consciousness of what else was in the room; the completeness that was there.

To explain the Tzimtzum let us use an example of a man who is sitting in a room and has everything that is good in the world, both physical and spiritual. Suddenly the lights go out and his memory disappears. This is the Tzimtzum. At this point, his reality is that there is only darkness and there is nothing good in this room; there is nothing good for him. Then the process begins with the *Kav* (line); the flashlight turns on. First there is a little bit of light and he shines it on a little diamond. He now has a new realization: *"Yes, there is a little bit of something here."* He does not have the complete awareness of what truly is there; he is beginning to have a little awakening.

Just as Rav Ashlag says the Endless World never changed, the room in this parable is the same in the beginning, the same when the lights go out and the man has amnesia, and it will be the same when he finally lights up the whole room. The reality remains the same only his perception of the reality, his illusion of what is happening, of what he has is what changes.

The Ein Sof, the reality of perfection and complete revelation of Light, does not change. What changes is only the way the Vessel, the way we, perceive the Endless World. The reality of the room filled with diamonds where the best of everything exists does not change, the man's perception of darkness and emptiness does not affect the reality of what is in the room. His perception only influences his own experience; this is all it can do. Therefore the Vessel through the Tzimtzum and through the Kav, and through everything else that occurs afterward, does not influence the Endless World at all, all it does is create illusionary realities for itself. These illusionary realities are necessary because only through these illusionary realities is there room for us to reveal and transform our Desire to Receive from a Desire to Receive to a Desire to Receive for the Sake of Sharing. But this necessity is only from our perspective, from the Vessel's side. The Light in the Ein Sof does not need any of these Worlds and therefore it is not influenced by any of these Worlds. The reality and complete perfection of the Endless World remain forever. The Vessel wanes; it goes dark, it reveals a little bit of Light, it reveals a little bit more Light— but this does not influence the Endless World.

2. **Then:** This action should not be understood according to its superficial meaning—as a human action would be—wherein one first acts this way and then in a different way thus withdrawing from the former action since there is no greater materialization than this. But He is not eventful or changeful, Heaven forbid, as is said, "I, God, do not change…." (Malachi 3:6) And even though we do not relate to His Essence but to the Light extending from Him, nevertheless, His Essence undergoes no change, no occurrence nor any motion. Since He is totally restful, the same is stipulated of His Light extending from Him, as long as it does not reach the state of becoming the Emanated being; namely, as long as it does not reach the state of being clothed in Vessels because only then does It go out of the category of His Essence to become the category of a new Emanated being that receives from Him.

We have already explained that all this newness applies mainly to the Vessel of the Emanated, namely the aspect of the Desire to Receive in the emanated, where even though this desire is metaphysical it is surely a New Form and is an Occurrence because, by definition, it does not apply to His Essence. This is not so with the Light that is clothed within it, which is not new since it is drawn from His Essence as Something out of Something. Nevertheless, the affect of the Supernal Light in the measurement of the Vessel—namely the aspect of how the Vessel is affected and receives from the Supernal Light—is also an aspect of newness, since it is surely an occurrence.

Know that all the new forms and the evolvement of the said levels are only in relation to the Vessel being affected by and receiving from the Supernal Light because this alone is susceptible to changes and to multiplicity.

However the Light on Its own is always in a state of absolute rest since it extends from His Essence. Understand this well and remember this throughout the study of this wisdom, literally with each and every word.

The only thing that changes is how the Vessel experiences the Light of the Creator. The Light of the Creator never moves; never changes, never leaves, and never comes back. It is constant, it is constantly revealed everywhere. In all of Talmud Eser Sefirot, when we discussed the Tzimtzum of the Light, the Light did not go away! Now we are discussing the Light coming back in a *Kav* (Line), yet the Light is not coming back in a Kav! What is being referred to here is only how the Vessel perceives that Light.

Even though the Vessel said that It did not want to experience the Light, the Light was still there. It is like the parable of the man sitting in the room, who has everything he will ever need, both of a physical and spiritual nature, and he decides that he wants to earn what he has, and asks to have amnesia so that he will not know what is in his room. The room never changes, the treasures never change, the perfection never changes, the Endless World never changes. What changes is only how the Vessel perceives the Light. This is why the Rav always said that consciousness is the most important thing. The Endless World is everywhere, all the time. Our perception, our connection to the Endless World, meaning our consciousness of the Endless World is the only thing that ever changes.

This revelation from Rav Ashlag is one of those concepts one cannot help but be so excited about. For thousands of years, when people attempted to study the secrets of the Torah without having this explanation, it would be considered Idol Worship because they could think that the Light of the Creator had left. Rav Ashlag tells us here that if one thinks that the Light of the Creator left, obviously inferring that the Light of the Creator is not perfect, this consciousness disconnects one from the Light of the Creator. Therefore, the danger of people studying Kabbalah without having the explanation of Rav Ashlag is that people can begin to think that the Creator changes. This thinking, this consciousness is very dangerous because this consciousness means that the Endless World is not everywhere; and we know consciousness influences reality.

This is why for so long the kabbalists did not teach just anyone. When Rav Ashlag came to Jerusalem and went to one of the kabbalistic schools in the Old City, he became very upset because when he asked the people, "What does the Tzimtzum mean?" They must have answered him saying, "Well, the Vessel says 'I don't want the Light here,' and the Light of the Creator responds with, 'Ok, you don't want the Light here, let Me take it away.'" If one understands it like this, then this person is doing tremendous damage because what they are saying, with their consciousness, is that the Creator went away. What a tremendous gift it is that we have access to Rav Ashlag's revelations.

---

From this explanation you will understand well that the Supernal Light does not stop illuminating upon the emanated beings for even a moment, and it does not fall into the category of Occurrences or New Forms, Heaven forbid. Rather, it is in a state of complete rest. And the whole idea of the Tzimtzum and the departure of Light mentioned here applies only in relation to the Vessel, namely the Middle Point, being affected and receiving. This means that even though the Supernal Light did not cease illuminating, nevertheless the Vessel now did not receive any of the Light's illumination because it diminished itself, namely it reduced the Desire to Receive in it so as not to receive in its Fourth Phase, which is the very Middle Point, but only in the three previous Phases in it, in which the Desire to Receive is scant, and the Desire to Share is more dominant (see section 14, with the words, "now you can understand...").

Thus, the Supernal Light was not at all influenced by the Tzimtzum nor did it change His way, Heaven forbid. But just as He illuminates in the Ein Sof, He also illuminates during the Tzimtzum, after the Tzimtzum, and in all the Worlds, even in the World of Asiyah (Action), without any interruption even for a moment. But the Vessels themselves are the ones that create all these changes because they receive just according to their measure, namely the measure of the Desire to Receive within them, as explained.

---

This teaches us that we, at any moment in time, can connect to the Endless World. Very often as we begin studying the Talmud Eser Sefirot and learn about all the Worlds that are created and all the changes and the processes that occur, it can sometimes make us think that we have to do something. For example, concerning the Holidays, we learn from the Ari in the Gate of Meditations, about the different meditations for Sukkot and what we have to do to awaken the Surrounding Light of the Sukkah or to awaken the Inner

Light from the Etrog, Lulav, Hadassim, and Aravot. All these processes are complicated and necessary, however we should not forget for one moment that the reality where the process of connecting to the Light of the Creator is complicated is a construct of the Vessel. We, the Desire to Receive for the Self Alone, the Ultimate Vessel in the Endless World, decided and wanted to go through this process. And this process does not influence the shining of the Endless Light, everywhere, all the time—which means that we can connect to that Endless Light anytime, anywhere.

There are many places in the Talmud where it discusses how with one action, a person can get everything. How is this possible? The Ramchal (Rav Moshe Chaim Luzzato) speaks about the different stages and processes a person has to go through to achieve perfection. Therefore how are we to understand that with one action a person can get everything? This is because the Endless World is always here. Yes it is difficult to connect to the Endless World while we are in the middle of the process, nonetheless once we understand that there are constantly two realties that exist at the same time—one is the reality of the perception of the Vessel where there is lack and there is work that needs to be done; and the other is the reality of the Endless World that never changes, it is a reality of a constant shining, a full completeness of the Light of the Endless World—a person can connect to that Endless World, at moments or through one great action. Therefore, the Talmud says that a person, through one action, can get everything.

It is very dangerous to think that the Tzimtzum and all of the Worlds that occur afterward have any influence on the Light of the Creator. And if a person begins to think that any changes occur within the Light of the Creator, the Light of the Endless World, then it is dangerous to study Kabbalah. No change occurs in the Endless World. In the Endless World, the Light of the Creator is in constant peace, and is constantly shining everywhere. Everything we discuss is only as the Vessel perceives the removal, the concealment of the Creator's Light, but not the Essence, not the truth of what is happening with the Light of the Creator.

> From these words you will understand what the Rav [the Ari] said: "**He drew down from the Endless Light (Ohr Ein Sof) a single straight Line,**" meaning that the place of the space itself, namely the Vessel that was emptied from the Light of Ein Sof, caused this drawing of the Line

from the Light of Ein Sof, due to the diminishment that became new in its Desire to Receive. For now, after contracting its Fourth Phase, the measure of the amount of its receiving is called a "Line;" that is, in relation to its previous receiving in the Fourth Phase, which filled the whole place. But now, when it does not have this great Desire to Receive, but only the former Three Phases of desire in which the Desire to Receive is scant, as said, the Vessel is considered as though it receives from the Endless Light (Ohr Ein Sof) only one Line of Light. And the entire place [and space] of the Vessel remains empty and vacant of Light, because this thin Light it now receives does not suffice to fill the whole place of the Vessel. This happened to it because of the lack of the Fourth Phase, which it diminished, as mentioned.

Thus it has been explained that the Supernal Light was not interrupted at all due to the Tzimtzum, nor did it change at all to be drawn as a single Line. Rather, all this great change took place due to the diminishing of the Vessels of Receiving so that now they can receive only a very small amount called "Line" from the Endless Light (Ohr Ein Sof)—that is, according to the degree of its desire, for it does not desire more than that degree; understand this well.

If literally translated, it seems that the Ari is implying that the Creator had a desire to do something—to draw a Line of Light, a limited amount of Light. However, the Creator is not doing any of this because the Creator never changes. The Light of the Creator always shines in a simple way, all the time. It is the Vessel that is creating these changes because the Vessel now wants to receive a limited amount of Light, which means the Vessel chooses not to perceive or receive the totality of the Light." Therefore the Vessel establishes that there be a Line, a *Kav*, which does not mean that there is a physical line but rather that in comparison to everything of the Endless, there is now only a limited amount of fulfillment, only a limited amount of Light that is being revealed because the Vessel does not want to receive anymore. The Vessel does not want Its desire fulfilled anymore. Once the Vessel decided that Its greatest desire not be fulfilled, there was the revelation of the *Kav*.

As Rav Ashlag continues to emphasize, when we refer to the word *Kav* we should never think that what is being discussed are the geometric shapes of lines and circles. Rather the concept of the *Kav*, which was revealed after the Tzimtzum is referring to a limited revelation of Light, of fulfillment not a shape of a line. This is the meaning of *Kav*.

To use a simple example, imagine the Vessel is like someone who goes on a diet. Before the diet, this individual does not care what they eat: steak, bread, pasta, etc. They then decide that although they really enjoy the pasta, meat and bread they will restrict the fulfillment and only eat vegetables. With this decision this individual can eat and receive some foods but the level of fulfillment is less. I think most of us who have tried diets of one kind or another know that the level of fulfillment that one receives from this eating plan is obviously limited. This is what the Vessel has decided.

The Vessel chose not to fulfill its greatest desire but instead to only fulfill the much lesser, lower Desires to Receive, which are the First Phase, Second Phase, and Third Phase. The Vessel chose to not allow Itself to receive all of the Light that the Creator reveals because It wanted to create a process of correction.

---

3. **From Its Circular Light:** The meaning of the image of the Circle was already clarified (Chapter 1, Section 19). [The Ari] is implying to us here that even after the Tzimtzum, the Supernal Light remained in the image of a Circle, which means without distinction between the levels; and all Four Phases are equal in rank in It (see Chapter 1, Section 19). The reason, as was mentioned before (in the previous paragraph), is that occurrences or newness do not apply, Heaven forbid, to the Supernal Light; look there carefully. And all these types of new aspects that are mentioned relate only to the Vessels.

---

What the Ari did using geometric shapes to deliver complex concepts is an unbelievable feat. Whenever the word "Circle" is used in the Writings of the Ari, it refers to the perfection of the Endless, meaning a place within which Light shines everywhere regardless of levels of desire, regardless of levels of connection. As Rav Ashlag says, "...even after the Tzimtzum the Supernal Light remained in the image of a Circle." This is an amazing concept. As far as the Creator is concerned the Supernal Light does not perceive any changes; there is never better or worse, never bad or good because Light shines everywhere regardless of whether there is a great Desire to Receive or not. In our world, as we perceive it, whether a person is disconnected from the Light or whether there is no desire, a lesser Desire to Receive, the Light of the Creator never changes. The Creator does not have any desire to give more or less Light to a Vessel that has more Desire to Receive. We, the Vessel, have created this construct within which if we have a great Desire to Receive we become disconnected. The Light of the Creator never changes. As Rav Ashlag says here: "Occurrences or newness do not apply, Heaven forbid, to the Supernal Light... all these types of new aspects that are mentioned relate only to the Vessels."

The Baal Shem Tov speaks about a very important concept: if we see something that disturbs us, it means that there is something of that quality within us. If we see someone who has anger and that bothers us, it means we have a problem with anger. If we see someone with jealousy and it bothers us, it means we have a problem with jealousy. The Baal Shem Tov teaches that we will never see something bad in someone else unless we have that element within ourselves. For example, in the Torah it says that Isaac loved his wicked son, Esau. Isaac saw nothing bad in him. Therefore Jacob had to steal the blessing. The Zohar asks: what does it mean that Isaac did not see the bad in Esau? Was he blind? Was he unwise? Esau, as we read, was not a good person. The answer is that we only see a negative quality in someone if we have that fault within ourselves.

The Baal Shem Tov also teaches that even if we hear about a tragedy somewhere or if we hear that someone died, even on the other side of the world, it is because there is something that is lacking in the work we are doing that allows the situation to happen. Isaac was not at fault with regard to the way Esau turned out. Isaac did everything right in raising Esav. Nonetheless, Esau had his own process to go through, and because Isaac was not at fault in whatever darkness or negativity existed in Esau, he could not see it. It was not a negative blindness; it was blindness due to Yitzchak's perfection. He had no fault in the failings of Esau, which is why he could not see them. From this we learn that if we see a fault in someone else, we have it within ourselves to one degree or another; even if it is indirect or seems illogical. For example, we hear about murders all the time and thank God, most of us are not murderers. How can it be then that we are exposed to it? There is a spiritual principle that stipulates that embarrassing someone is like murder. Therefore, if we hear about murders, perhaps the quality of embarrassing someone is a fault within us. If we hear about a crime or incident it does not necessarily mean that this is exactly what we do, however, if there is something bad that we see in someone else, if there is something bad that we hear about or see in the world, there is an element of that that has to do with me.

The Endless Light sees no bad; it sees no bad in the Desire to Receive for the Self Alone. It sees no bad in anything in this world. The Light of the Creator is in constant peace, shining everywhere. It does not care about higher or lower; the Desire to Receive or Desire to Share—the Endless Light sees only good. This is an awareness we can connect to: whenever we see good in another person; whenever we work hard to not see the bad in someone else we connect to an element of the perfection of the Endless World. Conversely, in connecting to the lack in other people in seeing the darkness or the bad in other people, we are, to a certain degree, disconnecting from this concept of the Endless World.

One of the many gifts of the Kabbalah Centres is that anyone who walks into the Centre—to whatever degree of connection they are at, are both welcomed and not judged. There is no one way that a person needs to do the work. Every person can connect on different levels. And no one should judge a person nor compare people's process, thinking: *this person is doing X and Y and the other is doing X and Z, therefore one is better than the other.* Once we start judging, meaning believing one is better and one is worse, we disconnect from this concept of the Endless Light.

---

4. **From Above Downward:** Do not forget that this does not signify, Heaven forbid, concepts that are likened to a physical place. Rather, that which is more pure is called "Above," while that which is coarse and inferior is called "Down." And as said earlier (Chapter 1, Section 6) that all that can be understood about the extending of the Light from the Emanator and its process of becoming an Emanated, mainly relates to the newness of the Difference of Form in the emanated, namely the aspect of the Desire to Receive that is new in it, which does not exist in the Emanator. For this reason, the Emanated is considered distant, coarse, base, and low in relation to the Emanator since its Difference of Form from the Emanator causes all these and separates it from being an Emanator into being an Emanated.

---

Know also that this Difference of Form, namely the Desire to Receive, is not manifested all at once but rather it is slowly formed in the sequence of the Four Phases, and its form is complete to its utmost growth only in the Fourth Phase. Therefore, the conclusion is that whatever has the scanter form of Desire to Receive, namely the first of the Four Phases, is considered closest to the Emanator and is the most important, elevated, and pure, since its Difference of Form is not as great as that of the next Three Phases. The Second Phase, in which the Desire to Receive is greater than that of the First Phase, is considered further away from the Emanator, coarser, baser, and lower than the First Phase and so on until the Fourth Phase, which is the furthest from the Emanator, coarsest, basest, and lowest of all. This is what the Rav [the Ari] meant in saying that the Line was drawn **"from Above Downward,"** namely from the First Phase to the Fourth Phase (not including), which is the lowest of all.

This mentioned idea of above and below is now a new reality with the emergence of the Line since before the Line illuminated, that is, during the Tzimtzum, there was no distinction of up and down as mentioned before (Chapter 1, Section 19). Yet after [the Vessel] received the Light in the aspect of only a Line, meaning it did not receive it with all Four Phases, but only with its first Three Phases, while the Fourth Phase remained dark without Light, only now the Fourth Phase is revealed to be the inferior, coarser, and a lower phase upon which are set the Three Phases that precede it in being purer and closer to the Emanator, as said. This was not so during the Tzimtzum. When the Light departed from all Four Phases all at once, there was not yet this distinction between the Phases, as said (Chapter 1, Section 19).

In reading the words of the Ari: **"The Light shines from above downward,"** it is easy to start thinking in physical terms; meaning the Light comes into the Vessel in this way. Of course this is absolutely not what is being discussed here as the Light never moves. The Light does not travel from Above downward. What is being described here is the way the Vessel perceives the Light: the First Phase, which is the lesser desire, has a perception of more Light; and the Second, Third, and Fourth Phases, respectfully, feel further away. The difference between the literal understanding of the words of the

Ari and the way in which we comprehend them—based on Rav Ashlag, is completely different.

In the earlier sections, Rav Ashlag explained at length that the only difference between Light and Vessel is that the Vessel has this new concept of a Desire to Receive. And as the desire becomes stronger and more pronounced the Vessel's Light becomes more and more different from the Light of the Creator. And since this new Desire to Receive is innate within the Vessel, the Vessel is considered further away from the Creator. The Difference of Form that occurs to the Vessel is what separates it; it is what moves it further away, not in physical distance but in differences of spiritual essence. Rav Ashlag explains at length that the Light of the Creator does not come directly into a Vessel of a great Desire to Receive, instead It goes through a process of Four Phases and only at the Fourth Phase is the great true Vessel—the Desire to Receive—revealed.

One of the key concepts that will be made clear throughout the Talmud Eser Sefirot, is that the work is in the Fourth Phase. Very often, there are some who are willing to remain with a limited desire, a desire of First, Second or Third Phase. There are people who are willing to go through life with fulfilling a limited amount of their desires.

The work that we are meant to do is not within the First Phase, the Second Phase or even the Third Phase; the work that we are meant to do is within the Fourth Phase—the greatest desire. If we go through life and do not awaken a greater and greater desire, we are not doing the work. If we are satisfied, if we think that within our realm we are okay, then we are not doing the work because the work is only in the Fourth Phase, in the great desire. This is why there has to be a constant awakening of a greater and greater desire if we are to be sure that we are doing the work.

2. **The Upper Head of the Line**[5] **is drawn from the the Endless (Ein Sof) Itself and touches It.**[6] **But the conclusion of this Line, down at its end,**[7] **does not touch the Endless Light (Ohr Ein Sof).**

5. **The Upper Head of the Line:** This refers to the First of the Four Phases, as mentioned in the previous paragraph.

6. **And touches It:** The First Phase, which is the upper head (or beginning), is closest to the Endless Light (Ohr Ein Sof), meaning to the Emanator. Therefore, it is considered as touching Him, since the dissimilarity in the Difference of Form of the First Phase is not apparent to the point that it can be separated from the Emanator, as said.

7. **Down at its end:** This indicates the Fourth Phase, which is farthest and lowest of them all, as said (Chapter 2, Section 4), for now it does not receive the Supernal Light and thus is not touching the Endless Light (Ohr Ein Sof) but is separated from It.

Clearly the Ari is not talking about physical closeness or physical touching, but rather a Similarity of Form and Difference in Form. This is how we understand the new reality of the Line (Kav). There are elements of the Kav that are still in unity with the Light of the Creator and there are elements of it that are in complete separation from the Light of the Creator, which is the great Desire to Receive.

We are not discussing two different Vessels. We are speaking about one Vessel within which there a part that is completely connected to the Light of the Creator and one part that is completely disconnected and separated from the Light of the Creator. This helps us to understand the concept that each one of us can have a part of us that is pure and in connection to the Light of the Creator, and we have a part of us that is complete filth and completely disconnected from the Light of the Creator. The Light and the darkness found within each of us is an unbelievable disparity; extremely opposite in parts.

What is important to realize and remember is that no matter how disconnected those parts of us are, this does not diminish the parts of us that are in complete unity. Thus when we do something of a negative nature related to the Fourth Phase, related to the great darkness, to the great Desire to Receive for the Self Alone, this does not in any way diminish or take away from that part of us that is still in complete unity with the Light of the Creator. Even when we fall, having done actions of complete separation from the Light of the Creator, it does not mean that the other part of us—the part that is completely connected to the Light of the Creator—is no longer connected; it is still there. This is really the battle that we face in life. It is not so much that we fall, it is that when we do fall, the negative side wants us to forget about that first part, the real part of us that is in complete unity with the Light of the Creator.

What we learn from the reality of the *Kav* is that although there is a part of it that is completely dark, completely disconnected from the Light of the Creator, there is still the never changing part, the First Phase of it, which is in complete unity with the Light of the Creator. And each one of us has this connection all the time. The question is always: where is our consciousness? Is our consciousness focusing on the part of us that is in complete disconnect from the Light of the Creator (which is what the negative side wants us to do)? Or is our consciousness thinking about the part of us that is in complete unity with the Light of the Creator? As the Baal Shem Tov teaches: wherever our mind is, that is where we are. Therefore, what we have to do is strengthen and awaken our understanding and connection and knowledge of that part of us that is in complete unity with the Ohr Ein Sof (Endless Light).

3. The Light of Endless (Ohr Ein Sof) is drawn and extends downward through this Line.

4. In the place of that space, He emanated, created, formed and made[8] all Worlds.

8. **He emanated, created, formed and made:** This alludes to the Four Worlds called: Atzilut (Emanation), Briyah (Creation), Yetzirah (Formation) and Asiyah (Action or Making), which include all the Worlds that are in countless details. These Four Worlds are drawn from the mentioned Four Phases: from the First Phase comes Atzilut, from the Second Phase comes Briyah, from the Third Phase comes Yetzirah, from the Fourth Phase comes Asiyah.

5. Before these Four Worlds,[9] the Endless (Ein Sof) was "He is One and His Name are One,"[10] in such wonderful and concealed unity. Not even His closest angels[11] have such ability, and they have no conception of the Endless (Ein Sof), since no mind of any created being can comprehend Him, since He has no place, no boundary, and no name.[12]

9. **Before these Four Worlds:** They are called Atzilut, Briyah, Yetzirah, and Asiyah, as said (in the previous paragraph), and they include the entirety of all the Worlds. Before all these, that is, before the Tzimtzum, these Four Phases were not considered as one above the other, as said (Chapter 2, Section 4). Rather, they were in a state of simple unity, as mentioned (Chapter 1, Section 12), without any difference among the Phases and between Light and Vessel but rather in a state of "He and His Name are one," as mentioned earlier—study there well.

10. **He is One and His name are One:** "He" indicates the Supernal Light, and "His Name" indicates the aspect of the Desire to Receive that of necessity is there, as said (Chapter 1, section 12, starting with: "We should not ask." Study that carefully). *Shemo* (His Name) has the same numerical value (346) as *Ratzon* (Desire), alluding to the Desire to Receive.

11. **Not even His closest angels:** In other words, now, after the Worlds were created, even angels, who are creatures that are closest in their spirituality, have no conception of the Endless (Ein Sof).

Before the Tzimtzum, the Light and Vessel were in complete unity. Yet we cannot understand how the Light and Vessel can be one because seemingly if you have purity and you have darkness, they should not be unified as one; if you have only sharing and only receiving, they should not logically be unified as one. However in the Endless World, there was a complete unity. This is how Rav Ashlag explained it earlier. Nevertheless, here the Ari is speaking about the fact that even the angels cannot comprehend the Endless World because they come from the World after the Tzimtzum.

Nonetheless we are meant to connect to the level of Ein Sof. We, therefore, can achieve something the angels can never achieve. We humans can achieve a connection to the Ein Sof, to the Endless World, but the angels cannot connect to Ein Sof because it is not understandable to them; meaning it is so far beyond what they can achieve.

---

12. **He has no place, no boundary and no name:** Since the state of, "He and His Name are One" exists in the Ein Sof, and no place or Vessel is recognizable there at all, as said before, therefore no mind of any created being can conceive it, since there can be no conception of Light without Vessel.

---

The first thing that we notice is that this is a little different from the explanation Rav Ashlag gave earlier. Earlier Rav Ashlag said: "And even though there is necessarily some Difference of Form between them, between "He" and "His Name," as explained, nevertheless this is not active there at all. And even though we do not understand this, it is so without any doubt. And the sages have said about this that the Ein Sof cannot be thought of or grasped at all, since this issue is beyond our mind." (Inner Light, Chapter 1, Section 12)

Here in the quote above, Rav Ashlag is saying that neither we nor the angels can comprehend the Endless World because we cannot comprehend Light without Vessel. It is important to know that there is always more than one true reason why anything occurs, especially in all spiritual matters. There are more than two reasons why we cannot comprehend the Endless World.

It says about the Ari that because there were so many thoughts coming to him all at once, he was not able to write anything down. For example, if the Ari wanted to explain why we cannot comprehend the Endless World, ten thousand reasons came into his mind, because if something is true there are a million and one reasons why it is true. Regarding lies there is never a good reason. Yet for good, for the truth, there are a million and one reasons why. Therefore, if the Ari was going to write down why it is incomprehensible to us and the angels that "He and His Name are One" he would not be unable to write down only one reason because ten thousand other reasons would come. Part of the *Ruach haKodesh* (Divine Inspiration) and the great assistance that Rav Ashlag had in revealing the Talmud Eser Sefirot, is that he knew which reason to give.

In the book The Wisdom of Truth, Rav Ashlag writes that there are certain righteous souls that are able to conceal, condense, limit and therefore reveal the wisdom. This is one of the great gifts that Rav Ashlag gives us in the Talmud Eser Sefirot. Because we experience a limited amount of consciousness and a limited amount of revelation, it is easy for us to write things down. However, to have both a constant flow of awareness and consciousness, reasons and understanding and on the other hand the ability to limit it to writing like Rav Ashlag had, is something that is a tremendous gift and what he brings to us needs to be appreciated.

Another idea to consider is that Rav Ashlag is telling us that we unfortunately cannot comprehend Light without Vessel. In simple terms, we cannot consciously and/or unconsciously comprehend the idea of doing something and not receiving something in return. Light without a Vessel means revealing Light without having a desire for it to come back to us in any way, shape or form. All of us, to one degree or another, are within the realm where there has to always be a return on anything that we do. We need to see the result, either right away or afterwards. Needing to see the result is the reason why we cannot comprehend revealing Light without receiving anything in return.

This is something that we have to work on, not simply because it is the spiritual thing to do, but also as Rav Ashlag makes very clear here, if we want to connect to the Endless World it requires us to reveal Light without Vessel, sharing without any anticipation, without any desire that something, anything will come back to us. This is the way we can connect to the Endless World. As long as we remain within the realm—where most of us are—of only comprehending Light with Vessel, sharing and receiving, we cannot truly connect to the Endless World. We can receive elements of it. We can receive this consciousness of the *Kav*, where there is a limited amount of revelation, yet to truly connect to the Endless World is impossible without coming to a level of Light without Vessel, sharing, giving without anticipating anything in return.

The third idea discussed by the Ari is that "no mind of any created being can comprehend Him." One of Rav Ashlag's main teachings is this concept of: "Certainty Beyond Logic" (*emuna lemala min hada'at*). What does this mean? Rav Ashlag explains that if we want to be a *tzadik* (a righteous person) we have to see only goodness; we have to see the Creator only acting in a good way. What then are we to think if we see someone in pain? What do we do when we see someone experience illness? There is no logical way—at least within the realm that most of us exist—to explain logically how this or that situation is from the Creator, and that the Creator is expressing goodness.

If we see someone in pain, if we see suffering, if we see something bad, as Rav Ashlag explains, it means that we are making ourselves a rasha, disconnected by seeing darkness. What we need to do is have Certainty Beyond Logic, which means: *I don't understand how this is good, but I believe this is good.* And when we develop Certainty Beyond Logic it is another way with which we connect to the Light of the Creator, and specifically the Light of the Ein Sof, the Endless World.

The Ari explains that our mind, explicitly our brain cannot comprehend this but if we do our work and find ways when things do not make any sense and we push ourselves towards Certainty Beyond Logic—as Abraham our Father did at the Binding if Isaac—this is another tool we can use to connect to the Endless World.

Thus what Rav Ashlag and the Ari are giving us—along with all the other great revelations—are two tools to connect to the Endless World. One, do actions of Light without Vessel. Do actions of revelation of Light, specifically without having any desire for anything good in return: not a good feeling; nor a spiritual connection; and certainly nothing physical or ego based. Actions that are Light without Vessel are actions of complete sharing without receiving anything in return; this is an aspect of a connection to the Endless World.

Two, to connect to the Endless World, requires work with Certainty Beyond Logic, beyond our consciousness, beyond our mind. As long as our work is within the realm of our mind, within the realm of our knowledge, we cannot connect to the Endless World. For us to connect to the Endless World, we have to find ways to work with Certainty Beyond Logic. When we go beyond the logical mind we can begin comprehending and connecting to the Endless World.

# INNER OBSERVATION (HISTAKLUT PNIMI)

Before anything, we need to know that wherever we deal with spiritual matters divested of time, space, and motion, not to mention when dealing with the Divine, we do not have the words with which to verbalize and express ourselves, since our entire vocabulary is based on imagined sensory perception. How can we use them in a place where the senses and the imagination have no power?

Take, for example, a subtler word such as "Lights." It too is likened to, and borrowed from, sunlight or the light of a pleasurable feeling, and the like. How then can they be used to express Divine matters? Surely they offer the reader nothing truthful. Needless to say, this is the case when revelations need to be made through these words printed in a book or in a dialogue concerning this wisdom, as is the custom with studies of any wisdom. Then, if we fail even by one word that is unsuitable for its purpose, the reader will immediately become confused, unable to make heads or tails of the entire issue.

It is not that we are unable to explain things using roundabout language because we can explain concepts pretty well with physical language, however it would not be truthful, it would not be exact. It is no coincedence that the wisdom of Kabbalah is called the "Wisdom of Truth." This means that the only way a person can truly come to understand this wisdom—and get a sense of a deep connection to the Light that is the essence of this wisdom—is if the person is completely truthful. If we are capable of lying to another person then we are capable of lying to ourselves, and we are capable of lying to the Creator. Therefore, truth is paramount to the ability to connect to this wisdom. There is no such thing as lying in one area of our life and not in other areas.

There are many lessons in this explanation by Rav Ashlag, and one of them is appreciation for the truth. Rav Ashlag is saying here that with any language that we have at our disposal—even using a hundred words would not suffice. If we try to explain an emotion, for example love, we can use physical words. But is there really a word or even a group of words that can truly capture and explain the meaning and experience of love? If an individual approaches someone who has never felt love and tries to use vocabulary to explain the emotion, it is almost impossible to describe it truthfully. It is possible to express it in an approximate manner. Therefore, the language that we use is capable of explaining things as an approximation; however in discussing this wisdom it is not enough to be approximate. This wisdom is exact, and the language has to be precise.

Rav Ashlag is telling us that there is an innate problem using language to explain these concepts. Because all language comes from the realm of the five senses it cannot explain truly spiritual matters, truly Godly matters with exactness.

Most of us live our lives in the realm that is an approximation of the truth and this wisdom. Kabbalah is not a wisdom that can be approximately true. It has to be precise, perfect and true. Rav Ashlag is telling us that if we write about Kabbalah and one word is not exact and to the point, the reader will be completely confused and will not be able to make sense of this wisdom. This represents a big problem in that the language we speak is a language that is incapable of truthful and exact explanation concerning matters of the true spiritual Worlds.

Therefore, the kabbalists chose for themselves a special language that can be called the Language of the Branches, since there is no entity, nor any power of that entity in this World that does not extend from its root in the Upper World. On the contrary, the origin of every entity in this world starts in the Upper World, and then it evolves down into this World.

Everything in our world has a Supernal Source. This is true about all physical objects and all words. Words in language have a Supernal Source. Nevertheless the way we understand the words in our world is clearly very far from their origin in the Supernal Worlds, yet there is a complete connection between them. The singular difference is that the words we use are of a much lower level. Take the word "table," for example. A physical table is connected to the Supernal Source, meaning the Light that is the table, however the Difference of Form between the physical table and its spiritual Source is great. Although it is one and the same, and connected, tethered directly to its spiritual Source, it is down-graded and therefore of a much, much lower reality.

When we consider the example of souls—there are souls of the righteous that are completely connected to the Light of the Creator and then there are souls that are the lowest of the souls called the "animalistic Nefesh," the animal soul that people can have. The animalistic Nefesh and the highest souls of the righteous that achieve their perfection are from the same Source as they are both soul. Obviously one is tremendously elevated, purified, connected to the Light of the Creator and one is much, much lower—but they are the same, they are of the same source. With this Rav Ashlag is saying that everything in our world is connected to the Supernal Worlds. However, the problem is that everything in our physical world is of a much lower level of emanation.

Thus the sages found a ready-made language, without effort, with which they can convey their comprehension to each other, orally and in written form, from one generation to the next. They [accomplished it by] using the Names of the Branches in this World, where each Name is self-explanatory, as in pointing with a finger to its Supernal root in the system of the Upper Worlds.

The problem is that when we hear the word "table" we think about the table we see in front of us. When the kabbalists think about or use the word "table," they are thinking about and referring to something much more elevated— the Source of Light that becomes manifested in our world as "table." The true kabbalists know its true meaning. They know that it is never describing a physical table—it is indicating the table's Supernal Source. When kabbalists hear and use the word "Light," they know it does not concern all the things we think of when we think about light but instead is denoting its Supernal Source. This is a very important concept to understand.

That said, the kabbalists did not create a new language, they actually used a language already there, which, by its nature, is obviously very confusing to those who are not kabbalists and do not have a clear vision of the Spiritual Sources of everything in our world. This caused tremendous misunderstanding throughout the generations of people who have tried to understand Kabbalah. If we truly grasp this concept, it gives us an appreciation for how impossible it would be to study Kabbalah on our own and the great merit we have in what Rav Ashlag did for us by revealing the Supernal Sources of things. Because of Rav Ashlag's vision, we are able to explain what the kabbalists had written before.

What we hopefully appreciate is that there is no way that the words we understand, when we read from the Writings of the Ari, the Zohar, the Torah, are anywhere close to the truth because neither the words of the Torah, nor the words of the Zohar, nor the words in the Writings of the Ari, are referring to the physical objects and meanings.

Rav Ashlag explains that the reason he called his commentary on the Zohar "The Ladder" (HaSulam) was to open doors and give us pathways; it was not his purpose to reveal everything. The Sulam is an opening to understanding, and once we train our mind to think in the way Rav Ashlag writes, we can understand the much deeper levels of the Zohar. The purpose of our study is to reveal Light and train our mind to see these connections.

The same can be said about Rav Ashlag's work, Talmud Eser Sefirot. The purpose of this study is to train our mind to think like the kabbalists do. The purpose of this study is to help us to connect to the Language of the Branches, to connect our consciousness, our mind, to the true understanding of this language. In learning the Language of Branches we are learning a new language, as Rav Ashlag said. When one learns a new language it might begin by learning a specific group of words and then expanding our vocabulary to learn the rest of the language. A smarter way, a more logical way to truly learn a language is to begin by learning the truest meanings of words. And if you understand the truest meaning of words you can then truly understand things.

But as Rav Ashlag says, it has to be clear to us that the only way we can begin to truly understand the writings of the kabbalists is to first understand how blind we are, how impossible it is for us to comprehend the writings of the kabbalists on our own. When we open up the words of the Ari, **"Before the creation of our world the Supernal Light filled the entire reality,"** our ego will want to tell us, "Well, ok maybe I don't understand everything, but I can make sense of it," and with that thought we are lost. The first stage is to understand that there is no relationship between the way we understand words and what the kabbalists truly meant when they wrote them.

Thus with this, your mind can remain at ease as you shall so often find in the books of Kabbalah puzzling expressions that are even sometimes alien to the human spirit. The reason is that since they have already chosen this language with which to express themselves, namely the Language of the Branches, as said, how can they omit a particular branch and not use it due to its lowliness, thus not expressing through it the desired concept while at the same time there is no other branch in our world that they can use instead. Because, just as two hairs are not sustained by one follicle, no two branches are traced to one root. Also it is impossible to wipe out the spiritual term stipulated by that lowly expression. Moreover, that loss will cause a flaw and great confusion throughout the expanses of the wisdom, for we have no other wisdom among all the disciplines in the world, in which subjects are so interrelated by way of cause and effect, reason and consequence, as the wisdom of Kabbalah, in which subjects are closely knit from beginning to end like one long chain.

Therefore, there is no freedom of choice here to exchange or switch between these Names, a bad one for a good one. Rather, we should always precisely use the same branch that points to its Supernal Root. We should also speak of it at length, until we provide the accurate definition for the understanding of the learning readers.

For instance, when the kabbalists talk about the Supernal Source of a dog, they use the word "dog." Although "dog" may seem to be a silly word to be used in discussion of spiritual matters, nonetheless there is a Supernal Source to the physical manifestation of a dog that we see in our world. Therefore, the kabbalists do not have the choice to say, "Well it is a weird word to use when we're talking about Supernal matters, let us try to find a more spiritual word, a more appropriate word." They cannot do this any longer, because it is an exact science and therefore an exact language.

This is why we find subjects and stories in the Torah and in the Books of the Prophets that seem to be inappropriate. Every physical thing, every physical object has a spiritual Source. If the kabbalists are talking about that spiritual Source, they have to use the physical word of that manifestation because every physical object in our world has a direct Source. Therefore, if they want to discuss a Source, the kabbalists would then have to go down into our world and say, "What is the lowest physical manifestation of that Source? That is the word I have to use."

The true gift of the Talmud Eser Sefirot is that it can transform our consciousness completely, which Rav Ashlag says is not easy at all; in fact it is the most difficult thing to do. However, if we truly study the Talmud Eser Sefirot and we truly study Kabbalah as Rav Ashlag reveals it, we will get to see the true world, the reality of our world, and that view then takes us to so many other levels, levels where with everything we see in our world, we see its Source; we see the Light that is within it. This is the level that the kabbalists attained; they achieved the level where they do not see tables or chairs or water or cups, they saw a Supernal Source. And every single one of us can tune our mind into the Language of the Branches—seeing physicality at the same time as we are able to directly link it to its Source. This has a tremendous benefit and one of the purposes of this study.

This study is so difficult because it is never going to be enough to hear it and know it, hear it and understand it. It requires a retraining of our minds. The benefit is that we then start seeing everything in its true Essence. We then get to see everything in its true Source.

This is the nature of a true kabbalist. A true kabbalist is someone who achieves the level of seeing everything as it is connected to its Source, and therefore sees Light in everything. There are many stories about the kabbalists that would have conversations with people, speaking to them about business or all manner of mundane things of the physical world. Yet, what they were truly doing was revealing Light—they were talking about the Supernal Worlds. This is because when we talk about a business we think of its physical manifestation. When a kabbalist speaks about business, he knows its Supernal Source.

There are many stories about kabbalists whose students would observe them sitting and talking with people. These students would begin understanding and seeing the hints their teachers were giving—the true *yichudim* (unifications)—the true revelations of Light they would be revealing. Rav Levi Yitzhak of Berditchev was very famous for doing this type of work. He would have mundane superficial conversations with many people. But in essence what he was doing was using these words as tools to reveal Light.

The second stage of understanding, as Rav Ashlag says, is knowing there is no wisdom more difficult to grasp. This is why I strongly urge everyone to review these teachings many times because it is not about understanding, it is about retraining it in our mind. And one of the amazing gifts of this wisdom is that it trains our mind to think in true form of the Light of the Creator.

Indeed, those whose eyes have not yet opened to behold the Heavenly sights and still do not have proficiency in the relation between the branches of this World and their roots in the Supernal Worlds, abide here as blind people groping in the dark, since they do not understand even a single word according to its true meaning, as every word is a Name of a branch in relation to its root. They can only do so if they receive the explanation from a distinguished wise sage who presents himself by explaining the subject using the colloquial language, which is necessarily like translating into another language, that is, from the Language of the Branches into the spoken language. Then he could explain the spiritual term as it is.

This is why I toiled in my commentary to explain the Ten Sefirot— as the Divine master the Ari taught us—according to their spiritual purity divested of all tangible concepts in such a way that every beginner can approach this wisdom without failing in materialization and misconception. With the understanding of the Ten Sefirot, a gate will open to both observe and know how to understand the rest of the subjects of this wisdom.

In revealing the Talmud Eser Sefirot, Rav Ashlag shared with us the opening up of the Supernal visions that he held. The only way that we can begin to understand this wisdom is to truly have an appreciation for who Rav Ashlag was and more importantly the work that he did to bring this down to our level, because it is the one wisdom that is impossible to explain, and understand, to teach and to write about, unless you have clarity of vision, like Rav Ashlag had. In the Zohar, Rav Shimon speaks often about being very careful not to repeat anything unless you heard it from a true kabbalist because with regard to the wisdom of Kabbalah, which is a precise, perfect wisdom it is impossible to understand unless you have completely perfected yourself.

So to imagine that we could understand it on our own is obviously silly. We must appreciate what Rav Ashlag has done for us, the gift the Creator has given to us through Rav Ashlag because clearly Rav Ashlag had that opening up of the Supernal vision. Most of us probably cannot even imagine working an entire lifetime to truly come to an understanding of all the Talmud Eser Sefirot, yet the entire purpose of the Talmud Eser Sefirot, as Rav Ashlag writes here, is to open a doorway. Meaning, we have to perfect our understanding of the Talmud Eser Sefirot, know all of it perfectly because this is simply the entry point into the true study, into the true understanding. This gives us an appreciation for how much work there is for us to do. For Rav Ashlag, the full explanation of the entire work of Talmud Eser Sefirot was just an opening of the door for us. After we understand all of Talmud Eser Sefirot, then we can truly begin to study this wisdom.

One important concept I want to share is this: when the Zohar says, "Woe to those whose eyes are closed; woe to those who are sleeping," it is referring to all of us. Every single one of us is, to some degree or another, completely spiritually blind. This blindness eventually affects our understanding of the wisdom, and the way we see the world.

When we look at another person and we experience any type of animosity, hatred or lack of unity, it is because our eyes are blind. If we are able to have true vision, we would see only Light in the other person. Thus this does not simply concern the wisdom we are discussing here, this manifests in every area of our lives. We have to beseech the Creator to please open up our eyes in this way. Once we are able to understand the Language of Branches; to begin truly seeing; to slowly, slowly open up our eyes to this wisdom, it will transform our entire life.

I want to emphasize the importance of having the awareness to understand the blindness, the darkness that we are in and to appreciate the gift that we are given in our generation that this wisdom has been opened up to us and to beg the Creator to help us and make sure that we merit the level of *p'tichat einayim* (opening up our eyes), as Rav Ashlag explains in depth in And You Shall Choose Life.

# CHAPTER 1

> "Know that before the emanations were emanated and the creations were created, a simple Supernal Light filled the entire existence…" (Etz Chayim, Chamber 1, Gate 1, Branch 2). These words require an explanation, since before the Worlds were emanated how could there be a kind of place of existence that the simple Light filled entirely? Also, the idea of the rising up of the desire to be contracted so as to manifest the perfection of His actions – it appears from the words of the book that there was already something missing there, Heaven forbid. Also, the idea of the Tzimtzum taking place exactly in its Middle Point is very puzzling, since he has already said that there is neither beginning nor end there. How then is there a center? These issues are indeed deeper than the sea, and therefore I must explain them at length.

At this point, many of us who have gone through at least the first section may think we understand. And maybe we do have a very, very limited inkling of it. However, even a perfect comprehension of what is written is only an opening to gaining full awareness of the true meanings of these teachings and of these words. There is a great danger of our ego convincing us that we know it already, thus we have to always remember that even if we think we understand it perfectly (which most of us probably do not), the words of the Ari and the words of Rav Ashlag, are like a shell covering the true essence of the words. Only the constant thought and work of trying to fathom more and more opens up those layers more and more.

> There is nothing throughout the entire existence that is not included in the Ein Sof. The opposite Concepts [that are perceived] by us are included in Him in the secret of One, Singular, and Unified.

1. Know that there is no essence of any entity in the world, either perceived by our senses or grasped by our mind's eye that is not included in the Creator, since they are all drawn unto us from Him. For is it possible to give what one does not have? This issue has already been well elucidated in the books. However, we need to understand [this issue as it relates to] concepts that for us are separate or opposite.

For example, the concept of wisdom is distinctly different from the concept of sweetness, as wisdom and sweetness are two distinct concepts. Also, the concept of the performer is surely different from the concept of the performance, since the performer and the performance are necessarily two distinct concepts. This is even more so with opposite concepts, such as sweetness and bitterness, and so on; they are surely distinguished separately, each one on its own. But with Him, wisdom, pleasure, sweetness and piquancy, performance and the performer, and other forms that are different and opposite—all this is included as one in His simple Light, without any distinction or difference between them at all.

We only need to look at our World to realize it is not so difficult to understand how one reality can encompass many different things. Our one world has trillions of things that are different and not alike; alike and separate. Therefore, the concept that within the Essence of the Light of the Creator there are different things is not difficult to accept, however, this is only one level. In going further, we can ask how all of these things are unified within the Creator? How is it that within the Light of the Creator, wisdom and sweetness, which are two completely different concepts—not opposite—but different become unified as one? How can the person doing an action and the action itself be unified as one? This is something we have to know and accept as truth even though we might not have the ability to comprehend. There is someone I teach these concepts to and every once in a while when we arrive at a very deep concept, they say that their head actually begins to hurt. I remember even the first time I learned this with the Rav—it was one of those concepts that was truly difficult to really internalize.

I hope everyone studying this takes the time to think about it because it is not a coincidence Rav Ashlag addresses this here in one of the first ideas that he shares with us in the Inner Observation. If we spend the time to truly think about this concept, it gives us a level of penetration into and comprehension of what the Endless World is about.

There is the mistake one can make in thinking that the Endless World includes everything in different forms. This is not what Rav Ashlag is saying. **The Endless World includes everything in one unified form.** And this too is a concept, which is probably beyond our ability to comprehend. But at least we can take the time to realize what that means in our mind and then, if possible, we can begin to think about it and try to internalize it. It is almost a meditative experience. It is a transcendence of our consciousness to be able to grasp this obviously very important concept.

---

Rather, it is all according to the concept of One, Singular, and Unified (*Echad, Yachid uMeyuchad*). "One" indicates that it is equally even. "Singular" refers to what is drawn from Him, since even all the multiplicities are by Him as a singular form, like His essence is. "Unified" indicates that even though He performs a multitude of actions, it is one Force that performs them all, and they all return and reunite again into one Single Form. This Single Form encompasses (lit. swallows) all Forms that appear through His actions. This matter is very subtle and not every mind can endure it.

---

Rav Ashlag says, "This is a very subtle concept that not everyone's mind and everyone's brain can comprehend." This is the literal translation of those words. With this I think that what Rav Ashlag is saying is that it is not only within the mind that we can truly comprehend this concept, rather it is one of those ideas that can only truly be understood through the *soul*; through a transcending of the mind. Earlier we discussed the idea of going beyond our understanding. This is one of those concepts that cannot really be understood even on a basic level without taking the time to think about it and allowing it to penetrate beyond our mind and thought.

Rav Moshe ben Nachman, the Nachmanides of blessed memory, also commented upon the subject of His Oneness according to the secret of *Echad* (One), *Yachid* (Singular) and *Meyuchad* (Unified), with the following words (from his commentary on the Book of Formation, Chapter 1, Mishnah 7): "There is a difference between One, Singular, and Unified. When He unites to act as one Force, He is called Unified. And when He divides in order to perform His action, each part of Him is called Singular. But when He is equally even He is called One." End of quote of his pure language.

**"He unites to act as one Force"** means He acts to bestow goodness as befits Him being Singular, and there is no change in His actions. And when **"He divides in order to perform His action"** namely that His actions are different one from the other and it seems, Heaven forbid, that He is doing good and doing evil, then He is called Singular, since all His different actions have one outcome: to do good. Thus we conclude that He is Singular in each and every action and does not change through His different actions. And when He is equally even, He is called One; namely, One points to His Essence, where all manners of opposites are equally even, as said before. And as Maimonides [Rav Moses ben Maimon] said, "With Him, the Knower, the Known, and the Knowledge are one." For His thoughts are much higher than our thoughts and also His ways from our ways.

Unified (*Meyuchad*) means that although we see things in our world that do not seem to be manifestations of a Desire to Share, we should know—with certainty beyond our understanding—that everything is a manifestation of the Light of the Creator. There is no difference. There is no negative manifestation. If anything, we are either only seeing a part of the manifestation or we do not understand the manifestation because everything is Unified (Meyuchad). Singular (*Yachid*) represents the idea that everything that is already manifested in our world is from the same Source, a Source of goodness. And therefore even if we do not see it or we cannot fathom it yet, all is Singular; it has one singular purpose, one singular manifestation, which is to do good. The word One (*Echad*) represents the Essence of the Light of the Creator, within which all the opposite realities are one single reality.

The Thought, the Cause, the Consciousness behind every cause, which is the Light of the Creator, is good (a Desire to Share), and therefore all manifestations have to be good. Even when we do not see it in our world, nonetheless we have to have—Certainty Beyond Logic—that sometimes we do not see. We might not see how it is good or that it is good, and this is one level of this concept. The more difficult part to understand is that within the Essence of the Light of the Creator not only is everything good, but everything is also one. We can understand that one person does different actions that are good: for instance, I can give charity (*tzedaka*) to a person and this is a good action. I can give a person a ride home, which is another good action—both are good actions, but they are two separate actions. Yet within the Essence of the Light of the Creator those are one unified action.

As Rav Ashlag says, this is a very subtle and deep concept and one that I really hope we all take the time to think about. It is no coincidence that Rav Ashlag places us here in the first section of the Inner Observation because one of the effects of taking the time to think through this concept and struggle with it is that it detaches us, a little bit, from the ego of our understanding. And there is no real way to manifest and truly connect to the Light of the writings of the kabbalists without creating a little bit of a detachment from our Desire to Receive for the Self Alone and the ego of our understanding.

---

**Two distinctions of sharing:**
**before it is received and after it is received**

2. Go and learn from the Manna eaters. Manna is called "bread from the sky," since it did not materialize when it was clothed in this world, and the sages said that each one tasted in it what they wished to taste. It turns out that it of neccessity contained opposite forms, that is, one savored a sweet taste in it, while the other savored a spicy and bitter taste. The Manna itself, however, of neccessity included both opposites together, since nothing can give what it does not have. If so, how can there be two opposites in one thing? Yet, it must be that it is void and divested of both tastes. It only included them in such a way that the material receiver can differentiate for himself the taste that he desires.

In this manner you will understand every spiritual thing, which is in itself singular and simple, but does include all the multitude of forms in the world. And when it reaches a physical and limited receiver, then the receiver will make out of it one form separate from the myriad of forms that are united in that spiritual entity. According to this we should always distinguish between two aspects in His abundance. The first is the form of the Essence of the Supernal Abundance before it is received, when it is still a simple and inclusive Light. The second is after the abundance comes to be received, by which it acquires one separate and partial form, according to the quality of the receiver.

This concept of learning from the Manna eaters by Rav Ashlag has a very important practical manifestation. We restrict every aspect of the Light of the Creator that is revealed to us because whatever joy or fulfillment we have in our lives is simply an aspect of the Light of the Creator. Every part of the Light of the Creator has the potential to reveal everything. But we restrict or constrict that revelation.

If we enjoy only one thing—and that is how the Light of the Creator is manifested for us—we are restricting that Light from manifesting in a million and one other ways. Thus with that limited joy, that limit of fulfillment that we allow ourselves to manifest, we are restricting the Light of the Creator. We are telling the Creator, "In this moment, I want to taste sweet, so although this Light that You will manifest now can manifest sweetness and Light and bitterness and beauty, I only want to feel sweetness." We restrict the infinite Essence of the Light of the Creator. What we should understand from this is that throughout our lives it is we who are restricting, we are limiting our connection to the manifesting Light of the Creator. We limit the Creator, Who both wants to and is capable of revealing all that is completely unlimited all the time. To whatever degree we are limited, to whatever degree our understanding, our connection, our scope is limited, to that degree we limit the Light of the Creator.

This knowledge should give us the desire to open up our limitations, and not to confine how we want the Light of the Creator to manifest. There is not one part of the Light of the Creator that manifests as sweetness and another part of the Creator that manifests as beauty, and a different Light of the Creator that manifests as joy. Every aspect of the Light of the Creator that manifests in a particular way has the potential within it to reveal all other things as well—but we limit it.

The level of consciousness the *tzadikim* (righteous souls) attain is that they constantly feel the Light of the Creator, unrestricted, unconstricted. They do not limit the manifestation of the Light of the Creator in the way that we do. It is really both a beautiful concept and one that should awaken within us the desire to truly reveal the Light of the Creator in an unlimited way. Everything that is revealed to us: every aspect of joy, fulfillment, beauty, sweetness is a Light of the Creator that we, as the receiver have restricted. We are literally constricting and binding the Light, not allowing it to reveal its full potential. The more we open ourselves up to a true connection to the Light of the Creator, the more we remove the barriers we have placed on the Light of the Creator that is already revealed.

There is no such thing as a Light of one kind of blessing or a Light of another blessing or Light of this idea or that idea. There is only Simple Light. However, when we (the Vessel) manifest a limited Light, the Creator has to respond to our constricted desire by negating all other aspects of this Light and only manifest a tiny aspect of this Light.

After a righteous person leaves this world they go to what is called *Olam Haba* (the World to Come). In that World, the righteous person is liberated from the restrictions of the Desire to Receive of the body and they can truly appreciate the complete Light of the Creator. However what about the person who also merits to go to the World to Come when they pass but while in this world does not truly appreciate a connection to the Light of the Creator? What if their joy comes from money, or comes from food, or from something else? For this person, fulfillment in the World to Come has to be limited because they have not expanded their Vessel to receive the true abundance of the Light of the Creator, and therefore in that World even the Light of the Creator will have to continue to be restricted.

In the next world, everybody sees the next person's connection to the LIght and is embarrassed by it. Imagine sitting around with people who are able to truly partake of all the Light and for us the Creator has to do a lot of work to restrict all that amazing Light to make it fit into our limited vessel. We would be embarrassed. This is why in the Talmud it says: "Each and every one is burned from [embarrassment at the size of] the canopy of the other, [and says:] 'Woe for this embarrassment, woe for this disgrace, [that I did not merit a canopy as large as his].'" (Bava Batra 75a)

What we need to do while in this life is to begin to understand that every aspect of the Light of the Creator has everything. There is no limited Light and there is no aspect of the Light of the Creator that manifests only one thing or another. When we limit our desire for the Light to specific areas where we think we need or want, those are the areas where the Creator has to unfortunately force and constrict Light and revelation. On the other hand as we develop and begin expanding what we desire, expanding our desire for a true connection to the Light of the Creator, then the Creator can start slowly, slowly giving us of His Light, needing less and less to restrict and constrict that revelation. This is an amazing idea, one that if we truly understand, will hopefully give us that push to deeply want to change in our connection and therefore in our feeling of the Light of the Creator.

---

**How we can understand that the soul is part of Divinity.**

3. From this we reach an understanding of what the kabbalists said concerning the Essence of the soul. In their words, the soul is truly a part of the Divine Above and is no different whatsoever from the "whole," except that the soul is a "part" rather than the "whole." This is likened to a rock hewn from a mountain. The rock and the mountain are essentially the same and there is no difference between the rock and the mountain except that the rock is only a "part" of the mountain while the mountain is considered the "whole." This is the summary of the words of the kabbalists. These words are seemingly utterly puzzling, and it is most difficult to understand how we can discuss differences and fractions of Divinity to the point of likening them to a rock hewn from a mountain. We can understand a rock being hewn from a mountain by an axe and mallet. But in Divinity, how and in what manner can they seemingly separate from each other?

---

In The Wisdom of Truth Rav Ashlag speaks about the concept of cleaving (*dvekut*), saying that if we take a moment to appreciate what this concept means we will be astounded: Our soul (meaning what we have within us) and the Creator, are exactly the same. The Essence that every single one of us has within us, is exactly the Essence of the Light of the Creator. Imagine the amazing abundance of this. When we understand what this means, we also recognize the pain that our soul goes through every minute of every day as it has to restrict its revelation.

Whenever the Creator has to manifest limited Light to us, He has to restrict all the other great potential the Light has to reveal the Light in this specific way. Our soul restricts this revelation through our actions and through our lack of work. The Kabbalists say that if we would hear the painful cries from our soul we would not bear it. Now we can understand why we would be astounded: there is awesome, unfathomable Light within every single one of us, and we continue to restrict this revelation through our Desire to Receive for the Self Alone and through our selfishness.

On the positive side, we need to truly appreciate who we are. Our soul is exactly the Light of the Creator: the power that created this entire world, the power that will bring the Resurrection of the Dead, we have all of that. But unfortunately we continue to hide it; to force it to conceal its revelation.

---

**The spiritual is separated through Difference of Form, just like the material is separated by an axe.**

4. Before we begin the explanation, let us clarify the principle of the notion of separation that applies to spiritual beings: Know that the metaphysical [aspects of] people differ from each other through Difference of Form alone. That is, if one spiritual being acquires two Forms for itself, it is no longer one but two. Let me explain it to you using the example of an individual's soul, which is also spiritual, as is well known that its form is simple (also unclothed), since this is a spiritual law. Certainly there are as many souls as there are bodies, which shine in them, yet they differ from each other by the Difference in Form in each of them. This is in accordance with what the sages said that just as people's faces are not the same, so too their opinions are not the same. And the body has the ability to differentiate the soul's form, to the point of distinguishing each soul unto itself, this one being good and that one bad, etc., according to their different forms.

Now you see that just like a material thing is separated, cut and divided with an axe, with a movement to create a distance between one part to another, so too is a spiritual entity separated, cut and divided due to Difference of Form, one part from another. And the level of the difference, is the level of the distance between one part from another. Remember this well.

This concept is one of Rav Ashlag's great revelations: Concerning spiritual entities, Difference of Form separates and Likeness of Form brings them together. This concept of Difference of Form and Likeness of Form is not revealed in the Zohar or the Writings of the Ari. Although, of course the Ari, and Rav Shimon in the Zohar knew these concepts.

This is one of those concepts about which we can say "if we only came to this world to hear this one secret, it would be enough," as is written in the Zohar in many places. In my opinion we are spoiled, in that we hear these concepts all the time, knowing that Rav Ashlag speaks about Difference of Form and Likeness of Form—but in truth, any one of us could have studied the Zohar and the Writings of the Ari for the next one hundred years and would never have arrived at this concept. It really makes one appreciate the revelation and clarity of Rav Ashlag, which he, of course, received from the Light of the Creator.

---

**How a Difference of Form can be depicted
in the Creation in relation to Ein Sof.**

5. All this is only supposed in this world, relating to [the base level of] people's soul (Nefesh). But as for the soul itself (Neshamah), of which it was said that it is a part of Divinity Above, it is still not clear how it can be so different from Divinity to the extent that it is called a "part" of the Divine? Do not argue that this is through Difference of Form. Heaven forbid this should be said, for we already clarified that Divinity is Simple Light that includes all manners of multiplicity of forms and opposites of forms in the world in His simple unity, according to the secret of One, Singular, and Unified, as said. And if so, how can we imagine the aspect of Difference of Form in a soul that it should be different from Divinity, and hence be distinguished and acquire the name "part" of Him.

In truth, this question applies mostly to the Light of Ein Sof before the Tzimtzum. The existence in front of us—all Worlds, higher and lower—is distinguishable into two categories. The first category is the structure of the entire existence the way it is before the Tzimtzum, when it was boundless and infinite. This category is called the Light of Ein Sof. The second category is the structure of the entire existence that emerged from the Tzimtzum and Below, where everything has boundary and measure.

---

This category is called the Four Worlds: Atzilut (Emanation), Briyah (Creation), Yetzirah (Formation) and Asiyah (Action).

As we know, no thought can grasp His Essence whatsoever, and He has no name or appellation, for how can we define by name that which we cannot conceive? Every name implies conception, indicating that we grasp something that name denotes. Surely, in this case, there is neither name nor appellation applying to His Essence at all, and all the Names and Appellations merely reflect His Light that extends from Him. Hence, before the Tzimtzum, the extension of His Light that filled the entire existence without any boundaries or end, is called by the name: Ein Sof (Endless). According to this we should understand how the Light of Ein Sof became defined in Itself, no longer being part of His Essence, to the point where we can define it by Name. This is the same difficulty we raised in relation to the soul, as said.

**A commentary on the words of the sages: "Therefore work and toil were prepared for the souls to earn their reward; because he who eats what does not belong to him, cannot look into the eyes of the other."**

6. In this lofty place, to understand, even very slightly, we need to discuss it at length. Let us investigate the axis of the entire existence before us and its general purpose. Is there a doer without a purpose? So, what is this purpose, for which He established the entire existence before us in the Upper Worlds and the Lower Worlds?

The sages have indicated several times that all Worlds were created solely for the Israelites, who fulfill the Torah and the Precepts, and so on, and this is well known. Yet we need to understand the question that the sages raised in relation to that: if the intention in creating the worlds was to give pleasure to His creatures, why then should He have created this physical world, which is foul and full of sorrow. Without it surely He would have been able to give as much pleasure to the soul as He wished to, so to speak. Why then did He place the soul in such a foul and contaminated body?

They answered this question, saying, "He who eats what does not belong to him will be ashamed to look in the face of the other." (Talmud Yerushalmi,

Tractate Orlah Chapter 1 Halachah 3 Page 6a) This means that in every free gift there is the defect of embarrassment. In order to prevent this defect from the souls, He created this World, in which there is a reality of work. And in the future they will enjoy the toils of their own labor because they receive their own reward in exchange for their toil. Thus they are saved from the flaw of shame.

**What is the relation between seventy years' work and eternal pleasure; there is no greater free gift than this.**

7. These words of the sages are very difficult in every way. The first difficulty is that our main direction and prayer is "Bestow on us from the treasure of free gifts." The sages said that the treasure of free gifts is prepared solely for the greatest souls in the world.

It says in Midrash Tanchuma, Ki Tisa 27:

> The Holy One, blessed be He, disclosed to Moses all the treasures that were to be bestowed upon the righteous, each in reward for certain acts. Moses asked: "Whose treasure is this?" The Holy One, blessed be He, replied: "This is the treasure of those who give charity." Moses asked: "Whose treasure is this?" "This is treasure for the master of the law," He replied. "And whose treasure is this?" Moses queried. "It belongs to those who honor them," He said. Then he pointed to the greatest of the treasures and asked: "Master of the Universe, whose great treasure is this one?" "I shall give it to him who performs meritorious deeds. But even to the one who has no good deeds to his credit, I will give them as a free gift from among these," as it is said: "I will be gracious (achon) to whom I will be gracious" (Exodus 33:19) [achon shares a root with the word chinam, which means free].

From the story in this Midrash it seems that if we do a good action we receive from the limited source, and if we want to get the greatest Light we receive from the source that is unearned. The question then is, why do any good actions?

The answer the kabbalists give is that the people who receive Light because they assist orphans and widows, and the people who do other actions or connections, both receive from limited sources, because they are aware of the Light that they are revealing and the Light they should receive. However a person who does all actions—helping widows and orphans and makes all the connections and still understands that at the end of the day none of their work, nothing that they have done, makes them deserving of the Light of the Creator—this is the person who receives from the greatest Source. It is not someone who does nothing and asks to receive, it is for the person who does everything, and still knows at the end of it that they not deserve to receive. This person receives from the Source that is for free.

The first question Rav Ashlag asks here is: "Why do we say that the ultimate prayer is to ask even though we do not deserve, when the work that we need to do in this world is to earn what we will receive?"

---

The essence of their explanation is the most difficult, since they explained that there is a great flaw in a free gift, namely, the embarrassment of all those who receive a free gift, and to reconcile this He presented This World where there is reality of toil and work, so that in the World to Come they will receive their reward in exchange for their trouble and the toils of their own labor.

Their explanation is very puzzling. This is likened to a man saying to his neighbor: "Work with me for a little while, and in exchange I will give you of all the pleasures of the world and beautiful trinkets for the rest of your life." There is no greater free gift than this, since the reward is not equal to the work. The work is in this [physical] world, a transient world of no value in relation to the reward and pleasure of the eternal world. What value is there to the extent of a transient world when compared to magnitude of the eternal world?

Needless to say the quality of toil, which is insignificant when compared with the quality of the reward. As the sages said, "the Creator will endow each righteous person 310 Worlds…" (Tractate Sanhedrin 100a) You

---

cannot argue that the Creator gives them a small part of the reward in exchange for their work and the rest as a free gift. In this case, what good was brought about by the sages' reform? The flaw of embarrassment would remain with the rest of the gift. But their words should not be understood literally, since there is a deeper intent here.

When I first started studying Talmud Eser Sefirot, this was one of my favorite sections because it really goes to the core of the work. The kabbalists preceding Rav Ashlag, do not go into this point and they never explain it. It is such an incredible gift to have Rav Ashlag's explanations because what was completely dark before Rav Ashlag reveals it, becomes so clear and so obvious after he reveals it.

> The entire existence was emanated from, and created by, one Thought; this Thought is the doer and the action; it is the existence of the hoped-for reward and is the essence of the toil.

8. Before we start elucidating the words [of the sages], we need to understand the Thought of the Creator in creating the Worlds and the existence before us, since these actions did not manifest before Him by way of a multitude of thoughts, as ours would. For He is One, Singular, and Unified, as said. And just as He is simple, so His Lights that are drawn from Him are simple and unified, without any multitude of forms, as it says, "For My thoughts are not your thoughts, neither are your ways My ways..." (Isaiah 55:8) Understand, therefore, and realize that all the Names, Appellations and Worlds, Supernal and Lower, are all one simple, singular and unified Light. With the Creator, the extended Light, the thought, the action, the doer and all that the heart can think of and contemplate are, with Him, truly one thing.

According to this you will judge and deem it that with One Thought this entire existence was emanated and created, both Upper and Lower Beings, up to the culmination of everything at the End of the Correction. It is this one Singular Thought that activates everything and is the essence of all actions. It is the recipient of the ultimate purpose and is the essence of the toil. It is itself the existence of all perfection and the hoped-for reward, as the Ramban (Rav Moshe ben Nachman, Nachmanides) said about the aforementioned secret of One, Singular, and Unified.

We mentioned earlier that this is not something our mind finds easy to understand. We can probably even understand a person having different thoughts directed towards the same goal, but for all thoughts to be the same thought all the time, unified and simple, is something that is not easy to grasp.

What Rav Ashlag is saying here—as he will explain—not only is the Thought of Creation, the beginning moment and everything that follows of the plan all the same thing, it is also all the same simple purity. This is one of those ideas that we really should take the time to think about; it is both, philosophical and also practical. For instance, the Thought of Creation, and everything surrounding it—as we will learn about—as well as what we are doing right here, right now is exactly the same. Everything that occurs in our world after the moment of the Thought of Creation until the Final Correction, when we will achieve the removal of death, all of this is not only toward the same goal, but deeper than that, they are all the same thing.

There is a unity and a simplicity that is probably beyond our comprehension, nevertheless it is there, and this is what Rav Ashlag is referring to. He is simply not talking about the fact that all the process is leading toward the same simple goal but deeper than that, all of the actions and all the processes are still all the same.

Sometimes it's easier to explain what it is not, rather than what it is. For example, if I want to get from here to my house, I can walk for one block, take a bike for a second block, and take a car for the last three blocks. All of those actions are leading toward the same goal but they are clearly three different actions. Walking is one action, riding a bike is another action, and driving a car is a different action. One can say that all of these actions lead towards one unified goal.

This is one level, but it is not solely what Rav Ashlag is saying. What he is telling us is that in the purity of the Light of the Creator all of those actions are unified as one. How can that be when most of us probably cannot perceive this? Nonetheless, this is what Rav Ashlag is telling us. One thought, one goal is behind all the actions that occur, and on a deeper level, all the actions that occur are all unified, are all the same.

This is one of those concepts that cannot be achieved simply through hearing it and understanding, it is something that we have to think about; really run it through our mind. And we may not be able to capture it with our mind—but we can start sensing the simplicity. We can start sensing the simplicity where every human becomes unified. We can, even today, begin to see inklings of this reality. Everything that occurs in our world, whether it is things that seem to be negative or things that seem to be positive, or things in our lives and actions that we do, they are all leaning towards the same goal. On a deeper level, they are all the same. It is not an easy concept to grasp but it is a beautiful one that we should really spend the time to dwell on to at least begin to sense a little bit of it.

---

**The Subject of the Tzimtzum, explaining how an incomplete action came about from the complete performer.**

9. The reason the Rav [the Ari] spoke at length in the first chapters of this book about the first Tzimtzum is because this issue is extremely serious since of necessity even the corruptions and all manners of flaws derive and come from Him, as is written, "I form light and create darkness." (Isaiah 45:7) Yet flaws and darkness are a true opposite to Him. How can one derive from the other, and how can they coexist with the Light and pleasure that are in the Thought of Creation? It cannot be argued that there are two thoughts distinct from each other; Heaven forbid you should say or think such a thing. How then does all this derive from Him all the way into this World, which is full of dirt, sorrow, and great filth? And how can both be contained in the One Single Thought?

---

In The Wisdom of Truth, Rav Ashlag says that at a certain point there were philosophers who believed that there are two sources in our world: there was a source that does good and a source that does bad because that is a logical reality. If you see beauty and you see ugliness, you would assume that there are two causes for them, two sources for them. Yet Rav Ashlag tells us this cannot be; that there is One Source from which our world originated.

The beauty of what Rav Ashlag is saying is that it is not enough to say that they come from the same Source yet act in different ways to bring about the same Final Correction. Therefore on some level they are unified. On some level they are one. Thus, the work that the Ari did and the work that Rav Ashlag is doing here is to help us come to this understanding of how everything is unified; how even the darkness we seem to see in our world is somehow unified as one with the beauty, with the fulfillment, with the Light of the Creator.

Rav Ashlag is not answering any questions yet, he is only posing these very important questions.

# CHAPTER 2

---

### Expounding on the Thought of Creation

10. Now we will come to the explanation regarding the outline of the Thought of Creation, for surely the conclusion of an action exists first in thought, since even in a physical person of many thoughts, the conclusion of the action will first come in his thought. For example, when he deals with building his house, we understand that the first thought he had in this work was about figuring the structure of the house in which to dwell. Thus, a multitude of thoughts and a multitude of actions precede the final structure which he originally thought. He reached this structure at the conclusion of all his actions. You see then that the conclusion of an action exists first in thought.

---

The Zohar in Vayetze speaks at length about this concept. Although Reuven was physically the first born of Jacob, he was not really the first born because at the moment of conception, the thought of Jacob was not with Leah it was with Rachel. The Zohar tells us twice that thought is everything and that it is thought that creates. Obviously, there is a deeper understanding of this, nonetheless, the idea is that every manifestation can only be an effect of thought. If the thought was imperfect, the effect will be imperfect. If the thought was perfect, the effect has to be perfect. And in the creation of our world, the Thought of the Creator was obviously perfect, therefore all manifestations from that Thought are also perfect.

---

The conclusion of the action is the axis and purpose for which all was created, that is, to give pleasure to His created beings, as said in the Zohar.

---

The singular purpose of the creation of our world was to give goodness to the creations, which is maybe obvious to us, but if we read the writings of spiritual philosophers throughout time, this, seemingly simple idea is not found very clearly in most places. The Ramchal (Rav Moshe Chaim Luzatto) and Rav Ashlag speak about this very clearly.

Even in the Writings of the Ari, the Ari tells us that the purpose of creation was "...to bring to light the perfection of His actions and Names and Appellations." In other places, it says that the Creator created the world so that He should be called King. This phrase does not refer to the idea of "giving pleasure to humanity." Of course, we know what is meant. The meaning behind all of the different explanations given in many of the writings is that the purpose of creation is to achieve lasting fulfillment. It is however, an interesting point that even in the writings of the true kabbalists this idea was not so obvious and clear.

It is well known that the Thought of the Creator is immediately concluded and enacted; for He is not a human that requires an instrument of action, rather the thought alone concludes every action immediately. We understand from this that as soon as the Creator thought about the Creation, to give pleasure to His creatures, immediately that Light was drawn and extended from the Creator in its entire nature and stature with every height of pleasure He thought of. All this was included in that thought that we call the Thought of Creation.

For those of us who are truly involved in spiritual growth we need to keep two opposite levels of consciousness in mind. On one hand, we have to do the work and push ourselves to do more, and on the other hand, we have to know that ultimately it is the Creator who will do the work for us. As Rav Ashlag explains, only when we push ourselves to the maximum does the Creator come in and help. We do not discount the importance of the work.

Nonetheless, we often do not completely appreciate how truly necessary the Creator's assistance is in our growth and how powerful and simple that assistance can be. When a person is working to grow and transform, the Negative Side wants us to think that it will take many years to complete the process. The reality is that this does not have to be the case as the assistance of the Creator happens in the blink of an eye.

At the Centres, when we think about the work of changing the world, we begin logically listing the things we need to do and develop a timeline of how long it will take to accomplish this task. Will it take three years, five years? It is important to do the work and think in logical ways about what we are doing, yet at the same time it is equally as important and powerful to know, and not forget that "the salvation of the Creator is like the blink of an eye." The Creator's assistance can come in an instant and change everything. This is the logical way to have certainty that Mashiach (Messiah) can come at any second.

One of the songs of the Third Meal says: "He utters and it happens" (Hu sach vayehi). The instantaneous nature of the Creator's assistance is something we underestimate and need to cultivate certainty in. In a letter that Rav Brandwein wrote to the Rav, he explains that the difference between a righteous person and a negative person is that a righteous person is certain in his salvation. A person trying to connect to the Light of the Creator truly knows with certainty that both he and the world will achieve completion and that this completion can come at any second because the Thought of the Creator is instantaneous to manifestation and certainly the words of the Creator are instantaneous.

We need to know that yes we are doing all of the work and all of the study, which will probably take us another 50 years to achieve completion, and at the same time also know that we do not have to wait that long. If the Creator has a thought for me to be perfect now, I will be perfect instantaneously. If the Creator says, "I want this individual to be perfect," Hu sach vayehi "He utters and it happens"—in one second completion can come. When we have certainty that "the salvation of the Creator is like the blink of an eye," we draw that redemption and that assistance in that moment. When Rav Ashlag discusses here about the power and the instantaneous nature of the Thought of the Creator, it should give us inspiration in the assistance of the Light of the Creator in our spiritual work, and this consciousness is what draws it.

> Understand this well because this is where [the sages] told us to be brief. Know that this Thought of Creation we call the Light of Ein Sof since we have no sound or word to describe His actual Essence by any Name. And remember this.

This is one of the subject areas the kabbalists say not to talk about too much. And the question is why is it important to not talk too much about the pleasures that the Creator had in the Thought of Creation; the pleasures that the Creator desires and thought to give all of us? There are many different answers to this. And I would like to share two of them, both of which come from The Wisdom of Truth.

One answer is that we cannot appreciate the true magnitude of the pleasure that the Creator has thought to give us. There is a verse that says: "No eye has seen it, God, aside from You, Who will do for those who await Him." (Isaiah 64:3) The true nature of the ultimate pleasure, the ultimate Light, that we are destined to receive is something we cannot comprehend. Although we talk about cleaving to the Creator; we give our mind some words to hold on to, the true nature of this amazing Light, of this amazing pleasure, is something that we cannot comprehend because we are bound by our Desire to Receive for the Self Alone; we are bound by the nature of our bodies. Therefore to speak about it too much is pointless, because in reality we cannot truly understand it.

Therefore, what will happen in the days of Messiah is something they say we do not talk too much about. Why? Not because you are not allowed to talk about it. It is something we cannot truly comprehend. The prophets and kabbalists give us some inklings as to how amazing that true and lasting connection to the Light of the Creator is. But we cannot really understand it. "No eye has seen it, God, aside from You…." (Isaiah 64:3) We do not have the ability to truly comprehend the totality of the Light of the Creator. And, therefore, we do not talk about it too much. This is one answer, which hopefully, awakens our appreciation for what this unbelievable Light is.

Sometimes people ask what will happen when Mashiach (Messiah) comes? And the simple answer is that whatever we imagine as the ultimate height of pleasure, the ultimate height of fulfillment is not one millionth of one millionth of what will be. From the pleasures we experience in our world we can gain a very lowly taste of what is going to be. However, to truly comprehend it is something we really cannot do.

The second answer Rav Ashlag gives in The Wisdom of Truth is related to the revelation at Mount Sinai. The entire process the Israelites experienced in coming out of Egypt and specifically in receiving the Torah, was imparted in Moses' question: "Do you want to receive the Torah?" Meaning are you willing to accept "Love Thy Neighbor;" are you willing to accept the responsibility of caring for all the people? Because only if every single Israelite fully accepted the responsibility to care for all the needs of all of the others could "Love Thy Neighbor" truly become manifest in its totality.

At Mount Sinai, the Creator states, "And you will be for Me a kingdom of priests and a holy nation." (Exodus 19:6) Rav Ashlag explains that what the Creator was asking of the Israelites was to accept upon themselves "Love Thy Neighbor"—to take care of all the needs of all the other Israelites at the time. Rav Ashlag asks: "Where are we told what the good part of accepting this is? Why did Moses not give more explanation of the fulfillment that would come?"

And Rav Ashlag answers that Moses had to be cautious because if he had told them how amazing it would be, then they would accept the responsibility for the reward and Not For Its Own Sake. Rav Ashlag explains that the purpose of our spiritual work is that we do it only for the sake of revealing Light; only for the sake of achieving *devekut* (cleaving) to the Creator. If we begin the spiritual work for the sake of receiving a reward—receiving something at the end—the work would never transform us.

Therefore Moses was very careful in speaking to the Israelites about the importance of accepting the principle of Love your Neighbor as Yourself, and how its performance would enable the transformation of all of the Israelites. Moses refrained from discussing too much about the pleasures and the fulfillment that would come because their motivation, as Rav Ashlag explains, needed to be the understanding of the transformation that we need to go through to achieve dvekut, union with the Light of the Creator. However, if they began by thinking about the pleasures they would receive at the end—it this would interfere with the transformational power of the tools. This is the second reason and the explanation of the words "this is where [the Sages] told us to be brief".

Therefore Rav Ashlag says, one answer as to why we do not discuss it is because "No eye has seen it, God, aside from You" (Isaiah 64:3), meaning our mind cannot comprehend the totality of that pleasure, so why talk too much about it? Rather, give an inkling of it, as Rav Ashlag does, but do not talk about it too much. The second answer is that we have to be careful not to talk too much about it because the true nature of the work has to be for the purpose of transformation and sharing, not for the pleasure that will come at the end. If the work becomes too much about the pleasure that will come at the end, it interferes with the transformational nature of the work that we do.

**The Desire to Receive in the emanated, of necessity, came out of the Emanator's Desire to Share. [The Desire to Receive] is the Vessel within which the emanated receives His abundance**

11. This is what the Rav [the Ari] meant when he said that in the beginning **"the Light of the Endless (Ohr Ein Sof) filled the entire existence."** This means that since the Creator thought to give pleasure to the created beings, and the Light extended and came out from Him, so to speak, immediately this Light was engrained with the Desire to Receive His pleasure. Consider also that this desire is the entire measure of the extending Light. In other words, the measure of His Light and abundance is in accordance with its desire to have fulfillment, neither more nor less. Read this carefully.

Therefore, we call the essence of the Desire to Receive, which is engrained in this Light by the power of the Thought [of the Creator], by the name: "Place." This is likened to a man who has place [and room] to accept a pound of bread to eat, while another cannot eat more than half a pound. What place are we referring to? Not the size of the stomach but the extent of appetite and desire to eat. So you see that the extent of the place for receiving the food depends on the amount of appetite and desire to eat. Needless to say, this is the case with spirituality where the Desire to Receive abundance is the place for the abundance, and the abundance is measured by the extent of the desire.

**The Desire to Receive that is included in the Thought of Creation brought it out of the category of His essence to become categorized by the name Ein Sof**

12. Thus we learn how the Light of Ein Sof came out of the category of His Essence, of which we can utter neither word nor syllable, to be defined by the Name the Light of the Endless (Ohr Ein Sof), as said. This is because of the said distinction that this Light already includes the Desire to Receive from His Essence, which is a new form that is not included in His Essence in any way, Heaven forbid, for who can He receive from, Heaven forbid?! This form is also the entire size of this Light, as said. Read this carefully because it is impossible to elaborate here.

It is interesting to me that Rav Ashlag uses the following logic: He says that we know the Creator does not have a desire to receive because Who will He receive from? In our physical world, the fact that we cannot receive something from someone does not preclude us from having the desire to receive it. Therefore this logic does not really apply in our world. We often have a desire for things we cannot manifest.

If we truly understand that the Essence of the Creator is only goodness and a Desire to Share, it makes sense that there is no Desire to Receive within Him. Nevertheless, it is interesting that Rav Ashlag often adds this concept—the Creator cannot receive from anyone because when we understand the concept of the Creator and the whole process of Creation, it is impossible for the Creator to have a Desire to Receive because He is perfect and all that He is, is goodness and a Desire to Share.

---

**Before the Tzimtzum, the Difference of Form within the Desire to Receive was indistinguishable.**

13. Yet despite all its potency, this new form was undistinguishable to the point of being different from His Light. This is the meaning of what was said in Pirkei DeRabbi Eliezer that "Before the world was created He was One and His Name was One." "He" indicates the Light in the Ein Sof, while "His Name" indicates the "Place," which is the secret of the Desire to Receive from His Essence [a desire] that is included in the Endless Light (Ohr Ein Sof).

This teaches us that "He and His Name are One" means that "His Name" refers to Malchut of Ein Sof, which is the secret of the Desire, namely, the Desire to Receive that is embedded in the entire existence that was included in the Thought of Creation. Before the Tzimtzum, no change or difference was distinguishable from the Light in [this desire], and the Light and "Place" are virtually one. Because had there been any dissimilarity or lack in the "Place," in relation to the Endless Light (Ohr Ein Sof), surely there would have been two aspects there. Read this carefully.

---

We have learnt that the Creator created perfection in the Endless World. There, the Light and the Vessel—the Desire to Share and the Desire to Receive—were not only unified, there was no difference between them. Why is it so important that both Rav Isaac Luria (the Ari) and Rav Ashlag explain that in the Endless World there cannot be any separation, there cannot be two separate forms? The reason is because consciousness is everything and if we misunderstand the Endless World and think there is any separation or lack of unity there, this thought has influence and manifests. Therefore, it is so important to know that everything is manifest from perfection. We should never attach any imperfection to the Essence of the Creator, the Essence of the Endless World, the Endless Light—especially as we look at the world around us and see pain, suffering, separation, dirt, and filth. Because if we misunderstand and think that maybe there is some lack, some separation, even a good separation of the two different forms in the Endless World, then that consciousness of lack manifests; it manifests in our world; it manifests in our life.

Thus understanding the perfection in the Endless World is necessary and important for us, not only in a manner of study but also in a way of living. Because if we have any perception of lack in the Endless World, that would have to manifest in our lives and in the world. This is why it was so important for the Ari and for Rav Ashlag to make clear that in the Endless World there is perfection.

---

**Tzimtzum means that the Malchut of Ein Sof diminished Her Desire to Receive, and then the Light disappeared because there is no Light without a Vessel.**

14. This is the idea of the Tzimtzum: the Desire to Receive that is included in the Endless Light (Ohr Ein Sof)—which is called Malchut of Ein Sof and is the secret of the Thought of Creation in Ein Sof and comprises the entire existence, as mentioned—adorned Herself so as to rise and match Her form to His essence. She therefore diminished Her Desire to Receive abundance from the Creator, in the aspect of the Fourth Phase of desire, as said before. Her intention was that by so doing, the worlds would be emanated and created all the way to This World in such a way that the form of the Desire to Receive would be corrected and reverted to the form of sharing. Thus She would reach Similarity of Form with the Emanator.

---

This phrase from Rav Ashlag is important and beautiful: "The Vessel in the Endless World, adorned Herself so as to rise." There was no lack in the

Endless World that the Vessel needed to fill, it simply wanted to elevate its perfection and part of that elevation includes the removal of Bread of Shame. Nevertheless it has to be clear there was no lack the Vessel wanted to fill, it just wanted to perfect itself.

When we think about it all the pain, all the suffering, all the deaths all stem from these five words: "…adorned Herself so as to rise" they sound almost trivial, God Forbid. The Vessel in the Endless World—we in one form or another knew that we had to achieve perfection; to one degree or another we need to perfect the perfection. And it is this thought that precipitated everything we have in front of us.

It is important to remember that every time we say these words, every time we study these words, we reveal that Light in the world and bring our world one step closer to achieving that perfection. Therefore, when we say "the form of the Desire to Receive would be corrected and revert to the form of Sharing, we are saying that She, the Vessel, would reach a Similarity of Form with the Emanator. The thought of the Vessel, in precipitating the removal of the Light of the Creator, is the entire process. We are in the middle of the process but the Vessel saw the end of it. The Vessel saw the perfection of humanity; the transformation of humanity, of our essence, to a Desire to Share. We will become unified with the Light of the Creator. As we study this and as we speak about it, we reveal this Light in the world and bring the world and ourselves many steps closer to achieving this.

> After She diminished the Desire to Receive, the Light was gone automatically, as we already know that Light depends on the Desire (will) and the Desire is the place for the Light, for there is no coercion in spirituality.

The Light of the Creator never forces Itself to be revealed. When the Vessel desires the Light to be revealed, the Light is revealed, otherwise it is not revealed. There is no coercion. There is no coercion in the revelation of the Light of the Creator. This is one of the key revelations of Rav Ashlag. Certainly, as we read the Study of the Ten Luminous Emanations, and even as we read all the Writings of Rav Ashlag, these little spiritual laws that Rav Ashlag sprinkles throughout his work seem almost secondary to the amazing revelations of Rav Ashlag. All of these laws come from a complete understanding of our world, however, what is truly inspiring is knowing that whatever laws Rav Ashlag reveals to us, are only a small part of what was necessary in his explanations and that Rav Ashlag's understanding of the laws of our world were a thousand times more. We are meant to get there as well.

The purpose of studying the Ten Luminous Emanations is not simply to attain wisdom but to become "an overflowing stream." As we study more and connect more, each one of us, can get to the point where we can begin to understand the spiritual laws as well as appreciate the gift that Rav Ashlag gave us in revealing this amazing wisdom and along the way introducing us to a few of the spiritual laws that govern our world. But even more than that, it is important to remember that the true purpose of this study and the true purpose of the revelation of Rav Ashlag is to elevate us to a place where we can start seeing it ourselves.

# CHAPTER 3

### Explaining the Quarry (Origin) of the Soul

15. Let us now expound upon the subject of the Quarry (Origin) of the Soul, of which was said that it is a part of Divinity Above, and so on. We asked in what way and by which means the form of the soul differs from His simple Light to the point of being distinct from the Whole. Now it is clear that a great Difference in Form has indeed taken place in [the soul], for even though the Creator comprises all forms that might be thought of and imagined, yet after what is said above, we find one form that is not included in the Creator, namely the form of the Desire to Receive, for from whom shall He receive, Heaven forbid? Nevertheless the souls' entire creation took place because the Creator wanted to bestow pleasure upon them—which is the Thought of Creation, as said—hence of necessity the souls were embedded with this law: to desire and yearn to receive His abundance.

By this they are considered different from the Creator because their form has changed from Him. As we explained, a material entity becomes divided and distinct by means of movement and distance, whereas a spiritual entity becomes divided and distinct by means of Difference of Form. And according to the extent of Difference of Form between one to the other is the distance between them measured. And if the Difference of Form reaches a complete and entire opposition, then it is severed, and completely separated, to the point that they can no longer nourish from each other because they are considered foreign to each other.

# CHAPTER 4

> After the Tzimtzum and after the Curtain over the Desire to Receive
> was made, [the Desire to Receive] became unfit to be a Vessel of
> Receiving and left the System of Holiness. In its stead, the Returning Light is
> used as a Vessel of Receiving, while the Vessel of the Desire
> to Receive is given over to the Impure System.
>
> 16. After the Tzimtzum and the making of the Curtain over this Vessel,
> which is called the Desire to Receive, [the Desire to Receive] was nullified,
> and it separated and withdrew from the entire System of Holiness.

The Vessel in the Endless decided that it no longer wanted to receive by means of Desire to Receive for the Self Alone. If we are part of that original Vessel, why then can we not say: "I want to change the rules, I now want to receive in the way of Desire to Receive for the Self Alone, as the Creator thought in the Endless World, in the Thought of Creation." The reason is, as Rav Ashlag says, "Any desire in the Upper Worlds becomes a rule and law in the Lower Worlds." Meaning, the Lower Spiritual Realities cannot affect the Higher Spiritual Realities. Once a rule is set, once a desire is put into place, then it has to be manifested.

Therefore, the Contraction (Tzimtzum) and the Curtain (*Masach*) are two different concepts. The Tzimtzum is when the Vessel desired to become more perfect and asked the Creator to contract His Light—meaning, no more receiving in the way of Desire to Receive for the Self Alone. Once that occurred, there is no more Tzimtzum. Now there is *Masach* and the Vessel has no say in what occurs. There is the stopping of the Light of the Creator because whatever occurred in the Upper Realities manifests as a rule and law in the Lower Realities.

Rav Ashlag explains that in the Endless World, in the Thought of Creation, the Desire to Receive for the Self Alone was not a negative thing, it was the whole purpose of Creation. In the Endless World, the Desire to Receive for the Self Alone was perfect, but after the Tzimtzum, a new reality came about where the Desire to Receive for the Self Alone is the source of all darkness, pain and death.

In the book, The Wisdom of Truth, Rav Ashlag explains that many philosophers have struggled with the concept of how negativity can come from a good Creator? Their conclusion is that there has to be a good God and a bad God, "two domains." But what Rav Ashlag has done is explain how all darkness, pain, and suffering come into being from a perfect thought. After the Tzimtzum, once there is a *Masach*, the reality is that the Vessel cannot receive the Light of the Creator for the Self Alone, because "[the Desire to Receive] was nullified, and it separated and withdrew from the entire System of Holiness."

The Desire to Receive for the Self Alone at its core essence, in the reality of its creation, was not a negative or dark thing. It was the purpose of Creation; it was a beautiful thing. However because we—the Vessel—said we do not want to receive in the way of Desire to Receive for the Self Alone, we have caused, not the Creator, but the Desire to Receive to become a dark essence. Once that has occurred, the Desire to Receive was completely taken out of all states of holiness, of anything that has to do with the Light of the Creator.

In its place, Returning Light was established as a Vessel of Receiving (as will be explained in volume 3). Know that this is the entire difference between Atzilut, Briyah, Yetzirah, and Asiyah of Holiness and Atzilut, Briyah, Yetzirah, and Asiyah of Defilement. The Vessels of Receiving of the Atzilut, Briyah, Yetzirah, and Asiyah of Holiness are made of Returning Light, adjusted with Similarity of Form to Ein Sof. While the Atzilut, Briyah, Yetzirah and Asiyah of Defilement use the Desire to Receive that went through the Contraction, which is an opposite form to Ein Sof. They are thus cut off and separated from the Life of Lives that is the Ein Sof.

The reality is that the only way to receive Light from the Creator is through the concept of Returning Light, which means that we will only receive if there is a sharing taking place. The example Rav Ashlag always gives of accepting something to eat from a friend even though we do not really want to eat it; is a Receiving for the Sake of Sharing—meaning that the only reason we eat the meal is because we know the pleasure it will bring to our friend. This is the only type of receiving that is connected to the Light of the Creator; it is part of the System of Holiness.

It is important not to be confused by this concept. Sometimes people think the Desire to Receive for the Sake of Sharing means that I am going to receive with my true desire and I will find a way afterwards to share. This is not at the level that Rav Ashlag is discussing. He is speaking about where the only way we receive is if the receiving itself is for the sake of sharing, because after the Tzimtzum, after the *Masach*, no receiving in a Vessel that is purely for my own self can be part of the Light of the Creator.

Every time we enjoy only for ourselves alone, we are connected to the System of Impurity. Rav Ashlag explains that we are nourishing ourselves from the leftovers of the Klipot because there is no receiving in the Vessel of the Desire to Receive for the Self Alone in the System of Holiness. Anytime we have pleasure that is only for ourselves alone, every time we have a Desire to Receive for the Self Alone, great or small, we are using the Vessels of the System of Impurity.

Rav Ashlag says, "They are thus cut off and separated from the Life of Lives that is the Ein Sof." The obvious question then becomes: How do they receive Light, how do they receive sustenance? The answer is that it was set up in a way that as long as the process of Tikkun is occurring, as long as we are in the middle of the process of correction, the Worlds of Atzilut, Briyah, Yetzirah, and Asiyah of Impurity do have some Light that is given to them.

There is a concept mentioned in the Writings of the Ari and Rav Ashlag also explains it in the Sulam: There are 320 levels of sparks, 288 of them need to be elevated and corrected by humanity, and the last 32, which are referred to as the "heart (*lev*, 32) of stone" are kept in the System of Impurity, in the darkness. Once we complete the correction of all the other 288 sparks, the last 32 will be corrected automatically, without our involvement. This system was set up so that the System of Impurity has some Light, some sustenance aside from the sustenance that we, unfortunately, give to it whenever we act with our Desire to Receive for the Self Alone. The Rav explains that the Hebrew word *avera*, which usually translated as "sin" actually means a "transferring of energy" to the Other Side.

One of the amazingly powerful and beautiful concepts Rav Ashlag is revealing here is how the split occurred between Light and darkness, life and death. After all, the biggest question is: How did it come about from a Desire to Share? How did it come about from a perfect world? How did it come about from the Endless World? And the answer, thanks to Rav Ashlag, is logically very simple. Paradoxically the root of all pain, of all suffering, of all darkness in our world is not a bad thing; it is a good thing. The Desire to Receive, the Vessel, is something the Creator knew had to be part of our process; it is the singular purpose of the creation of our world. However, because of the amazing system that is set up, it had to become a place of darkness in this step of the process. This is why, at the end of the process, this goes back to be positive.

It is said that when *Mashiach* (Messiah) comes, the Angel of Death—Samech-Mem-Alef-Lamed, will become a Positive Angel—Samech-Alef-Lamed. Dietary restrictions will be removed, pork will be able to be eaten. After we finish the correction, all those parts of our world that are of the System of Impurity today—which in one way or another are of the form of the Desire to Receive for the Self Alone, upon which there was Tzimtzum—will revert back to being part of the System of Holiness.

I really hope we take the time to think about this and understand that at the core of the reality of our world there is a remarkable paradox. As Rav Ashlag makes clear, although today there are two systems, the System of Holiness and the System of Impurity, the one distinction is that the System of Impurity holds within it the purpose of Creation, which is the Desire to Receive for the Self Alone that is a positive thing. However in the realm we are in right now, which is the realm of the process, there has to be two separate forms.

At the end of the process, the System of Impurity will become transformed to what it really was in the beginning and will be at the end, which is part of the System of Holiness. And therefore, we will be able to do all kinds of things because these distinctions between System of Holiness and System of Impurity will no longer exist as the correction will have been done on the Vessel of the Desire to Receive. This is both a beautiful and also very important concept because it removes the judgment that one could have on the system.

> **Human beings nourish from the dregs of the Klipot (Shells),
> thus using the Desire to Receive like the Klipot do.**
>
> 17. Now you can understand the root of corruptions that was instantly included in the Thought of Creation, which was to give pleasure to

His creations. After the evolution of the Five Worlds, which include: Adam Kadmon, Atzilut, Briyah, Yetzirah, and Asiyah; and after the Klipot (shells) also appeared in the four worlds of Defilement, according to the secret of: "God has made the one with its opposite" (Ecclesiastics 7:14), we find before us the physical and sullied body, of which it says, "the inclination of man's heart is evil from his youth" (Genesis 8:21), since from youth he is wholly nourished from the dregs of Klipot (Shells).

The Desire to Receive for the Self Alone is not a negative thing in children because on a certain level they are in the world of the Thought of Creation and they have no choice at this point. Children live in a state where the Desire to Receive for the Self Alone does not separate them from the Light of the Creator. This is the power of children. When the Zohar says that the world is sustained by the "breath of the children" and from the words of spiritual study and prayer that come out of the mouths of children it is because they are pure. They are pure, not in the way that we might imagine—where children are perfect in the ways of Desire to Share. Of course, children are not. However, the Desire to Receive for the Self Alone that children have is of the World of Tikkun (Correction). It is not a form of separation.

This helps us to understand more clearly that the Desire to Receive for the Self Alone in its essence, is not bad, and at the End of the Correction it will also not be bad; children receive from that. What happens as a person grows up, and unfortunately, this refers to all of us to one degree or another, we still have to be sustained by the System of Impurity because whenever we receive enjoyment that is only for ourselves it has to come from the System of Impurity.

It is important that we do not beat ourselves up about it to a certain degree because it is understood in the Creation that every person will go through a process of transformation. And during that process of transformation, we will be sustained from the System of Impurity, from the Worlds of Impurity. It is not that important to beat ourselves up about every little enjoyment that we receive in the way of Desire to Receive for the Self Alone. What is important is that we are clear about it, meaning we know that whatever pleasure we receive that is only for ourselves has to sustain us from the System of Impurity, it is sustaining us from the Worlds of Impurity.

And what the Klipot (Shells) and Defilement are all about is the form of the Desire to Only Receive that they have in them. They have nothing whatsoever of the Desire to Share. Thus they are opposite to the Creator, for the Creator has no Desire to Receive at all, Heaven forbid, and His entire wish is solely to share and fulfill.

The Klipot are therefore called "dead" since due to their Opposition of Form to the Life of Lives, they are cut off from Him and contain none of His abundance. Accordingly, the body that is nourished by the dregs of Klipot is also cut off from life and is full of filth. All this is because of its embedded Desire to Only Receive and not to share, for its desire is always open to receive the whole wide world into its belly.

Rav Ashlag does not very often use the term "Desire to Only Receive," which is an extreme form of Desire to Receive. Typically we simply use the term "Desire to Receive." Most of us are somewhere in the middle of Desire to Receive and Desire to Share. The System of Impurity is the Desire to Only Receive, with no Desire to Share.

Death occurs when we are completely overtaken by the System of Impurity. Rav Ashlag says: "….they are severed from the Creator and they are literally dead." How does it happen? Every time we do an action of Desire to Receive for the Self Alone, we add one layer of detachment from the Light of the Creator, and one layer of attachment to the System of Impurity. And unfortunately this is a process that most of humanity undergoes throughout their lives.

However, at the end of a person's life, one does not necessarily feel completely overtaken by the Desire to Receive for the Self Alone. Unfortunately, one of the tools the negative side has at its disposal is to blind us to the reality of our soul. When most people leave this world, they do not feel they are completely of the Desire to Receive for the Self Alone. Rather, what happens is that as a person lives their life and day after day does an action of Desire to Receive for the Self Alone, they are detaching their soul from their body; detaching their body from the Light of the Creator—and the end of that process has to lead to death, not because the Creator punishes them but because this is the logic of the system. This is the result. Obviously there are righteous people (tzadikim) who pass away in a different manner.

What this should awaken in us is an examination of what we are doing. Literally, every time we act in a way of Desire to Receive for the Self Alone, we are cutting away one more piece of our soul's connection to life. Every action. If it is a small action, it is a small cut. If it is a big action, it is a big cut. If, Heaven forbid, we continue this process, what happens at the end has to be death. It is not that at the end, the Creator comes to us and says, "I am upset with you and am going to take your life." If throughout our lives we keep cutting away at our connection of our body to the Essence of the Light of the Creator, the result has to be death.

Tzadikim and people like Chanoch (Enoch) and Eliyahu haNavi (Elijah the Prophet) are different because they move in the other direction. Every day they created more and more attachment to the Light of the Creator through actions of Desire to Share. At the end of their lives, they were in complete Uniformity [Similarity] of Form with the Light of the Creator. Therefore, they lived forever. Living forever was not a reward they received at the end of their lives, it is a reality into which they brought themselves because of the actions of their lives.

This, at its core, is the reason of life and death, and it is the consciousness that we have to strengthen within ourselves, so that we, humanity, can achieve "the swallowing up of death forever (bila hamavet lanetzach)" (Isaiah 25:8) so that we can achieve immortality. However there is the work that goes with it; there is the consciousness, which as the Rav always says, is the root, the source. Without this understanding it is very difficult to truly achieve immortality, to understand the logic of the system. On the other hand, there are also the actions, with the constant everyday thoughts of: *"I am doing this action of sharing and by doing this action of sharing, I am attaching myself to the source of life, to the Life of Lives. And I know that if I live my life this way every day, I am attaching myself more and more to the Creator and I will live forever because I am detaching myself from death, from the System of Impurity."*

This is true both in physical life and death, and also in how we feel. Meaning, when we act in ways that are of Desire to Receive for the Self Alone, we are detaching ourselves from the Light of the Creator; we are detaching ourselves from joy; we are detaching ourselves from feeling good. Therefore if someone feels down, dark, sad, the reason is that either today or yesterday or the day before or a month before that, this individual did actions that cut away their connection to the Source of Life and Light.

The opposite is also true. When day after day, action after action, we attach ourselves more and more to the Source of Light, the Creator, the Desire to Share, which is the process of transforming a Desire to Receive to a Desire to Receive for the Sake of Sharing, we can connect to living forever. The Zohar says about Jacob, "Jacob did not die." The reason Jacob did not die is because he lived this process of constant transformation.

This is one of those concepts that has to become who we are. Rav Ashlag uses the term, "as if they are placed in a box." This is a concept that has the clarity to push us in our spiritual work; it is truly the root driver, and is the reason we push ourselves to transform the ways we share, and thus move us away from the Source of Impurity.

Therefore the wicked while alive are called dead since by changing their form from their root to the other extreme, and by having no aspect of sharing, they are severed from the Creator and they are literally dead.

They come to the point where they have completely detached themselves from the concept of giving. And fortunately or unfortunately this is not necessarily referring to a situation where a person goes through life being selfish and becomes worse and worse in their selfishness. Rather this is referring to one action of selfishness after another action of selfishness that may even be surrounded by actions of sharing. When there are a critical mass of actions of selfishness, of the Desire to Receive for the Self Alone, those actions in and of themselves will bring about death. To be clear this is not describing a person, who when 190 years old is so terribly selfish and there is no obvious giving in him. No! Heaven forbid. Rather this is referring to a person, who has some goodness, does some actions of a Desire to Share, and nonetheless has enough of a Desire to Receive for the Self Alone there that slowly cuts the cord and detaches the person from the Source of Life.

For example, it is like a person who is attached to the Light of the Creator (and therefore life) with a rope that is made up of 1000 little strings. Throughout life, this person can detach one string after another, after another, after another and then toward the last days of their life, snips the final string and detaches themselves from life and therefore, Heaven forbid, dies.

That said, a person who is within the realm of the Desire to Receive for the Self Alone, who acts selfishly on a regular basis—as unfortunately most of us do—can be in a state of being dead even while they are alive. How can this be? Because this person is within the process of dying. Even if actual physical death occurs fifty years or even 100 years in the future, this does not mean that the individual was living throughout that time. Unfortunately, if we are not truly, consistently transforming our selfishness—our Desire to Receive for the Self Alone into a Desire to Share—then even while we are alive, we are still in the process of dying, Heaven forbid.

What is a negative person? This is a person who is within the process of dying. What determines whether a person is within the process of dying? It is when a person is within the process of the Desire to Receive for the Self Alone, meaning they are not pushing themselves strongly and consistently to transform themselves that they are in the category of "the wicked while alive are called dead." This negative person, even in their lifetime, is considered dead because they are dying every day by detaching themselves one strand at a time from the Life of Lives; from the Source of Light, which is The Creator. The purpose of our lives is to do the opposite. To attach and keep attaching so that when a person is at the end of what would be their physical life, they are not detached from the Life of Lives and instead achieve the level of "the swallowing up of death forever (*bila hamavet lanetzach*)." (Isaiah 25:8)

And even though it seems that evil people too have some aspect of sharing, by giving charity and the like, it has already been said about them in the Zohar that every act of kindness they do, they do it for their own sake; for their main objective is themselves and their own honor; see there (Tikunei HaZohar, Thirtieth Tikkun).

Most of humanity, even in actions of sharing, even in actions of charity, are within the realm of the Desire to Receive for the Self Alone because there is something that they are expecting to see at the end. And if there are any expectations at the end of an action of sharing, then we are still within the realm of selfishness, the realm of Desire to Receive for the Self Alone and therefore still within the realm of "while alive are called dead." In our actions of sharing, even as we think we are acting in a way that is not selfish, we have to examine what is the real driving force behind our action; what is the real reason that we are performing this action because to whatever degree we still have expectations at the end of our action of sharing, this action is not taking me out of the realm of death.

Therefore, it is imperative that we not only refrain from doing negative actions, but it is also essential that we delve into our positive actions—the actions of sharing we think are the right thing to do—and figure out to what degree they are in the category of Doing It for Its Own Sake. To whatever degree our actions of sharing have an expectation at the end, to that degree they are still within the realm of "the wicked while alive are called dead," and we are detaching ourselves from the Light of the Creator.

The scary realization is that even actions of sharing can detach us from the Life of Lives, from the Light of the Creator, if at their core those sharing actions are for the purpose of receiving something at the end. This awakens us to the fact that It is not just that those actions are not helping us grow because they are not truly for the sake of sharing, or that in some way we expect to receive something from them, but unfortunately those actions can also, Heaven forbid, assist the process of detachment from the Light of the Creator because they are not considered actions of sharing. If the reason, the desire behind any action of sharing is for the sake of a desire to receive something at the end, they are within the realm of detachment from the Light of the Creator. So not only do those actions not lead to a connection, they can also be part of a disconnect, Heaven forbid.

It is so important to look within ourselves and our actions and our motivations behind our actions of sharing and try to cleanse them of Doing It for Their Own Sake, the selfishness that to one degree or another is attached to it. To whatever degree we think our actions of sharing are actions of connection to the Light of the Creator, are actually done with a Desire to Receive at the end of it attached to it, they are also detaching us from the Light of the Creator. Therefore, it is so important that we cleanse our actions of sharing as much as we cleanse our actions of Desire to Receive for the Self Alone.

---

But the righteous, who are occupied with the Torah and the Precepts not for the sake of a reward but in order to give pleasure to their Maker, purify their body this way and turn their Vessel of Receiving to the form of Sharing. This is in accordance with the words of Rabbenu HaKadosh (Rav Yehuda HaNassi): "It is revealed and known before You that even though I toiled in the Torah with my ten fingers, I did not derive pleasure for myself even with my little finger." (Tractate Ketubot, 104A) In this way they completely cleave to the Creator, since their form is absolutely similar to their Maker with no Difference of Form whatsoever. This is how the sages commentated on the verse, "…who say to Zion, you are My people (*Ami*; עַמִּי)" (Isaiah 51:16) interpreting it in the Prologue to the Zohar, paragraph 67, as, "you are in partnership with Me (*Imi*; עִמִּי)." The righteous are partners with the Creator, since the Creator commenced the Creation and the righteous complete it by reversing the Vessel of Receiving into a Vessel of Sharing.

There are two tremendously important concepts here: Firstly to be afraid of "every act of kindness we do, and ensure that we do it for its own sake. And secondly to be scared of the understanding that, unfortunately, many of our actions that we think are connecting us to the Light of the Creator, that we think are part of the System of Holiness, are in fact part of the realm that is "the wicked while alive are called dead" because even our actions that look like they are actions of sharing, are only for the self alone.

This reason true spiritual work is so difficult is because there is no external way of knowing whether a person is part of the System of Holiness or part of the System of Impurity. Two people can be doing exactly the same thing externally and one will be part of the System of Holiness and one will be part of the System of Impurity. Concerning ourselves, the only way to know which system we are a part of, is by constantly and honestly looking inside at our motivation as to why we are doing it. What is pushing us? What are we expecting at the end?

Rabbi Simchah Bunim of Peshis'cha said that in the Torah Esau is described as a "man of the field" (Genesis 25:27); he was a wild person, he was a negative person, he was a murderer. Esau was all kinds of terrible things. Therefore, as we read the Torah for the first few times, we get an impression of Esau as a very wild and negative person. Yet Rabbi Simchah Bunim of Peshis'cha says this is not true. If any one of us would look at Esau, we would see a tremendously spiritual person, a tremendously elevated soul. We would ask Esau for blessings because he would seem to be a great spiritual leader. Rabbi Simchah Bunim of Peshis'cha uses the example that may not be so common to us but among the Chasidim it is known that whoever gives the speech during the third meal of Shabbat is a very elevated soul. Rav Simcha

Bunim of Peshis'cha says that if we would go to Esau at the third meal, we would hear words of wisdom.

The idea here is that none of us can truly know who we are unless we look within. We can be doing actions of sharing from the moment we wake up in the morning to the moment we go to sleep at night; only giving, only sharing and it could still all be For Their Own Sake and not for the sake of another. If this is true, then even those sharing actions detach us from the Light of the Creator. They are not part of the process that attaches us to the Light of the Creator but rather they detach us from the Light of the Creator. Hopefully this is a scary and awakening thought.

The second idea that Rav Ashlag speaks about here is one of becoming a partner with the Creator in Creation. The Zohar, Prologue 67 says, "You are in partnership with Me." The Creator says to us that we are meant to achieve the level of partnership with the Creator. The Creator began the process of Creation but He cannot finish it. He is not meant to finish it. It is up to us, every single one of us personally as well as for humanity as a whole to complete the process of creation.

For instance, Abraham argued with the Creator, when it came to the destruction of Sodom and Gomorrah. He said, if there are 50 people or 40 people or 30 people or 20 people or even only 10 people, do not destroy the city. And the reason Abraham was able to do this is because he had committed his life to the partnership with the Creator. The more we see ourselves as partners, the more we act as partners, the more power we have within that partnership.

Imagine two people who decide to build a business together. One of them works all day and all night, invests all of his money, and the other partner comes in once a month to check the books. Obviously, over time, the partner who is doing all the work will say to the other, "I am doing most of the work, I have invested most of the money, I will give you a small piece of the profits but you cannot possibly come here and tell me how to run the business. You cannot tell me what to do, what merchandise to sell and what prices to sell at. It does not make any sense. It is obvious that you do not consider yourself a real partner in this business. I will not give you the right to make decisions and changes."

It is the same way in our partnership with the Creator. If we are truly dedicated to the partnership with the Creator, which means that we are honestly working on our own selfishness on our Desire to Receive for the Self Alone, and also doing as much as we can to change the world, then to whatever degree we are invested in this partnership, to that same degree we have power in that partnership, as is it written, "The Holy One, Blessed be He, decrees, and the Righteous nullify it." (Tractate Mo'ed Katan 16b) Imagine that the Creator can decree something, and the righteous person says, "No, you cannot do it God because I am as much of a partner as you are." This can only happen to the degree that we are truly invested in this partnership, both in our own spiritual growth and in the spiritual growth of the world.

The exciting and inspiring part is that the Creator wants us to be partners. The Creator says, "You are in partnership with Me." (Zohar, Prologue 67) He is saying to us, "Please be with Me in this partnership." And it is up to us to reveal and act based upon how much of a partner we are. If we are 30% partners, we have 30% say. If we are 40% partners, we have 40% say. This also affects the level and the power of our prayers. If we are complete partners, if we completely give of ourselves, then the Creator has to listen to us. There is no two ways about it. "The Holy One, Blessed be He, decrees, and the Righteous nullify it." (Tractate Mo'ed Katan 16b) Conversely the Righteous can decree and the Creator has to do it.

If we are completely committed to this partnership and that shows up in the way we do our work as well as how we work with others—then when we ask, the Creator has to make it happen. Yet we are a minority shareholder with only a little bit invested into the partnership, to that very degree our ability and our voice will be limited. Make no mistake it is exact; it is an exact degree. Fortunately or unfortunately, we can gauge our partnership with the Creator by how our prayers are answered and how our voice is heard. Know that we are meant to come to the point where we are equal partners with the Creator—50-50.

There is a parable regarding Moses that helps us to understand this concept. When the Creator" "became angered," Moses held onto the Creator's coat saying, "No, I will not let You do this." How does one achieve the level where we can tell the Creator, "No! Creator You say this person should die or that this should happen in the world and I say, 'No' because I am a partner. I live my life as a true 100% partner. I am completely dedicated to my own growth. I am completely dedicated to the growth and the transformation of the world."

This is not a zero sum game where a person is either a complete partner or no partner at all. It is a process that, God Willing, we experience throughout our lifetimes where today, if we are 3% or 5% partners or even 10% partners, tomorrow we will be 11% partners, and as we grow in that work we can come to the point where we are literally 50-50 partners with the Creator. When we come to this level, we can decree. A righteous person decrees and the Creator has to fulfill it. The Creator decrees, and a righteous person annuls it. We can tell the Creator what to do in a positive way and we can also tell Him what things not to do. The beauty of this is that the partnership becomes 49-51 percent partnership, where the Creator gives us the additional share and we can actually tell the Creator to do things, and can also stop the Creator from doing things.

This is a very exciting place to get to. Every single one of us can and is meant to come to this point. How do we achieve this? As Rav Ashlag makes clear it is through the process of true transformation of our Desire to Receive for the Self Alone to a Desire to Share.

---

**The entire existence is included within the Ein Sof and is derived by way of Something out of Something. Only the Desire to Receive is new and is derived as Something out of Nothing.**

18. Know that the entire aspect of newness, which the Creator presented in the Creation—which the sages said He produced as Something out of Nothing—only relates to the form of the desire to be fulfilled inherent in any created being. Nothing besides that was new in the secret of Creation. This is the meaning of, "I form light and create darkness." (Isaiah 45:7) Nachmanides (Rav Moshe ben Nachman also known as the Ramban) comments that the word "create" denotes something new, that is, something that did not exist before.

You can see that it does not say, "create light." The reason is that there is no newness to it, such as there is in producing Something out of Nothing, since the Light and everything included in the Light—that is, everything pleasant in the world that can be grasped by the senses and the mind—all this derives as Something from Something. This means they are already comprised in the Creator and therefore have no newness to them. Hence it says, "I form light" to indicate there is no aspect of newness or creation in it.

---

This is a beautiful idea. Whatever pleasantness, whatever Light we receive—in whatever Realms we receive it—has existed forever. When we connect to Light, when we receive Light, we are connecting to the Endless. We are connecting to the Realm that is beyond time, space, and motion. Even in the smallest things—whether a person receives enjoyment from food, from a friend, from his family, and/or receives enjoyment from prayer and from study, the sense one receives—the connection one makes is a connection with something beyond time. We are connecting to the Creator.

The Creator has not created this new Light for us to enjoy today. Whatever enjoyment we receive has been around forever in the Essence of the Creator, even before the Endless World. The only thing that is new is the Desire to Receive for the Self Alone.

It is amazing to know that now, with the help of the Creator, as we study, the Light that we feel is not something that just happened, meaning I am studying and enjoying this and I am getting the Light of the Creator as something new, as something that is only created now. No. This Light that we are feeling in this moment has been around forever. Before time. It is the Essence of the Creator that has never changed. The idea that we can and we do, to one degree or another throughout our lifetimes, make these little attachments to this Endless and even beyond the Endless, before the time level of the Light of the Creator is really an amazing and inspiring notion.

The greater our consciousness is, the stronger our attachment. Meaning, the next time we receive pleasure, the next time we receive a taste of the Light of the Creator, to one degree or another, we should say, I know and have this consciousness that now I am connecting to a Realm beyond time, beyond space, beyond motion. I am connecting to the Essence of the Creator, which has existed forever. The greater our awareness is of this connection, the greater our awareness is of what we are connecting to, the more powerful that connection will be, the more Light this process will reveal.

Therefore, every time we receive from the Light of the Creator, we have a decision to make: Are we going to deepen that connection by knowing where it comes from, what it is, and therefore strengthening it and growing it? Or are we going to detach it from ourselves? The other side to this is to know that because of the place from which this revelation comes, we have to treat it with respect. And therefore, whether it is the physical or certainly the spiritual things that we enjoy, it is important to realize the magnitude and the beauty of even a small sliver of that Light.

But of darkness, which includes everything unpleasant grasped by the mind or the senses, it says, "...and create darkness," (Isaiah 45:7) because He produced them virtually as Something out of Nothing, meaning that this is not found in the least, Heaven forbid, within His existence but became new now since the root for all these things is the form of the Desire to be Fulfilled included in the Lights extending forth from the Creator. At first, the form is dimmer than the Supernal Light and is therefore called "darkness" in relation to the Light. But eventually, the Klipot evolve and emerge from it, as well as the *Sitra Achra* (Other Side) and evil people, who are completely cut off from the Source of Life because of this [desire].

This is the meaning of, "Her feet go down to death...." (Proverbs 5:5) "Her feet" indicates conclusion, and [the verse] is talking about the feet of Malchut, which is the aspect of the desire to receive pleasure that exists in the extending of the Light of the Creator. Eventually what evolves from Her (Malchut) is the aspect of death to the Other Side and to those who nourish from and follow the Other Side.

The concept, "Her feet go down to death..." (Proverbs 5:5) is very important. It tells us that the end result of the Desire to Receive for the Self Alone is that it leads to death. This concept is something that we need to constantly drill into our consciousness because it gives us the totality of the picture. Meaning, every time we are about to act in a way that is of the Desire to Receive for the Self Alone, in a way that is selfish, in that moment we probably know, in some way that although we will enjoy this, it is not the right thing to do. However, what we do not see and do not have awareness or consciousness of is that the only place that this action can lead me is to disconnect from the Light of the Creator—into pain, suffering and death.

The reason we allow ourselves to do actions of Desire to Receive for the Self Alone, actions of selfishness, is because we do not have a true understanding of the concept, "Her feet go down to death..." (Proverbs 5:5) that the only path we can go on when we act with our Desire to Receive for the Self Alone is towards death, towards a disconnection from the Light of the Creator. Therefore, the next time, today as we are about to do an action of Desire to Receive for the Self Alone, we should stop and say to ourselves, *"Remember, although right now this might seem like a good and enjoyable thing, it will only lead me to one place, 'Her feet go down to death.' (Ibid.) It can only lead me to disconnect from the Light of the Creator, to pain, to suffering, to eventually death."*

Truly having an understanding of the totality of the picture—the cause and the effect—is one of the greatest forces of consciousness we can use to do battle with the Desire to Receive for the Self Alone because the Negative Side does not want us to see the end, but rather only see the moment that is right now: *"This action will give me some pleasure and enjoyment.* We have to be constantly reminding ourselves of the verse, "Her feet go down to death…." (Ibid.) The end result of an action of the Desire to Receive for the self alone will be toward death—maybe not today nor tomorrow or next week, month, or year.

Both the Talmud and the Zohar say that if a person is having trouble with their own Desire to Receive for the Self Alone, with their Evil Inclination, there are certain steps that one can go through. But eventually, if nothing works, "remind him of the day of death." (Zohar, Miketz 195) This is not just to scare us but to give us clarity because the Negative Side will always say, "Look at this great enjoyment you are about to have, go for it." What our evil inclination tells us is, "Do not look further; do not look towards the manifestation; do not look at what will happen at the end from this action."

If we want to maintain a connection to the Light of the Creator, we have to say to the Other Side, 'No, I will not be fooled by you telling me that in this moment I will achieve some sort of pleasure from this action of selfishness, from this action of Desire to Receive for the Self Alone. I know the end. I know the cause and the effect. I know the totality of the picture, 'Her feet go down to death….' (Proverbs 5:5) I know that this action can lead me eventually only towards disconnect, pain, and death."

Putting together this picture is one of the most difficult things for us to do because we are conditioned to simply look at what we have in front of us right now, and not put together the cause and the effect; the totality of the picture. Reminding ourselves that we cannot do actions of Desire to Receive for the Self Alone because the end of this action is death, has to be a constant work. Even though I see enjoyment from this right now (greater or smaller), I cannot allow myself to do this because I know, and remind myself that the end of this action, the end of this enjoyment, has to lead towards one place, towards death. 'Her feet go down to death….' (Proverbs 5:5)"

This is no longer a mystery; we now understand that we are either doing this work or we are not. To do the work we need to check in with ourselves at the end of each day, the end of each week, asking, "How many times today or this week when I was about to do an action of selfishness, of the Desire to Receive for the Self Alone, did I remind myself of "Her feet go down to death…" (Ibid.), of the totality of the picture that at the end only leads towards disconnect, pain, and eventually death?"

Most of us have to remind ourselves of this consciousness, making it a true and large part of our spiritual work, and thereby stopping ourselves from doing actions that can lead towards death. This is a tremendously important understanding and more important than that, it is a constant work that we should be doing.

> To us—being branches stemming from the Ein Sof—whatever
> is in our root is pleasurable, whereas whatever
> is not in our root is bothersome and painful.

19. However, one can say that this Difference of Form of the Desire to Receive has to, of necessity, be present in the created beings, otherwise how can they come out of the Creator and emerge from the category of the Creator to become the category of a created being. This cannot be imagined, except by the Difference of Form as mentioned above. Moreover, this form of the Desire to be fulfilled is the basic essence around the Thought of Creation, around which the whole Creation revolves. It is also the measure of the amount of goodness and pleasure of which we spoke at length before. For this reason it is [also] called *Makom* (Place). How can it be said that it is called "darkness" and that it goes down to the level of death, since it causes a break off and separation from the Life of Lives in the lower receivers, Heaven forbid. We should further understand what the great fear is that the receiver's experience due to the Difference of Form from the Essence of the Creator. And why is there great wrath and anger on this account?

Here Rav Ashlag asks one of the most fundamental and important questions regarding layers of consciousness: Why should we be, and are we, so fearful of the Desire to Receive for the Self Alone? Why are we so afraid of being in a difference of form from the Light of the Creator? Why are we fearful of the Desire to Receive for the Self Alone? Why is there so much discussion concerning the danger of being in a difference of form from the Creator, Whose Essence is a Desire to Share and we are of a Desire to Receive? This is a deep and philosophical question and there is a technical answer to this. The fear comes from the principle that like attracts like, and if we are in a Difference of Form from the Light of the Creator, we cannot receive the Light of the Creator, we cannot have joy, and we cannot have the fulfillment that is the Light of the Creator. This is the simple answer.

Of course, Rav Ashlag goes deeper. He says that while the former is a good answer as to why we do not want to have a Desire to Receive for the Self Alone, there is a deeper level. Here Rav Ashlag makes a very important distinction. The reason the technical answer is not good enough is because it only addresses one level. There is a deeper reason that is truly at the core of who we are and of what gives us joy and happiness. However before we dive into Rav Ashlag's answer, it is important that we be clear about what the answer is not.

The answer is not as simple as: If we are in a Difference of Form from the Light of the Creator, we cannot receive the Light. The Talmud says, "The cursed cannot cleave to the blessed." (Beresheet Rabbah 59:9) meaning, the Light of the Creator cannot come into a Vessel that has the opposite form—the Desire to Receive for the Self Alone—because like attracts like. In the spiritual realm, when things are in affinity with one another they can connect. This is why I am so scared. That is why I do not want and we should not want to have a Desire to Receive for the Self Alone. If I am not in affinity with the Creator, I will not be able to receive that Light of the Creator. This is one level of an answer that we would initially give. It is not a bad answer. It is a very strong technical answer.

However, what Rav Ashlag will now reveal is the core of this reality; the core of who we are and why we can never, ever, ever be satisfied with selfishness; why we can never be satisfied with Desire to Receive for the Self Alone. Even if the Creator created some sort of mechanism that allowed His Light to become manifest in a Vessel of Desire to Receive for the Self Alone, we still could never have been satisfied with that. This is what Rav Ashlag goes into.

In order to sufficiently explain to you this subtle issue, we need to expound first upon the origin of all the pleasures and suffering felt in our world.

Every once in a while, Rav Ashlag throws in the word "subtle" to indicate a thin distinction and a very important revelation that we should give thought to. When things are obviously dissimilar, most people can see the difference. Yet when there is a small distinction between things, when the difference is subtle, we need someone with more awareness to make things clear. For instance, there is a game where two similar pictures have twelve or so differences. At first glance the images appear to be the same, but if we make a point to look closely, the differences in them become apparent and sometimes they become obvious. In our life, the true solutions to problems are on this level of subtlety, on this level of focus of clarity.

When we look at a person who is tremendously selfish and full of the Desire to Receive for the Self Alone it is easy to see Light and darkness. But when we look at ourselves and we are involved in the spiritual work, helping other people, seeing becomes more subtle, there is a thinner distinction. In reality, even that slight distinction is a great separation. When we begin focusing in on ourselves and focusing in on our understanding, this level of subtlety is where true growth comes from.

To whatever degree we do good things, the Negative Side wants us to look at the generality so that we think of ourselves, "I am a good person, I do good things." Yet to start really looking deeply within ourselves, who we are, what we do, and why we do it, is something the Negative Side does not want us to do. This focus and clarity about ourselves is an indication of a person who is connected to the Light of the Creator. Another indication stemming from this is that a person who is connected to the Light of the Creator is one who desires to delve deeply into the subtleties, as Rav Ashlag does here. And of course it takes a kabbalist to reveal this to us.

You will understand this with the common knowledge that the nature of every branch will be equal to that of its root. Therefore, whatever is pertinent to the root will be loved and coveted by the branch, whereas whatever is not pertinent to its root will be shunned by the branch. It will not be able to bear it but hate it. This law applies to every root and its branch, without exception.

The Creator is the Root to all the creatures He created. Therefore all things contained in the Creator that are drawn directly from Him to us are enjoyable to us and please us, since our nature is close to our Root. But all things that are not present in the Creator and are not drawn directly from Him to us—except by the axis of creation itself—will be against our nature and it will be difficult for us to endure them. For example, we love rest and hate movement very much to the point that we do not make a single movement unless it is to attain rest. This is because our Root does not move but is in a state of rest, as movement does not apply to Him whatsoever and is thus against our nature and we hate it. In the same way, we love wisdom, strength, wealth, and all good qualities since they are included in the Creator, who is our Root. And we hate very much their opposite, such as stupidity, weakness, poverty, shame and the like; for these are not present at all in our root and are therefore detested and hated to the point of being unbearable to us.

One of the beautiful things of Rav Ashlag's revelations is that he goes to the root of everything. People who are into spirituality, and even those of us who are involved in the Centre, may understand things on some level, even on a deeper level, but we do not always push ourselves to go as deep as possible, to the core. The gift of Rav Ashlag's revelations is that he does not just explain, he goes all the way to the core.

The Talmud Yerushalmi mentions the fact that Bread of Shame exists. And although many know about the law of Bread of Shame in general, here Rav Ashlag explains *why* Bread of Shame exists. He explains that our soul is one and the same as the Light of the Creator, which means our innate essence is the same as the Creator's Essence, and the Creator's Essence is only to share and not to receive. Therefore whatever is not like the Creator, meaning not like our pure nature, will not, in the long term, make us happy.

This answers the question of why there is a discussion and a great fear of being in Difference of Form from the Creator. There is the technical answer we spoke of earlier which is: if I am in Difference of Form from the Creator,

I cannot receive His Light, which is not the answer to the deeper spiritual reason. For even if I could receive the Creator's Light, as long as I am in Difference of Form from the Creator, I could never be satisfied because I would be in difference of form from who I am. Each one of us are of the Creator, and because we are of the Creator, we cannot enjoy, we cannot have peace when we are in Difference of Form from the Creator as it is against who we are. This is a tremendous revelation and one that really needs to seep in; one we should think about.

The second level of this is that many of us still, unfortunately, enjoy things that are opposite to the Light of the Creator because we are not connected to who we truly are. This is a tremendous understanding. To whatever degree we are satisfied and not fearful of being in the state of Desire to Receive for the Self Alone, we are not true to who we are. The problem is if we enjoy being selfish, enjoy being of the Desire to Receive for the Self Alone we will not be able to receive the Light of the Creator; we will not be able to achieve lasting fulfillment. This awareness is great, but there is a deeper, more subtle understanding. And it is that we can never be happy with ourselves when we are being selfish because we have the same essence as the Creator.

Although we can find momentary pleasure—especially in our world of darkness, confusion and blindness—within the realm of the Desire to Receive for the Self Alone we can never be truly satisfied. Even if we could find a way to receive some sort of enjoyment through the process of being connected to the Desire to Receive for the Self Alone, it would never be true enjoyment because it is not true to who we are. If we enjoy the Desire to Receive for the Self Alone, we are not really who we are, and we are not living the reality of our essence. We can never be happy in this way. This is the source, the root for all pain, for all suffering that we feel in our world. It is not simply that we have pain and suffering in our lives and in our world because we are in Difference of Form from the Creator and, therefore, we cannot receive His Light—although that is true—nevertheless on a deeper, more important, more profound level, we can never achieve fulfillment as long as we are of the Desire to Receive for the Self Alone because that is not true to who we are.

This is also a way for us to gauge where we are on our spiritual path. As Rav Ashlag says, whatever is like the Creator is like us in our essence and thus we are happy with it. Whatever is not of the Creator—not of the aspects of peace, wisdom, strength—is not of our essence and therefore is something we feel uncomfortable about. Thus the question really becomes: is what we are doing something we do not feel comfortable with? Look around the world. Look at ourselves, are we not necessarily tremendously upset by lack of wisdom? If wisdom is an aspect of who we truly are and it does not bother us, to one degree or another, that there is a lack of wisdom this simply indicates that we are not in touch with who we truly are.

We should examine what is the Creator and what is us. How upset do we get whenever we act selfishly? How lacking are we of peace when we act with our ego, with our Desire to Receive for the Self Alone? To whatever degree we are okay with being selfish, with acting in a way of the Desire to Receive for the Self Alone, to that degree we are not in touch, in contact, in true uniformity with our essence; which is the essence of only the Desire to Share. As Rav Ashlag says the desire to share is the essence of all the good qualities in our world. When we allow ourselves to act in ways that are not congruous to our true essence, is an indication for us that we have not revealed enough or are not connected enough to who we truly are, to our true essence.

A very important question we have to ask ourselves is: How bothered are we by all the qualities that are not of the Creator and therefore not of our essence that are still within our lives, within ourselves? And conversely how okay are we with those qualities? To the degree that we are okay acting selfishly with our ego, is an indication that we are not really connected to who we truly are and to that degree we are not living the lives that we are meant to live, we are not really living our own life. This is a very important gauge and it is a question that we have to ask ourselves often. This is a tremendous revelation that Rav Ashlag gives us here. We should take the time to first of all understand what it means, and second of all its significance to our lives.

> However, we need to investigate how we can receive something not directly from the Creator but from the axis of Creation itself.

Fulfillment, joy, peace, wisdom, strength are all qualities that come directly to us from the Light of the Creator. Rav Ashlag reveals that there are also aspects that occur in our world that are not directly drawn from the Light of the Creator, and asks how this can be. This is an important philosophical question. How can it be that things occur and manifest within the process of Creation that are not directly drawn from the Light of the Creator?

In The Wisdom of Truth, Rav Ashlag speaks about ways of looking at our world, which are not true: one is that at the seed level there are two forces in our world—a force of good and a force of darkness. All that is good in our world comes from the force of good and all that is bad in our world comes from the force of darkness. Yet we know this is not true. There is only one Source, one Seed to our world and as there is only one Source and Seed to our world and this is revealed within the process of Creation, how is it possible that we draw realities and manifestations that are not directly from the Creator? How can there be pain? How can there be stupidity? How can there be weakness in our world?

Before we delve into the answer it is important to stop and realize the magnitude of the question. Because, although we could continue on with understanding the process of Creation as in there was a creation of the Desire to Receive for the Self Alone and, as Rav Ashlag said earlier, if we follow that train of thought all the way down to its logical conclusion, the more Desire to Receive for the Self Alone the more disconnect there is from the Light of the Creator, and eventually we will have to come to darkness, pain, and suffering. This way of thinking only explains the logical progression of the darkness created by the Desire to Receive for the Self Alone. It does not explain, on a deeper level, how is it possible that there can be anything in our world that is not from the Creator? How can one create something that is coming from you but is not you?

As it is with so much of Rav Ashlag's teachings, the beauty of this question is that one can sense here that this is not only a question about process but also a question about truth. And as this wisdom [Kabbalah] is the Wisdom of Truth, there has to be an entirety, a clarity, and answer to every question. Even if we could understand the progression of the creation of our world in a logical sense, we still have to understand, on a deeper level, how everything can still be coming from the Creator.

Rather what is this comparable to? It is like a rich man who summons someone from the street, provides him daily with food and drink and presents him with gold and silver—each day more than the day before. You will notice that the poor man savors two very different flavors simultaneously in these immense gifts. On one hand, he endlessly savors great pleasure from

> the excess of gifts. On the other hand, it is hard for him to bear the bestowal of so much good and he is ashamed while receiving it, and the many gifts bestowed upon him continually make him impatient. Surely the pleasure in the gifts comes to him directly from the generous rich man. However, the impatience that he experiences in the gifts does not come from the rich man that gives, but it comes from the very essence of the receiver as shame is awakened in him because of the act of receiving and from the free gifts. And even though this surely is caused by the rich man, it is indirect.

I believe the reason Rav Ashlag added that last line is because it is not enough to explain how the Vessel could feel a Bread of Shame—a sense of embarrassment from receiving not from the Creator. As he said earlier, if one receives without limit then that receiving will cause an internal sense of embarrassment that is not caused by the wealthy man nor is it attached to the wealthy man. Yet here Rav Ashlag is saying that the Creator does have a hand in this. There cannot be anything in our world that does not come from the Creator, whether in a direct way or in an indirect way. Therefore, Rav Ashlag had to explain and add this sentence: **"And even though this surely is caused by the rich man, it is indirect."** Although the sense of embarrassment, of the Bread of Shame that is felt by us, by the Vessel, is something internal and natural to receiving from a giver with no end, nonetheless there cannot be anything in our world that does not have its Source within the Creator.

Therefore, while we can explain very well how the Bread of Shame is a feeling only of the Vessel and has no attachment to the Creator, Rav Ashlag has to add, "No, there is some round about cause of the Bread of Shame by the Creator because there cannot be anything in our world that is not of the Creator. This is an important concept to internalize if we want to study this wisdom not simply in ways to understand, but also in ways of truth. As Rav Ashlag says, we need to understand that there is only one Source; even in speaking about Bread of Shame, which is a tremendously affected part of Vessel, there still has to be the Creator's hand within it.

> Since the Desire to Receive is not in our root, we feel ashamed
> and impatient because of it. This is why the sages said that
> in order to correct it, He "prepared" for us work and toil in
> the Torah and the Precepts in this World—to transform
> the Desire to Receive into the Desire to Share.
>
> 20. From this discussion we understand that all forms that are drawn
> indirectly from the Creator will convey the difficulty of patience in them
> and are against our nature. From this you understand that the new form
> that arose in the receiver, namely, the Desire to be Fulfilled is not really
> any flaw or defect relative to Him. On the contrary, this is the main axis of
> His creation; without it there is no Creation at all, as said. But the receiver,
> the bearer of this form, feels difficulty of patience on account of himself,
> since this form is not present in his root. Read this carefully.
>
> Now we are able to understand the reasoning of the sages that this world
> was created because "He who eats what does not belong to him will be
> ashamed to look in the face of the other." (Talmud Yerushalmi, Tractate
> Orlah Chapter 1 Halachah 3 Page 6a) Seemingly, this is very puzzling,
> as said.

Rav Ashlag quotes a section from the Talmud Yerushalmi: "If a person eats and does not work for his bread he is embarrassed to look at the face of the one giving to him;" this phenomenon is called Bread of Shame and it is often given as the reason for the creation of our world. The understanding is that we have to earn what we will receive. Rav Ashlag says, "Seemingly, this is very puzzling and not a good answer." No matter how long we live or how many lifetimes we experience, we can never earn endless Light because to earn endless Light one would have to work endlessly, and we are not going to work forever as there will be an endpoint to our work when Mashiach (Messiah) comes. Therefore, this system could never work. Since within this frame we will not work endlessly, we will not be able to receive endlessly.

So the answer to the question of how we solve the problem of Bread of Shame is not by working endlessly and therefore earning everything we will receive. As a matter of fact, the statement regarding how to earn what we receive is itself a false statement. Because the concept of Bread of Shame is not a problem that needs to be solved; we earn through working. When the kabbalists make this statement, they are not asking a question. It is not a question or answer about a process. I really hope this is clear because this is one of those points you can read and think you understand and completely miss the point of what Rav Ashlag is saying.

> But now their words please us, since they were talking about the Difference of Form of the Desire to be Fulfilled that is inherent in the souls, as said. For "He who eats what does not belong to him will be ashamed to look in the face of the other" (Ibid.) that is, whoever receives a gift is ashamed when receiving it because of the Difference of Form from the root, which does not contain this form of receiving.

I ask that you read this Inner Observation again and again until this is 100% clear. We can solve the problem of earning and yet not solve the problem of our essence. Meaning, if the Creator found a way by which we could earn the Light that He gave us, we still could not be satisfied because in earning the Light we would not have changed our essence. If we still receive in the way of receiving, we are still being opposite to our essence.

Imagine the Creator said, "I will give you 10 ounces of joy and fulfillment, and have gauged that 10 ounces of joy is worth 10 hours of work. Therefore, pray, study and do spiritual work for 10 hours." Now that we have earned this Light are we happy? We cannot be happy. We have dealt with Bread of Shame and have taken care of earning this Light, yet when we have to receive that Light, we cannot enjoy it. This is because simply receiving for ourselves alone is against our essence. We cannot earn receiving because receiving is against our essence. Even if we do all the work necessary to enable us to receive the gifts of the Creator, we cannot receive them. Our essence is a desire to share and we can never be satisfied with receiving even if it is earned.

This is a tremendous departure from how most of us understand this question and answer. First, the problem of Bread of Shame is not a problem of earning because even if we earn, we will not be satisfied. Therefore, the question regarding Bread of Shame is not how do we earn what we receive, but rather how do we completely transform how we receive pleasure? We think: "I will experience pleasure by receiving—I will take in but I have to earn it. So I will do the spiritual work so I earn what the Creator gives me." This is not the case. The above revelation from Rav Ashlag tells us that we cannot be happy or satisfied with receiving because we are beings of sharing, whether we are aware of this or not; whether we like it or not. That is who we are. We are beings of sharing. We can only be satisfied in sharing. We can only enjoy in sharing.

Therefore, what has to be done is to create a way where we completely flip the worlds around to where our pleasure does not come from receiving. Our pleasure comes from sharing. Here is a second and very important point: there is no problem in having pleasure. It is not that we come to a point where we only want to share and therefore, receive nothing. The issue is not in receiving pleasure. The issue is receiving pleasure by way of receiving. Once we get to the point where we receive pleasure in giving, which is a much greater level of pleasure, then we can receive pleasure endlessly.

Why is there no Bread of Shame when a righteous person gets to the level where with every giving there is a tremendous amount of joy? Why is this not a problem if the issue is simply with receiving? The answer is that there is no problem with receiving joy as long as it is within the right Vessel, within the right process, which is a Desire to Share. It was never a problem of having joy and fulfillment. The problem is in the way we receive this joy and fulfillment— if it is in a way of receiving that could never satisfy us.

I ask that you take the time to think this over. Review it until you achieve clarity regarding what you might have thought concerning Bread of Shame. The simplest way to think about this is that the purpose of the creation of our world was not to earn what we receive. Even if we give full payment for what we receive we still could not be satisfied. Receiving by receiving, even if earned, cannot satisfy us because our essence is the essence of sharing. The joy of receiving cannot be felt fully in a vessel that is a vessel of sharing.

I ask you to consider the fact that our entire thought process of how we receive joy is completely upside down. As we are blind to who we are, we think that taking in is what gives us pleasure. In truth, giving-out is the only way we can feel pleasure. Therefore the point is not in not having pleasure, or stopping pleasure, or finding a way around pleasure. The point is in the realization that because of who we are in our essence, sharing is the only true way we can receive pleasure.

For instance, if there is a person who enjoys eating great steak. He has a great steak in front of him and has the opportunity to go outside in the cold and share this steak with someone. He does not choose to go out to share because it is the better thing to do or even the right thing to do, he simply makes a very calculated decision based on examining what he will enjoy more, on what will give him pleasure. He comes to the conclusion that going out to share will give him more pleasure than eating the steak alone. This is not a spiritual decision. It is not a decision of better or worse. He is making a selfish decision based on what gives him more pleasure. And this is the point. We want to get to the level where the joy comes from the giving. It is a complete reversal of the Vessel that we are born with. Even if we understand that giving is a good quality to have, it is still something that is secondary to our nature because we are born and raised to think that pleasure comes only from the taking.

The purpose of our spiritual work is to transform ourselves to the point where our greater pleasure comes to us from actions of sharing. In this way our decisions to do sharing actions are not spiritual decisions or even decisions about the right thing to do, but rather they are simply selfish decisions. It just so happens to be that we enjoy sharing more than we enjoy something else. This is a very important switch.

I think we have all experienced the phenomenon where something of a physical nature that was not enjoyable for whatever reason, over time becomes fun to do. We teach ourselves, even in the physical realm, to enjoy things that previously we could not. We create a new Vessel to receive pleasure differently. This is the process that we are meant to do in this world—to create a new type of Vessel within ourselves, a new way to intake pleasure. When we achieve the point where sharing becomes our means of taking in, we achieve the level that Rav Ashlag is discussing here. Then we achieve transformation.

This is also the secret of bringing about real change in our world. Rav Ashlag writes in The Wisdom of Truth that the problem with people who try to bring about change to our world, even spiritual people, is that they cannot give enough "motive power," as Rav Ashlag calls it; motivational reasons for people to share all the time. Rav Ashlag uses the example of communism, which in and of itself is similar to the ultimate end point the world needs to achieve. A phrase that communism often uses is "every person acts or creates and does according to his ability and receives according to his need." This is ultimately the place the world is meant to get to; whereas part of humanity as a whole, each individual does as much as they can in creating sustenance, food, wellbeing, and takes in whatever they need. There is no limit for people to get what they need because there will be so much when we all come together and do all of the work—even physical things—for the rest of the world. Everyone will be able to take. There will be no more hunger. There will be no more lack for anyone in our world. This is the theory of socialism, of communism.

However Rav Ashlag says the problem is that if there is no absolute motive to do it, the system will break down; as was the case in the countries that have tried to implement communism. When a person gets to the truest level where he shares, not because he understands the philosophical reason why it is better to do so but rather because he arrives to the understanding that, "I want to have pleasure. I want to enjoy and sharing is what gives me pleasure." When we can bring ourselves to this point, as well as expand this understanding and consciousness to the world, that is the point at which the Final Correction occurs.

This very important distinction is not only the secret to our own fulfillment, it is also the key to bringing about the change that we desire for the world. When a person gets to the point when the sharing is more pleasurable than the receiving, they will not be able to stop sharing. This leads us to the principle that we are never meant to limit our pleasure. In fact the ultimate goal is not to come to the point where we limit our pleasure but rather to get to a point where our greater pleasure comes from actions of sharing. This is also a way to gauge how we are growing spiritually.

However when we do this work of transforming our Vessels to enjoy sharing, we have to be very careful that none of this pleasure goes into the Vessels of receiving—for instance, the good feelings that come from actions of sharing, like what people say about us or think about us. The Vessel has to become an entirely different Vessel. What needs to happen is literally taking out the old Vessel and bringing in a new type of Vessel—a Vessel that feels something else. It is not only enough to train ourselves to share, it is also important to train ourselves to realize where our pleasure from the sharing comes from. If our pleasure in the sharing still comes into the old Vessels, meaning Vessels that take in rather than Vessels that are purely enjoying the sharing, then we are still not getting to the point we are meant to arrive at.

> In order to correct this, He created this World, where the soul comes and clothes itself with a body. And through dealing with the Torah and the Precepts for the sake of giving pleasure to one's Maker, the Vessels of

Receiving of the soul turn into Vessels of Sharing. This means that from [the soul's] side, it does not wish for this outstanding abundance, yet it receives it in order to give pleasure to its Creator who wishes for the souls to enjoy His abundance. And since [the soul] is clean of the Desire to Receive for Itself, it is no longer "ashamed to look in the face of the other." (Ibid.) With this, the utmost perfection of a created being is revealed. The necessity and stipulation of this far-reaching evolution to this World will be explained later that this great work of turning the Form of Receiving into the Form of Sharing can only be imagined in this World, as shall be explained.

Rav Ashlag says our physical world and everything that occurs within it is a necessity for our spiritual work. **"...this great work of turning the Form of Receiving into the Form of Sharing can only be imagined in this world."** is a very important understanding to have. There is nothing in our world and there is nothing that happens in our life that is not for the purpose of assisting this transformation. It is important that we realize this. It is not just that the creation of our world was necessary in order to allow for us this transformation, it also means that every detail of our lives is geared toward that goal.

When we truly understand this, nothing that happens in our lives can upset or bother us because we realize where it is leading. It can be compared to the video games where there is a road and we are driving a vehicle on that road. Even if we turn the wheel all the way to one side or the other, the game keeps us on the road. We can turn the wheel as much as we like, we are not going to go off that road. Imagine there is a player who thinks he wants to drive in the other direction. He spends his entire life trying to turn the wheel and yet the car does not go there. Like the driver and the game, the entire purpose of everything in our world is to lead us here.

To a certain degree, many of us are trying to turn the wheel and the car all the way around in the game of life. It does not work. The road is forcing us in one direction. From the moment of Creation, the world and every specific thing that happens in our lives is leading us towards **"turning the Form of Receiving into the Form of Sharing."** If we are not aware of where we are being lead and we think that we want to go the other way, we will spend our whole life trying to do the impossible—turning the car around. Everything in our world and everything in our lives is meant to bring us toward this transformation of form. Without knowledge of the end goal, not only do we not get to where we think we want to go, we also do not enjoy the ride and the process because it appears to be the opposite of what we want.

Rav Ashlag is saying that everything that is in our world and everything that is in our life is geared towards this goal. If we are aware of this, we understand why things happen to us and we appreciate them. If we do not understand this and we do not understand that everything in our lives, every specific thing that happens in our lives is towards that goal and we try to fight it and change it, then we will never achieve fulfillment.

---

About the wicked, "And destroy them with double destruction" (Jeremiah 17:18); as for the righteous, "they shall possess a double portion" (Isaiah 61:7).

21. Come and see: [it says] about the wicked, "And destroy them with double destruction," (Jeremiah 17:18) because they hold the rope on both ends as this world was created with the total lack and void of all abundance and goodness, and in order to acquire possessions one resorts to movement. But we know, much movement is hard for people since it is an indirect derivative from the Essence of the Creator. Yet to remain empty of possession and goodness is also impossible since this is also contrary to the root, as the root is filled with all goodness. They therefore choose the pain of much movement in order to achieve their many possessions. But since all their possessions and property are for themselves alone, and when they already have one portion they want two hundred, we conclude that people leave the world with half their cravings unfulfilled. Thus they suffer on both ends—from too much movement and from sorrow over lack of possessions, of which they lack half.

But the righteous "possess a double portion in their land" (Isaiah 61:7) that is, after turning their Desire to Receive into the Desire to Share and whatever they receive is [only] in order to share, then they "possess a double portion." (Ibid.) For besides attaining the fullness of pleasure and the choicest possessions, they also attain the Similarity of Form with the Creator. Thus they are in a true state of cleaving and at rest since the abundance reaches them by itself, with no movement or work on their part.

---

What we learn from this section is that the motivation for what most of us see as the Desire to Receive comes from the Light of the Creator. Next time we have a selfish desire, a negative desire, we can realize that the seed of that desire stems from the Creator. The Creator wants us to know that there is both a way for us to have fulfillment and that we are meant to have it, so go ahead and do it. However many of us take that push, that motivation and go after the Desire to Receive for the Self Alone, and this step is where the problem lies. Nevertheless, the actual drive to fulfill ourselves, to take in more, to have more pleasure, comes from the Light of the Creator. It comes from our essence.

This is why Kabbalah is never about desiring less or deciding not to take in, deciding not to receive, because the desire for fulfillment, as Rav Ashlag explains, is true to our essence and nature. This is why it is an inborn trait of all of humanity. We are constantly thinking and working to bring in pleasure. The problem is when that desire is used to drive us toward things that fulfill our Desire to Receive for the Self Alone, and unfortunately this is 99% of the time, and we miss the point. The purpose of this drive, the purpose of this awakening of desire, is this process of transformation. It is to know that the only way that we can fulfill our innate, natural drive to achieve fulfillment is by going through this process of transformation in acquiring these new Vessels of Desire to Share. Nevertheless at its core, it is important that we remember that there is no way to hide from it. There is no way to hide from this Desire to Receive great pleasure. Nonetheless it is meant to drive us toward a transformation, toward a Desire to Share.

There is a story that is often told as an example of this: There is a poor man who has a friend who is very wealthy. The poor man visits his wealthy friend and tells him about a difficult situation the poor man finds himself in. He asks his wealthy friend for money. The wealthy man agrees no questions asked. "Come to my office tomorrow and I will give you whatever money you need." The next day the wealthy man waits in his office and his friend does not show up. It gets later and later in the day. At 6:00pm, the wealthy man leaves the office and goes home. That night, again, his friend arrives at his house and says, "Please can you help me? I am in a lot of trouble now. I need some money. Can you please lend me some money?" The wealthy man says, "Yes, I told you yesterday to come to my office and you didn't come. Never mind, come to my office tomorrow." The next day, the wealthy man goes to his office and his poor friend does not come. And this goes on and on and on.

The idea is, obviously this person is living in a very sad cycle, where the answer to his problem is right there waiting for him. He does everything that he needs to do in order to bring about the solution but he never completely manifests it. Unfortunately, this is the same process most of humanity goes through. We have the driving force, the true essence, the awakening of who we are that tells us to make sure that we achieve fulfillment. Make sure that we take in. Make sure that we achieve the level that is true to who we are—a level of constant joy, constant fulfillment. But we forget the last step, which is the transformation that is necessary (and there is no way around it).

Therefore, what we can do is start taking this motivation and transforming it; using it first to achieve understanding, followed by doing all the actions necessary for our transformation. This is a very important key concept. Rav Ashlag says that it is the understanding of how we can achieve not only our own transformation, but the transformation of our world. Once we achieve this level, and even throughout the process, we achieve a true "motive power" to complete the transformation of our world.

# CHAPTER 5

> **The Thought of Creation stipulates that all the details in existence**
> **derive one from the other till the End of Correction.**
>
> 22. Now that we have merited the previous [explanation], we can somewhat understand the mightiness of the Singularity of the Creator, Whose Thoughts are not our thoughts, etc. All the multiplicity of things and forms that we can understand throughout the existence before us is to the Creator unified in one single thought, namely, the Thought of Creation "to bestow fulfillment to His creations."

Ultimately, we are meant to achieve a level of love toward the Creator. For example, the Rambam (Rav Moses ben Maimon) says that a person has to take the time to look at Creation and say, "Wow, what an amazing Creator. I want to get close to Him. I want to cleave to Him." It is actually an important part of our spiritual work to go out and look at the physical creation that is our world and be in awe of it, and then through this awe awaken a desire to cleave to the Light of the Creator. However, as he often does, Rav Ashlag stresses the importance of awakening a love of the Creator through understanding the greatness of His singularity.

Billions and billions and billions of actions—of causes and effects—all stem from and are One Unified Thought, which is the Thought of the Creator at the point of creation, which is the Singular Desire to Share. Everything that we learn in the Study of the Ten Luminous Emanations and everything that is in our world is all unified in that One Thought. We should take the time to think about this concept. There was no second thought. There was no second step. It is One Single Thought and everything that occurs after the One Thought ties us all the way back into that One Thought. What Rav Ashlag is saying here is that everything that occurred throughout the process of Creation up until today, and everything that will occur from today onward until the Final Correction, is all unified in One Thought. And it is important that it is unified within the One Thought. It is this simple.

In the beginning of this study the Ari (Rav Isaac Luria) says that the Light of the Creator is a Simple Light because if this Light is true, it has to be simple.

Therefore, everything of our world goes back to that one singularity; one coming together. It is important we realize that everything in our world, the entire process of Creation and everything that we are studying here, is really only One Thought.

This Single Thought encompasses all of existence in utter unity until the End of the Correction, for it is the whole Purpose of Creation, as said. It is the Performer, namely, the Force that performs on that which is performed, since that which is only a thought with Him, is an absolutely stipulated law unto the created beings. And since His intention for us is to give us fulfillment, of necessity the notion of receiving His good abundance was activated in us.

One of the beautiful things about learning Ten Luminous Emanations from Rav Ashlag is that in addition to the study, Rav Ashlag also goes through a process where he teaches about the spiritual laws that govern our lives and the world. One of them is: A desire in the Upper Worlds, is a law in the Lower Worlds. Whatever is a desire within the Cause, is something that that Cause wants to occur. Once it manifests in the Lower Worlds, it becomes an unchangeable law.

Before the Tzimtzum, the Vessel said, "I want the Light of the Creator to be removed. I do not want to receive based on my Desire to Receive for the Self Alone. I only want to receive once I have accomplished a Vessel of Sharing." This was a request and desire of the vessel in the Cause stage. The Vessel had the choice to go either way. But once the Cause decided that this is what It wanted, further down the line, the vessels that came into effect afterwards do not have a choice anymore. They can no longer receive in the Vessel of Desire to Receive for the Self Alone.

So this gives us important insight into the power of being a parent or a teacher—of being a cause in any effect. If our spiritual work and desire are complete, whether it is a child or student, we give this over to our effect in a complete way, in a way that becomes a law, which in a positive sense is a very important and positive aspect of giving over.

The reason why we, as Vessels, were created with a Desire to Receive, is not so much that the Creator desires a vessel, so He created a vessel, as would naturally be assumed. No, this is not the case. Since the Creator is the Desire to Share, automatically, whatever occurs next—the effect—has to include within it the Law of Receiving. This is an important distinction. Very often when we think about the process of Creation we understand it as the Creator has the Desire to Share and then he goes about creating a Vessel to Receive. This is one way to view it but it is not the true and complete way to see it. The true and complete way to see it is that once there is a Desire in the Cause, once the Creator Desires to Share, the Vessel automatically, and by law, must have been created. That is the obvious and necessary and indisputable next step.

It is also the action; that is, after this Law of Desire to Receive fulfillment was embedded inside us, then we define ourselves by the name of action because through this Difference of Form we are no longer part of the Creator but become created; from actor we become the action, as said.

And it (the Thought of Creation) is the toil and work since due to the Force activating that which is activated, as said, the yearning to receive grows increasingly within us with the unfolding evolution of the Worlds, culminating in a separate body in this World, which is in invert proportion to the Life of Lives because it is incapable of bestowing anything outside of Itself, and this brings death upon the bodies as well as all kinds of suffering and toil for the soul, as shall be discussed further.

Because of the injection of the Desire to Share from the Creator's side into the Vessel, the Desire to Receive within us, within the Vessel, becomes greater and greater. It is like Newton's first law of motion—sometimes referred to as the law of inertia. An object at rest stays at rest and an object in motion stays in motion with the same speed and in the same direction unless acted upon by an unbalanced force. It will stay in motion until another force pushes against it. Once the Creator has had the Thought of Creation, then within the Vessel is instilled the seed of a Desire to Receive the Light of the Creator. Nevertheless it does not end there because Cause will affect forever unless something new occurs.

What is so beautiful about this whole explanation—and this is what Rav Ashlag wants to clarify—is that everything that occurs is One Essence. The entire essence of our world, the entire essence of everything that has occurred, is occurring and will occur in our world and in our life is One Essence—the Thought of Creation. There is nothing in our world that is not the Thought of Creation from the most positive thing, the Essence of the Light of the Creator, to the most negative thing that we can imagine. Pain, suffering and death is all part of the Thought of Creation. It is all part of that One Singular Essence.

What Rav Ashlag is making clear is that even pain, even suffering, even death, and everything in between, as well as complete fulfillment, is of the same Essence. It is the Essence of the Thought of Creation. It is the Essence of Desire to Share completely to the creations. Hopefully, this overwhelms us with the idea that there is no way out. We can try to think within our own selfish desire to receive for the self alone that we can somehow be separate and somehow make our own path but there is no way. There is no way to get away from the essence of what everything in our lives concerns, which is the Thought of Creation. Whether we see something as the greatest good or we see something as the greatest negativity, it is all the same thing. It is all the Desire to Share; it is all the Thought of Creation.

That said, the first idea that has to become clear in our mind is that if we are not in the process of completing this Thought of Creation, we are fighting against a force that is impossible to fight against. It is the force of nature. The single Force of not only physical nature but behind literally everything there was, there is and there will be is this Thought of Creation, and there is no way to fight against it. There is no way to run from it. There is no chance to come to a life that is not dedicated to this continuation of the Thought of Creation, to a continuation of the transformational process of both ourselves and the world, not because it is the good or best part of our world but because it is the only thing that exists.

In The Wisdom of Truth, Rav Ashlag explains that the Final Correction is inevitable. Our only choice is how it will occur. Will it be with the Way of Torah, which is the path of transformation or will it be in the Way of Suffering? And one of the reasons there is no choice, is because that force of nature began and continues forever. **The force that is bringing the process to its end is embedded everywhere and in everything.** It is impossible for us to fight it. Unfortunately, at times we stupidly think that we can go against that Force, in one way or another. This is what causes all of our frustration, all of our pain, all of our disappointment in life because we do not have a complete understanding that there is no running away from this process. It is imbued and embedded in absolutely everything in our world. And everything that occurs in our lives is only of that essence, is only to bring us towards that impossible will to fight, that impossible nature to fight. This is the first idea.

The second idea is that within everything that happens to us there are two essences, which is clearer to see when there is difficulty and pain. Within every reality there are the lies that we see, which are for example, this person or this situation is causing me pain. This is the basic false level of everything that can be compared to waves on the surface of the ocean. Then there is the true essence of everything that is occurring to me, that is a cause to me, which is the True Reality and the essence of the Thought of Creation.

When we begin to truly know this it means that everything that happens to us in our life, everything that someone else does to me, everything that happens to me beyond my control, has within it two essences. One is the essence of falsehood, meaning "this is causing me pain, this is causing me suffering, this is uncomfortable. I do not want this to happen. I do not know why it is happening. And then there is the true essence of it, which is this is part of the process to bring me towards lasting fulfillment. When we have this understanding we not only connect to the True Reality and therefore, have probably more peace and more fulfillment in the moment, we actually draw closer to that ultimate fulfillment, we actually draw closer the End of the Correction, the Final Correction. This is an important idea.

This is such an amazing concept, it cannot be said too many times, so I will say it again: As Rav Ashlag explains, everything that happens to us, from the greatest good to what is perceived to be the greatest negativity, has two essences. One is the essence of falsehood that we unfortunately see with our physical eyes, which the ego and the Desire to Receive for the Self Alone and the Other Side want us to see. We can perceive this as the greatest thing, which is separate from the Thought of Creation or we can think this is a terrible thing: "I do not know why it is happening. I am not sure why it is happening. Why is this person doing this to me? Why do I find myself in this situation?" This is the false level of reality of everything that happens to us. Then there is the truth of what happens to us in our lives. The true essence of why it is happening is the Thought of Creation.

Now, there are two powers to this understanding. The first power is that when we truly come to the realization that this is happening to us because it is bringing us closer toward the Final Correction, we experience a certain level of peace, and gain a level of awareness. But more importantly, this awareness has the power to draw ourselves, and also the world, at least one step closer, or to whatever degree closer, to realizing the Final Correction. It is like a diamond in the sand that we can hardly see, yet if we take the moment to really pay attention and uncover it, we can take it as our own because now we have earned it. But if we just see a glimmer and pass it by, we have missed a tremendous opportunity.

The Midrash makes the events surrounding the Israelites exodus from Egypt sound very dramatic. As they come to the desert, the Egyptians were behind them, trying to kill them. And was also all manner of wild animals trying to kill them from all sides. And, of course, the very great ocean in front of them. They came to a point where there was no way out; a point where they had two realities to connect to: the reality that this is a terrible situation—death behind them, death in front of them, death on all sides, or the reality of knowing this is part of the process of the Thought of Creation and that somehow within this process we are going to reveal the Thought of Creation.

And because enough of the Israelites brought 100 percent of their consciousness to this understanding—this is part of the process of the Thought of Creation, they were able to reveal the 72 Names of God. They were able to reveal the miracle of the Splitting of the Sea. Because they were able to break apart the falsehood of this world and see the true essence, which is the Thought of Creation within this situation, it allowed them to reveal the miracles.

---

This is the grounds for the work of the Creator with the Torah and the Precepts. For through the illumination of the Line on the contracted space, the Holy Names, the Torah and the Precepts come forth.

And by means of the toil in the Torah and the Precepts with the intention to give pleasure to the Creator, our Vessels of Receiving slowly transform within us into Vessels of Sharing. This is the whole desired reward. As long as the Vessels of Receiving are not yet corrected, we cannot open our mouth wide to receive the abundance of the Creator for fear of the Difference of Form based on the meaning of, "He who eats what does not belong to him

---

will be ashamed to look in the face of the other," (Talmud Yerushalmi, Tractate Orlah Chapter 1 Halachah 3 Page 6a) which was the reason for the first Tzimtzum, as said. But as we correct our Vessels of Receiving so they would be for the Sake of Sharing, we make the Vessels aligned with their Creator and worthy of endlessly receiving His abundance.

Before we recite the Birkat HaMazon (Blessing after the Meal) we cite a section in Psalms that says: "Then our mouth will be full of joy…." (Psalms 126:2) This refers to the time of the Final Correction. The idea is, and it is an important understanding, we know the Creator desires to share with us completely and endlessly all the time and if we do not have a vessel, unfortunately, we cannot receive this Light. Only as we complete the process of transformation and achieve a vessel of Desire to Share can we truly open ourselves up to receive from the Light of the Creator. Once that transformation occurs, the Light that we receive is the same essence of the Desire to Share that was in the Thought of the Creator at the time of creation—the Thought of Creation.

It is important that we remind ourselves that the Study of the Ten Luminous Emanations is not only to gain understanding but is also actually an awakening of Light. This is why it is vital that every time we study, we think of the words of Rav Ashlag as he refers to the awakening of the Final Correction. As we say these words, we actually reveal this Light. And as we think about them, the Light of the Final Correction goes out into the world. Thus this is not simply a process of study but rather, as we say the words and think them, we are actually bringing the world a step closer to the Final Correction. Rav Ashlag explains in the Introduction to Ten Luminous Emanations (And You Shall Choose Life) that we are awakening the Surrounding Light, the potential Light and shining it down into our world.

So you see that all those opposite forms throughout the Creation before us; namely the form of the actor and the action (Cause and Effect), the form of the damages and the corrections, the form of work and its reward and so on, are all included only in this unique Thought of the Creator in utter simplicity, namely "to give fulfillment to His created beings" accurately, neither more nor less.

This is an essential concept to internalize. Deuteronomy 4:35 says, "…there is none beside Him." There is nothing except the Light of the Creator, which means there is nothing except the Thought of Creation. There is nothing else. When we see someone and we think that there is something that is wrong with that person or we say that this person has a negative trait, what we are doing is separating ourselves, not the person, but ourselves from the Essence of the Light of the Creator, from the Thought of Creation because we are saying there is something different—there is the perfection of the Thought of Creation and there is this negativity.

To help us grasp this concept, Rav Ashlag quotes a known story in the Gemara: One of the sages sees a person who is ugly. The sage says to him, "Wow, you are ugly." Keep in mind that he is talking in spiritual terms. And the person responds "Why do you say this to me? Speak to the Essence Who created me." The idea here is that if we see something ugly, if we see something negative, we are disconnecting ourselves from the truth, from the Essence of Creation, the essence of our world. The Essence of everything around us is one, which is the perfection of the Thought of Creation. If we see darkness and negativity, if we see something wrong in someone else or even within ourselves—to a certain degree—we are disconnecting from the true essence of our world because the essence of everything in our world is one.

Similarly, all the myriad of concepts is also included in that Thought: both the concepts in our Holy Torah and external wisdoms, and all the myriads of creatures and Worlds and the different conducts in each, all these derive and extend from this unique Thought as I shall explain later in its place.

Everything. Wisdom. Understanding. Science. Art. Math. The spiritual work. All spiritual wisdom's have only one essence. This is one of those thoughts that we truly have to run through our mind again and again until it becomes part of our essence, as Rav Ashlag says. There is nothing in our world that is separate from the Essence of the Light of the Creator. Part of our spiritual work is to come to this understanding, to this consciousness that everything is the Thought of Creation. Everything is an effect of a Desire to Share completely to His creations. Once this consciousness becomes truly part of our essence, we do not see the negativity in other people. We do not see negativity that comes into our lives. We do not even see darkness within ourselves. We see only the essence of all of it.

In the Torah Portion of Beshalach, it says "Then Moses will sing…" (Exodus 15:1), which is future tense. This verse is telling us that we are meant to come to the point where we see the future. What is the future? The completion of the process. The goodness of everything. This too is one of the concepts that we should take the time to let percolate in our minds because as we do so it elevates us and connects us to the truth and Essence of goodness, of Light, of fulfillment of the Thought of Creation in everything. It is a powerful, necessary, and important consciousness that we need to develop within ourselves, where we come to the point that this is all we see. This is all we understand. We see the truth and essence within everything. It is a beautiful, crucial, and necessary step of consciousness.

---

**Malchut of Ein Sof means that Malchut does not bring an aspect of finiteness there.**

23. From the above said we understand the words of the Tikunei HaZohar concerning the Malchut of Ein Sof, concerning which thresholds were agitated with astonished voices wondering, "Could it be possible to pronounce the name Malchut in the Ein Sof? If so, there are also the first nine Sefirot, and so on." It becomes clear with our words that the Desire to Receive that is of necessity included in the Light of Ein Sof, as said, is called the Malchut of Ein Sof. Except there Malchut did not create an end and limit to the Light of Ein Sof, since the Difference of Form due to the Desire to Receive was not yet revealed in Her (in Malchut). This is why it is called Ein Sof (Endless) because Malchut does not create an aspect of finiteness there. This excludes after the Tzimtzum and below, where an aspect of finiteness was formed in each Sefirah and Partzuf by means of Malchut.

---

What is so imperative for Rav Ashlag to explain is that in the Thought of Creation everything has to exist. Even the reality of there being a Vessel, which then later manifests as that which creates darkness, creates pain, creates suffering. It has to be in existence in the Endless World. It has to be in existence even in one way or another in the Creator, in the Thought of Creation because if it is not true, if there are these new processes that began out of nothing, after the Tzimtzum, this means that there is some separation between us and what happens in our world and the Creator. And this cannot be.

This is a beautiful idea if we can truly understand it. There is nothing in our world that is not tied all the way back up into the Creator. Tied all the way back up into the Thought of Creation. And what that means is that there is nothing in our world that cannot be used as a tool to go back to the Creator. Everything that occurs in our world, the worst darkness, the worst pain, the worst difficulty has a link up, a thread that connects it to the Light of the Creator.

Many of the teachings from the kabbalists are tied to this lesson. However, before we discuss two of them, it is helpful to grasp that this consciousness of knowing that everything in our world, certainly good things, but even the most negative things, even the most dark things, are linked up to the Essence of the Light of the Creator. This knowing, this awareness and consciousness links everything back up to the Creator.

The kabbalists, especially the Baal Shem Tov and his students speak about the sweetening of judgments. And when the Ari (Rav Isaac Luria) speaks about sweetening judgments, he discusses the concept of elevating, explaining that when we elevate judgments to their Source, we sweeten them. During the Prayers there are meditations to elevate judgment. The whole process of the Shofar on Rosh Hashanah is about elevating judgment. This sounds like a very high spiritual concept, but another way to do it as explained by the No'am Elimelech (Rav Elimelech of Lizensk) is with consciousness. When we as individuals think about judgment or negativity in the world, and in our mind we know that this is not separate from the Light of the Creator, we are elevating it. As the Zohar says Malchut to Binah—elevating judgments up to understanding—and by elevating judgment up to understanding, we sweeten that judgment.

When we consciously elevate difficulty, darkness and connect it to its Source knowing that nothing can become separate from the Light of the Creator, we sweeten that judgment. So besides revealing the Light of the Creator there, through that process we also transform it. And the greater my consciousness, the more connected I am, the more my power to really change that situation around.

Rav Ashlag takes all this time to reveal to us that everything in our world flows from the Light of the Creator and therefore, there has to be a Malchut in Ein Sof. There has to be this aspect that is the Vessel, what we call the Desire to

Receive within the Endless World because there cannot be anything in our world that is completely detached from the Light of the Creator.

There is a famous teaching from the Seer of Lublin (Rav Yaakov Yitzchak haLevi Horowitz) regarding Exodus 33:6, where following the golden calf incident it says about the Israelites: "And the children of Israel divested themselves of their adornment at Mount Choreb," meaning that they lost all that Light they received at the revelation of the Ten Utterances. The Seer of Lublin explains that between the time of the sin of the golden calf and the loss of the Light of the Ten Utterances, there is a gap. It is not immediate. Moreover, it says, "and they mourned" (Exodus 33:4); there was a sadness that came upon them, and then afterwards it says that they lost the Light of the Ten Utterances.

The Seer of Lublin explains that if they had not become sad, meaning felt detached from the Light of the Creator after and because of the prior sin of the Golden Calf, they would not have lost the Light that they had received at the Giving of the Torah. It was only because there was a three step process. They transgressed at the sin of the Golden Calf, they became sad about it and, thereby, thinking that they had detached themselves completely from the Light of the Creator. This sadness made them lose their Light. If they had only sinned at the Golden Calf and did not fall into sadness, into thoughts of detachment from the Light of the Creator, they would not have lost their Light from the Revelation at Sinai.

This is an important idea. There is nothing that we do, even the most disgusting, negative action that we can do that will completely detach us from the Light of the Creator. This is why Rav Ashlag spends so much time explaining that there has to be a Malchut in Ein Sof. Yes, it is not the same Malchut that we have here, it is not the same darkness and negativity that we have here but its linkage up to the Endless World, its Source, has to be. Therefore, no matter how far a person falls, this link is always there. This knowledge is something the Negative Side does not want us to know. It wants us to think that if we did a negative action, we have completely detached and this consciousness of complete detachment is the way the Negative Side takes us over.

There cannot be complete detachment from the Endless World. There cannot be anything that exists in our world that is completely new and separate from the Light of the Creator because if that were true there can be things in our world that are not linked back up to the Endless World. This is an essential idea and these are just two of the lessons that we learn from it. First, we can elevate and sweeten judgment by having this consciousness, and through strengthening in this consciousness. And second, there is nothing that can be done with regard to ourselves and in the world that will completely detach us from the Endless World, and this consciousness keeps and strengthens our connection.

# CHAPTER 6

**The Desire to Receive cannot appear in any entity unless it goes through Four Phases, which is the secret of the four letters of the Tetragrammaton (Yud-Hei-Vav-Hei).**

24. Let us expand a bit further on this subject in order to understand well the finiteness that was formed due to Malchut. Let us preface this with a law set by the kabbalists and brought in the Zohar in the Tikkunim (Corrections): There is no Light great or small, neither in the Upper nor the Lower Worlds, that is not arranged in the order of the four-letter Tetragrammaton, Yud-Hei-Vav-Hei. This issue is in accordance with the rule, brought in the Etz Chayim ("Tree of Life"), that there is no Light in any World that is not clothed in a Vessel.

Explanation: I have already clarified the difference between the Essence of the Creator and the Light extending from Him. The only difference is that the Desire to be Fulfilled included in His Extending Light constitutes a Difference of Form from His Essence, since there is none of this Desire in Him. In that way, the Extending Light is defined by the Name "Emanated Being"—since due to this Difference of Form, the Light is no longer part of the Emanator but is considered part of the Emanated. It is also clarified that the Desire to be Fulfilled included in the Light of the Creator measures the amount of the Light's greatness as well. It is called the Light's Place, which means it receives the abundance of the Creator according to the amount of its Desire to Receive and its yearning—not more nor less, as said.

This is a concept that we have heard many times, as Rav Ashlag explains here, the Light is revealed according to the Desire of the Vessel—no more, no less. The greater the Desire, the greater the Light that is revealed. The amount of Light revealed within the Vessel is dependent on the Vessel's Desire to Receive. Many of us think we even have a Desire to Receive the Light. We recognize that we have a Desire to Receive things of this physical world and, for those of us who are involved in the spiritual work, we believe that we also have a Desire to Receive the Essence of the Light of the Creator. As we read this we begin to understand that this idea has to be a lie because if we had a true Desire to Receive the Light of the Creator we would have It [the Light]. If we do not have the Light of the Creator it is because we do not have a true Desire to Receive the Light of the Creator.

There is a teaching from Rabbi Eliyahu Di Vidash in his book *Resheet Chochmah*, which says that one cannot have two desires. If a person has a desire for the Light of the Creator as well as a desire for something else, it is not going to work. Sometimes we think we have a desire for the Light of the Creator but we also have a desire for other things. In *Resheet Chochmah*, Rabbi Eliyahu Di Vidash says that this is impossible. One cannot expect the desire for the Light of the Creator to become manifest if we have a desire for other things.

We not only have to think about awakening and strengthening our desire for the Light of the Creator, we also have to work on diminishing our desire for other things of a physical nature because the two desires cannot live together. For instance, fire and water cannot co-exist in the same vessel. Therefore, the idea that we also have a desire for the Light of the Creator is a patently obvious lie. As Rav Ashlag says, "If we had a true desire for the Light of the Creator, we would have the Light of the Creator."

The reason we lack the Light of the Creator is because we lack desire, and this lack of desire is caused by either a simple lack of desire for the Light of the Creator or a desire for other things. Even if in our mind we do not see it this way, to whatever degree we unconsciously and in reality have a desire for other things, we have a much more limited desire for the Light of the Creator. Therefore, part of the work, aside from the work of awakening a greater and greater desire for the Light of the Creator, is to diminish the other desires, to whatever degree we can because the other desires are going to put out the flame of desire for the Light of the Creator, and thus we cannot manifest it.

Another aspect of this is that in discussing spiritual matters we are speaking about matters that last. If the Light of the Creator is going to become manifest, it has to be in a Vessel that lasts. Sometimes people get very excited about their spiritual work, they have a great desire for the Light of the Creator, yet a month later it becomes diminished. Clearly, it was never a true desire because a true desire will not disappear.

There are three reasons as to why the Light does not come, even though we think we have a true desire.

First is that we may be lying. We do not really have a desire.

Second is that we have other desires. As Rabbi Eliyahu Di Vidash says, because there cannot be the existence of two desires, those other desires—whether through our consciousness or lack of consciousness—will diminish the desire for the Light of the Creator, even if we do not feel it. We either have a desire for the Light of the Creator or a desire for other things.

And third is that the desire is not a true lasting desire. We think we have a desire for the Light of the Creator, however, if this desire does not remain as strong in a month or in six months, we did not really have the desire. I have heard it said, "I don't know what happened. For a long time I was excited, and I had a real desire, and then it went away." The reality is that if it went away we never truly had a desire. Because the Creator works within the World of Truth, if we have a desire and the Creator knows it is not a true desire, meaning that in a few months it will wane, the Creator cannot fill that Vessel because it is not a true Vessel; it is a Vessel with holes. And to pour Light into that Vessel is worthless.

It is important that we try to understand what it is about our Vessel that is not a real Vessel, and therefore does not allow the Light of the Creator to become manifest. Whatever, at this moment, feels like a real Vessel and desire but is not being filled is not a real Vessel. It is important not just to be disappointed or upset that our Vessel is not being filled, we also have to understand the reasons that make our Vessel not a true Vessel. Rav Ashlag says that a true Vessel does not just mean that in a flippant way we say, "Oh yeah, the Creator, I really, really, really want you to fill me with Your Light." It has to be a true lasting Vessel. It has to be a Vessel that does not have other competing desires and it has to be a Vessel that will last.

It was also explained that this subject of the Desire to Receive constitutes the entire aspect of newness that took place with the Creation of the Worlds by way of Something out of Nothing. Only this form alone is not included, Heaven forbid, in the Essence of the Creator; and it is only now that the Creator presented it for the sake of the Creation, which is the secret of: "I… create darkness," (Isaiah 45:7) since this form is the root of darkness due to the Difference of Form in it; it is therefore dimmer than the Light extending within it and because of it.

From this you can understand that all Light extending forth from the Creator is immediately considered as having two aspects. The first part is the Essence of the Extending Light before the form of the Desire to be Fulfilled was revealed in it. The second part is after this form of the Desire to be Fulfilled was revealed in it. Then it became coarser and a little darker due to the acquisition of the Difference of Form, as said.

One of the real advantages of studying from Rav Ashlag is that we begin to understand that everything has a layer within a layer within a layer. If we look through a spiritual microscope at the formation of a Vessel, we would see different layers. As science delves deeper into the moments before the Big Bang, investigating the tiniest measurements of time to see how our world came about, parallels between what they discover and the true spiritual process will emerge. This is what Rav Ashlag does here—parsing deeper and deeper into the process that led to the creation of the Vessel, which is the spiritual and therefore root of the physical process of our world coming together.

On a complete side note, one of the reasons we can understand language is that our mind can dissect time into much smaller moments than we think. We tell time with our conscious mind in seconds, but our unconscious mind can deconstruct seconds and that breakdown allows us to understand speech. This is the reason why when we hear a person talking, even if they speak quickly, we can hear when a word begins and our mind knows where to put those stops.

Were it not for our unconscious mind's ability to parse seconds and time measurements into smaller and smaller pieces, we would not be able to understand language. It is truly beautiful when we begin thinking about the way the human mind is set up. The ability that the Creator gave us to be able to parse moments of time into smaller and smaller increments gives us many things, and one is the ability to understand speech.

Nevertheless, what Rav Ashlag is discussing here is the parsing of the creation of the Vessel. He explains that if we examine the process of a Vessel becoming created, we would see that there are really two stages. The first stage is the process as the Light begins to become manifest into a Vessel, even though the Vessel is not there yet. The second stage is when the Vessel begins receiving the Light of the Creator. The Rav often spoke about the idea that when we throw a rock into a lake, change begins to occur in the water even before the physicality of the rock has impacted the water, which is another aspect of physical matter.

If we think about it logically, there is the Light and the Vessel. The Light should remain Light until the Vessel receives it. Yet Rav Ashlag is saying here that even as the Light is ready to come into the Vessel, before it enters the Vessel, it is already starting to change. The idea that the change begins to occur before the actual cause of the change happens is a beautiful concept when we understand it.

Therefore, Rav Ashlag says that the Light begins to change even before it gets into the Vessel. Yet logic dictates that there is Light and there is Vessel and that only the second that the Light comes into the Vessel does the change occur and it [the Vessel] becomes separate from the Essence of the Light of the Creator. Meaning, if we could parse every millisecond into the greatest degrees it would still be 100% Light until it first touches the Vessel. However Rav Ashlag is saying that this is incorrect, the Light begins the process of changing even before it becomes manifest in the Vessel.

> The first part is the secret of the Light, whereas the second part is the secret of the Vessel. There are therefore four distinguishable Phases in any Extending Light that concern the activation of the Vessel. The form of the Desire to Receive, which is called a Vessel in relation to the Extending Light, is not completed at once but by way of Activator and Activated (Cause and Effect). There are two parts in the Activator and two parts in the Activated; these are called Potential and Actual in the Activator and Potential and Actual in the Activated. Altogether there are Four Phases.

The basic idea is that there is Light and Vessel and that within the process of Light and Vessel, the Light becoming Vessel has a cause and effect, and the Vessel becoming Vessel has a cause and effect. What Rav Ashlag reveals in this discussion is the process of a Vessel becoming a Vessel. It is important to understand the process of the Vessel becoming a Vessel because to the degree our consciousness understands the process of becoming a Vessel, to that degree we can create a Vessel. One reason we lack a true Vessel is because our consciousness does not comprehend a true Vessel. This is not necessarily a logical process but it is a spiritual one. The more our mind works through the process of a Vessel becoming a Vessel, the greater our ability will be to create a greater Vessel.

One of the gifts that Rav Ashlag gives us is not only the tools and understanding of transformation, but also by explaining the spiritual process of a Vessel becoming a Vessel, we will transform. That said, as we begin delving deeper into the Four Phases of a Vessel becoming a Vessel we will unconsciously become a better Vessel. This study actually gives us the ability to become a greater Vessel.

It is important that we appreciate this gift because as our mind works through the process by which a Vessel becomes a Vessel, we change spiritually. It gives us a greater ability to awaken a stronger Vessel. Earlier we spoke about three reasons why the Light of the Creator does not come, even if we have a desire. This is the fourth reason. We lack the ability to truly create a great Vessel because our mind does not understand the greater degrees of Vessels becoming Vessels. It is important to know that as we think about it, as we study it, our awakened understanding changes us spiritually. It gives us the ability to create a greater Vessel.

---

**The Desire to Receive is established in the Emanated Being only when the latter awakens to receive on its own accord.**

25. The reason is that the Vessel is the root of darkness, as said, which is the opposite of the Light. It therefore must be activated gradually in steps by way of cause and effect. This is the secret of: "Water conceived and begot darkness" (Midrash Rabbah, Exodus Chapter 15) because darkness is a progeny of Light itself and receives from it by way of pregnancy and birth, which are like potential and actual.

---

The Book of Formation describes the four elements: fire, wind, water and earth. The Midrash Rabbah (that Rav Ashlag is quoting here) explains that everything that is formed in our world—both physically and spiritually—comes from those four elements. When it refers to the element of water, the Midrash Rabbah says that water birthed darkness. What does this mean? Water represents the Light of the Creator and, in a slow process, water birthed the darkness in our world. The Desire to Receive has to be included within the desire of the Creator to reveal His Light. However, when the Desire to Receive is initially revealed it is not darkness; it is a little bit darker than the Light. Then as it continues to become a reality, it becomes completely dark.

Rav Ashlag is telling us here that going from Light to darkness can never be an instantaneous quick process. It always has to be a slow process. This is what the Midrash Rabbah is referring to and it is an important spiritual understanding for all of us. When a person goes from connection to disconnection—from being connected to the Light of the Creator to being disconnected from the Light of the Creator—it is almost never an immediate process. The Midrash says the Negative Side is like a spider that weaves a web slowly. The Evil Inclination comes into a person and starts small with a voice that says, "Do this…"—usually it is something that is not terrible and certainly not the worst thing in the world. Then over time, the Negative Side, the ego, the Desire to Receive for the Self Alone, completely overtakes the person. And at that point the person does not know any more that they are disconnected.

The Evil Inclination, the Desire to Receive for the Self Alone, does not have the power to tell us that one day we are a very connected person and the next day we are the most disconnected person, not at all connected to the Light of the Creator. However there are many different parables in both the Zohar and the Talmud that explain how the Negative side overtakes the person. Sometimes the Talmud refers to it in the way of a spider weaving its web. Other times the Talmud talks about it like a guest who comes into your house and stays one day and then the next time he comes he stays two days, and so on, and so on, until he sets up shop.

The Ramchal says that the most dangerous and saddest part about a person who is completely disconnected is that he does not know that he is disconnected. He does not know because the process was slow. A slow process leads to a little less excitement today, a little less excitement the next day, until eventually, at the end of the process "Water conceived and begot darkness." (Midrash Raba, Exodus Chapter 15) A connection to the Light of the Creator can slowly but surely create darkness; slowly but surely create a disconnection from the Light of the Creator.

As Rav Ashlag says here, going from Light to darkness has to be a slow process. And this is the process that occurs in the creation of our world. Meaning, the Desire to Receive that has to be included in the Light's Desire to Share is not darkness; it is the first step, which is only slightly different than the Light of the Creator. Eventually at the end of the process of going after the Desire to Receive for the Self Alone there is a complete darkness; is the complete disconnection from the Light of the Creator.

So darkness comes from Light, which is something important to keep in mind all the time. One of the things this concept teaches us is that there is nothing in our world that is not of the Creator. Even the greatest darkness has a source in the process of Creation, in the Light of the Creator. The darkness we see in our world has its source in the Light of the Creator. The Zohar speaks about the concept of: "I will be with him in distress." (Psalms 91:15); that the Creator says "I am with you in the difficulty. I am with you in darkness." No matter what darkness a person finds himself in, no matter what disconnect a person finds himself in, he has to know, we have to know that the Light is there too.

Now we understand the logic of the idea that the Light of the Creator is always found in darkness. Even when a person is at their lowest point, the Light of the Creator is there. However, now we understand the logic of this, and hopefully this knowledge strengthens our consciousness. Of course, the Light of the Creator has to be in the darkness because darkness came from Light. Whatever darkness we feel in our own lives or that occurs in our world, has to be an eventuality of the Light of the Creator, in one way or another. Therefore, even within that darkness, the Light of the Creator exists. This consciousness has the power to remove the outer layers of that darkness. As the Baal Shem Tov says, once a person knows that the Light of the Creator is within him and with him in the darkness, this knowledge already takes away the darkness.

When we find ourselves in a situation of darkness, great or small, the Negative Side does not want us to realize that the Light of the Creator is not only there, but has to be there with us. The Evil Inclination wants us to think, *I am so disconnected now, I am in a place where this is darkness, the Light is on the other side and is not connected to me.* Yet this is not so, whenever there is darkness, the Light of the Creator is there. The Baal Shem Tov says that the awakening of the consciousness that the Light of the Creator is in that darkness, removes that darkness. This awareness has the power to remove that darkness.

The reason is that of necessity the Desire to Receive is immediately included throughout the Extending Light, as said, except it does not amount to be called Difference of Form until this Desire is clearly set in the Light.

For that to happen, the aspect of the Desire to Receive included in the Light on the part of the Emanator does not suffice. The Emanated Being itself must reveal the Desire to Receive in it, in actuality, on its own accord. In other words, it must draw abundance from its own desire, more that the amount of Light that extends in it from the side of the Emanator. After the Emanated [Being] is activated through its own initiative by increasing the amount of its Desire, the yearning and Desire to Receive are set in it, and the Light can consistently be clothed in this Vessel.

Rav Ashlag tells us here that a Vessel (a Desire to Receive) can only become manifest once it is awakened by the Vessel itself. A simple example Rav Ashlag uses is this: A person visits someone at their home. The host makes the guest a special dish that the guest has never tasted before. If the guest is hungry, he has a Vessel, a desire to receive food. Howeve the guest has never tasted this particular dish. The host asks the guest if he wants to eat. The guest is hungry and does not want to insult his host so he accepts whatever the host has made. The guest then eats the food, and it is the most amazing food he has ever tasted, now when the guest asks for this food in the future, he has a true Vessel for that food.

When the host first asked his guest, "Do you want to eat?" there was some measure of Vessel there. The guest is hungry and wants to eat. But does the guest have a strong and specific desire for this particular food? The answer is no because he does not know what it is or what it tastes like. After he tastes it, once he has awakened a true desire for himself for this delicious food, is the only point when the guest's desire for this food is considered a true Vessel. Only when the Vessel awakens the desire for the Light on its own can it be considered a true Vessel.

This reveals a very important spiritual lesson. A desire that is not a truly manifested desire is something we see in people who are starting their spiritual journey, as well as in people who are further along in their spiritual process whereby their connection, even their excitement to the Light of the Creator is an externally affected desire. Although there is some awakening from within, it is not an owned desire. The unfortunate reality is that if our desire for the Light of the Creator is not a wholly, completely manifested one that we have affected and brought about on our own, it cannot last; it will not last.

About Abraham and Sarah it is written, "...and the souls that they had acquired in Haran...." (Genesis 12:5) Throughout their lives, Abraham and Sarah, did what we do at the Centre. They travelled the world speaking to people about the concept of the spiritual work that one should take upon themselves. And they were successful. Thousands of people all over the known world at that time changed their lives completely. They were inspired by Abraham and Sarah to start living a spiritual life focused on transforming the Desire to Receive for the Self Alone into the Desire to Share. And as we continue reading the stories of the Torah, Isaac, Jacob, and the 12 Tribes—a relatively small group—carry on this work throughout history. And in Egypt, the group of 70 people became 600,000. Yet we never again read about "...the souls that they had acquired in Haran...." (Ibid.) What happened to all of the souls that Abraham and Sarah awakened in Haran?

The answer is that while Abraham and Sarah awakened people's desire, this awakening of desire was not owned by the people they awakened. It was always an effect of the inspiration, Light and teachings of Abraham and Sarah. Because there was no continuation because those tens of thousands of people did not own the Vessel, the Vessel evaporated. This is something that, unfortunately, we see often—people inspired, connected, and doing the spiritual work but it is clear that they are inspired by external forces and It is not owned by them.

The question I ask is this: If there was no Kabbalah Centre in the world, Heaven forbid, and we did not have the support that we have, would we still be doing the work? This is a good way to know whether the Vessel is owned; whether one truly owns this Light. Just because a person is doing the work and inspired to do the work does not mean much in the long run. It is important to remember that there will never be better teachers than Abraham and Sarah, never! Nonetheless, they could not affect the creation of a true Vessel. As Rav Ashlag says, the Vessel has to awaken the desire and own this desire itself. We cannot create a Vessel for someone else. We can inspire, we can help and we can support.

Because the Vessel can be lost as well, a question we have to constantly be asking ourselves is: Do I own my Vessel? Is my Vessel affected by external forces—even good forces? It is not a bad thing for someone who does not have an inner connection, an inner certainty, an inner commitment, to get support. It is not a bad thing while we are still weak to have assistance to push us. However this can never be what our connection is about, what our Vessel is about. If we do not own the Vessel on our own, it will not last. We see this from Abraham and Sarah and their students, and we see it today.

Do we own our Vessel? Do we have an internal commitment and understanding of our desire? Is it our own? One simple way to think about it is this, "If everything in the world was literally against me doing this work, would I still be doing it?" If the answer is yes, then we own the Vessel—at least for now. Many of us to one degree or another lack this desire and it is important to know what we lack so we can ask for it.

Rav Ashlag explains that one purpose of darkness—one main reason we go through times of disconnect is to awaken a desire and appreciation for the Light. If the Light of the Creator was always with us we could never awaken a true desire or appreciation for that Light to become manifest. This is why it is important to constantly ask ourselves these questions so we come to a true understanding of where we are: Do I own my Vessel? Am I affected externally? And is this the reason that I am doing what I am doing? If we do not delve deeply into our own Vessel, we can never beg the Creator to give us a true Vessel. If we allow ourselves to maintain a shallow Vessel (that is a Vessel that is not created completely by ourselves) and do not beg the Creator to give us a true Vessel, then the Creator cannot give it to us.

Lastly, concerning this subject, Rav Brandwein told the Rav that there is always a deeper and deeper level to this Vessel, even once we own it. As we will learn, there is a Malchut for Malchut, meaning a Vessel in the lowest World. Then there is a Malchut for Zeir Anpin, a Malchut for Binah, a Malchut for Chochmah, and there is the Malchut of Ein Sof. Thus even once we own the Vessel we can still go higher. Who does not want to go higher? We have to constantly be searching within ourselves. How much do I own my Vessel? And to whatever degree we lack true ownership we have to beg the Creator to give it to us.

Rav Ashlag continues, **"The emanated being itself must reveal the Desire to Receive in it, in actuality, on its own accord."** What this means is that in a Vessel that is not a true Vessel, the Light can go in and Light can go out but Light cannot remain. Therefore when we say that we have to own our Vessel it means we have to make sure that our conviction and our work is internally motivated. The problem with not having this conviction is not just that one day we will completely lose it but more importantly, even as we are still connecting and doing the work the Light cannot be in us consistently. There will be ups and downs in our commitment, in our excitement and in our dedication because our Vessel is not a true Vessel. Light can come into a non-true Vessel but it cannot stay there consistently.

This is a tremendous secret that explains why a person, in his spiritual work, has moments of ups and downs. It is because there is no true Vessel there. There are two problems with not having a true Vessel: one is that it can go away completely (as we learned from the students of Abraham and Sarah); and two, while the externally affected Vessel is still there, the Light cannot remain in that vessel all the time—the Light goes in and out, in and out. Even while the Light is there, it is not a true Vessel. Rav Ashlag says that as long as a person does not truly own the commitment to the work of transformation and is not internally motivated, then even when that person is in a good place there will be ups and downs. An uncompleted Vessel is still a Vessel and to whatever limited extent that Vessel has Light, it cannot hold onto it all the time. This is a very important idea.

It is true that the Light of Ein Sof extends, so to speak, by means of the mentioned Four Phases as well until the ultimate measure of Desire on the part of the Emanated itself, which is the Fourth Phase, since without which it would not have left the aspect of His Essence to be established as a Name unto itself, namely Ein Sof. However, with all the omnipotence of the Creator, the form did not change at all due to the Desire to Receive, nor was any difference registered between the Light and the Place of the Light, which is the Desire to Receive pleasure as said, and they are actually one.

The beauty of studying Talmud Eser Sefirot is that that when we study the phrase, "before the creation of our world He was One and His Name was One," (Pirkei DeRabbi Eliezer) we touch that unity. We connect to that perfection. This something that we need to keep reminding ourselves of. In the Introduction Rav Ashlag says that the reason it is so important to study the Ten Luminous Emanations is not for the understanding but for the connection. When we learn about perfection, we are connecting to that perfection, we are touching that perfection.

And this is what is said in Pirkei DeRabbi Eliezer that before the world was created, He was One and His Name was One. This repetition of "He and His Name" is difficult to understand. For before the world was created, what did His Name have to do there? It should have said that before the world was created He was One. But this alludes to the Light of Ein Sof—before the Tzimtzum—for though there is an aspect of Place there and there is Desire to Receive abundance from the Essence of the Creator, there is still no difference or distinction between the Light and the Place, and "He is One," namely, the Light of Ein Sof; and "His Name is One," namely the Desire to be Fulfilled that is included there without any differentiation at all, Heaven forbid. Understand the allusion of the sages that Shemo (His Name) has the same numerical value (346) as Ratzon (Desire), namely, "the Desire to be Fulfilled."

**The entirety of the Worlds in the Thought of Creation is called the Light of Ein Sof. The entirety of the Receivers there is called the Malchut of Ein Sof.**

26. We already explained about the idea of "the conclusion of an action exists first in thought," (from Lecha Dodi, by Rav Shlomo Alkabetz) which is the Thought of Creation that extended from His essence in order to give fulfillment to His created beings; that with the Creator, Thought and Light are the same thing. With this it is understood that the Light of Ein Sof that extended from His Essence encompasses the whole existence before us until the destined End of the Correction, which is the conclusion of the action. To the Creator, all the created beings are already concluded with all their completion and pleasure that He wanted to fulfill them. This complete existence with all that is required is called the Light of Ein Sof, while their entirety is called Malchut of Ein Sof.

# CHAPTER 7

> Although it (the Vessel) was contracted only from the Fourth Phase,
> the Light left the first Three Phases as well.

27. It has already been explained that the Middle Point, which is the secret of the inclusive Point of the Thought of Creation and is the secret of the Desire to be Fulfilled in it, adorned itself in order to make its form aligned with the Emanator even more. Even though from the part of the Emanator, due to his omnipotence, there was no Difference in Form, nevertheless the Point of Desire felt something drawn indirectly from His Essence. This is likened to the story about the rich man; look there. It therefore diminished its Desire from the aspect of the last Phase, which has the utmost magnitude of the Desire to be Fulfilled in order to add in cleaving in the aspect of drawing directly from His Essence, as said before. Then Light was emptied from all aspects of the Place, that is, from all Four Phases in the Place. And even though it diminished its Desire from the Fourth Phase alone, the nature of spirituality is that it cannot be divided into parts.

Here Rav Ashlag reveals an amazing spiritual law: **"The nature of spirituality is that it cannot be divided into parts."** Anything that is truly spiritual, anything that is truly of the Light of the Creator, cannot be divided into parts. In studying from the Ten Luminous Emanations, it is a beautiful thing that we not only learn about the totality of the picture that Rav Ashlag gives us—what came before Creation, what came during the process of Creation, what will be in the end—we also learn the spiritual laws that govern the points in the process. These spiritual laws are overarching rules. This particular rule is one that is true all the time: The true spiritual nature of anything is that it cannot be divided into parts.

What does this mean for us? On one level, here specifically, what Rav Ashlag is talking about is that the Vessel said, "The only desire I want to restrict, the only desire with which I can no longer receive is a complete desire." For example, in a situation where a person has not eaten all day and has a true desire for a specific food, at a particular time, this desire is an ultimate desire. If a person is not hungry today but enjoys this food, this is a lesser level of that desire. And, of course, there are lesser and lesser degrees of that desire.

The true Tzimtzum, the true restriction that the Vessel decided to establish was only on the perfect, ultimate desire—when we are starving and want a particular food. What Rav Ashlag is revealing to us is that the decision to restrict the desire made it so the Light had to be completely removed. It would be impossible for the Light to stay in this section and not in that section. This is how it relates to the process of Creation. The spiritual law is that spiritual entities, spiritual essences cannot be divided into parts. And another important lesson to our current, continuous spiritual growth is that we can never be in a situation where we are half and half.

Zohar, Emor 129 states that the Creator says, "Open to me an opening no wider than the eye of a needle and I will open to you Supernal Gates." What the Zohar is telling us is all we need to do is create a small opening, a small action, and with that can come great change. The Kotzker Rebbe (Rabbi Menachem Mendel of Kotzk) asks, "Since the Zohar does not use superfluous or extraneous words or just choose examples by accident, why did the Zohar exactly choose the example of a small object as the eye of a needle?" If the Zohar was only trying to tell us to open a small opening, to create the smallest of actions, so that the Light of the Creator will come in and create the great change, it could have used other examples of small things; it could have used a grain of sand. The eye of a needle is but one example. It could have said "Open to me an opening no bigger than a grain of sand and I will open to you Supernal Gates."

The Kotzker Rebbe answers that the difference between the smallness of a grain of sand and the smallness represented by the eye of a needle is that although they are both small, nevertheless the eye of a needle represents a completeness. Although the opening of the eye of a needle is small, it is a complete opening. It is not a limited opening. This teaches us is that in our spiritual work although all that is expected of us is a small opening, nevertheless the opening needs to be complete. It needs to be a complete being, a complete essence. The Light of the Creator cannot be manifested in fragmentation, in parts. There has to be a complete essence, a complete reality.

The Kotzker Rebbe uses the concept of the Mikveh as an example of this spiritual law. According to the Halachah, the spiritual law concerning the Mikveh, if even one hair is outside of the water at the time of immersion, the Mikveh will not work. It is not enough to be 99.9% immersed in the water of the Mikveh. One has to be completely submerged under the water. If even a small hair, only 0.00001% of our physicality is outside of the water of the Mikveh, it invalidates the entire mikveh. Why is this? Rav Ashlag explains that a revelation of a spiritual essence cannot occur in parts. It is either a complete revelation or there is no revelation. It is a complete opening or no opening. The eye of a needle represents this. The mikveh represents it.

There is a section in the Book of Prophets where Elijah the Prophet asks the Israelites at the time "How long will you keep hopping between two opinions?" (I Kings 18:21) In Elijah's time there were those who did the spiritual work but also took time to do all manner of negative things as well. They would go through both doors. They would go to both places. With his question, what Elijah the Prophet was telling them, and us, is you cannot make a spiritual connection at the same time you make a complete spiritual disconnection. Here Rav Ashlag says, very clearly, **"...the nature of spirituality is that it cannot be divided to parts...."**

In our current work, the lesson to internalize is that to whatever degree we are parsing our spiritual work, it is not complete. We may think we can compartmentalize it, we may think we can divide it and connect here or disconnect there but it is impossible, not because it is wrong or because it is not "the ultimate way" but because, as Rav Ashlag says, spiritual nature does not happen in parts. Either it happens or it does not happen.

We are either consciously connecting or we are disconnected. There is no middle ground. There is no connecting in parts. There is completeness in the spiritual system. This is true both, in the process of Tzimtzum, and also in our constant spiritual work. There cannot be a situation where we are partly connected and partly disconnected. There cannot be a situation where we are partly making an opening and partly not making an opening.

True spiritual connection, true spiritual opening, has to be complete. It can be as small as the opening of an eye of a needle nevertheless it has to be complete. The Light of the Creator cannot be revealed in parts or in disassociated fragmented sections. Therefore, if we want to truly know if we are making openings, if we want to truly know if we are connecting to the Light of the Creator, we have to ask ourselves the question: Do we think that our work can be divided into parts? Do we think, to whatever degree, that our consciousness can be divided into parts? And if we think that it can, we are truly not making a connection because it is a spiritual nature.

The beautiful thing about Rav Ashlag's revelation is that it is not simply right or wrong, it is the spiritual nature. If our life, our consciousness, our work is not in tune with this spiritual nature, then there is nothing else that we can do. It is not about trying or doing more, it is either in uniformity, working within the laws of spiritual nature or it is not. This concept is also a good way for us to know where we are in our personal spiritual connection and spiritual work. If we think that we can do the spiritual work in parts, disassociating certain parts of our life and consciousness, then we are not in keeping with this spiritual law, which is, **"...it cannot be divided into parts...."**

---

*Then a Line of Light again was drawn from the first three phases, while the Fourth Phase remained a vacant space.*

28. Afterwards, the Light of Ein Sof again was drawn to the place that was emptied, however it did not fill the place in all Four Phases, rather just the Three Phases, as was the Desire of the Point of Tzimtzum. Thus it came about that the contracted Middle Point remained hollow and empty, as the Light only shone until the Fourth Phase, not including, and the Light of Ein Sof ceased there.

---

The spiritual law that comes into effect after the Tzimtzum is that a Desire to Receive for the Self Alone at its greatest level can no longer be fulfilled. Nevertheless a lower level of desire can be fulfilled, meaning that if we are not starving and we like this food, this is a lower level of desire, a type of Vessel that can be filled. However the ultimate level of desire, which we call the Fourth Phase—the ultimate, complete desire and Vessel can never be fulfilled anymore.

We now exist within the reality where a direct path from desire to fulfillment no longer exists. In this reality, as Rav Ashlag explains, the only way desire can be fulfilled is through the process of Ohr Chozer (Returning Light), which is the process of transforming a Desire to Receive for the Self Alone into a

Desire to Receive for the Sake of Sharing. When we within can transform any one of our desires into a Desire to Receive for the Sake of Sharing, then that desire can be fulfilled. Whatever desire we do not transform, and still keep within the realm of the Desire to Receive for the Self Alone, this Vessel can no longer be fulfilled within the process of correction. Now the Light comes back in and the Vessel realizes: "I can receive Light as long as it is not to my greatest desire but my greatest desire to receive can no longer be filled."

The subject of the Phases being included within each other, which applies in the Supernal Worlds, shall be explained later on. With that you shall understand that the Four Phases are included within each other in such a way that all Four Phases exist in the Fourth Phase itself. Thus, the Light of Ein Sof reached its first Three Phases, and only the last Phase in its Fourth Phase remained empty without Light. Remember this.

This spiritual law that dictates every spiritual level, every spiritual layer, includes within it all the other layers, governs everything in our world—not just this part within the Creation process. For instance, within Keter all the other Ten Sefirot are included. Within Chochmah there are all the other Ten Sefirot. Everything is included in everything. Rav Ashlag explains clearly throughout the Ten Luminous Emanations that it is very dangerous to start viewing the Creation process as either Circles within Circles or as Lines in Circles but instead only as one containing the other because every aspect, every level, contains all the other levels.

There are endless connecting Circles. If we look at it as a geometric pattern it is not just one Circle covering another Circle, covering another Circle but rather it is Circles that are both outside of each other and inside of each other. Every level is included in the levels above it and included in in the levels below it. Even Keter has the Ten Sefirot. Chochmah has the Ten Sefirot. Binah has the Ten Sefirot. This means that within every Desire to Receive there are the other levels, whether the greatest Desire to Receive or the lowest Desire to Receive.

Let's use the example of having the greatest Desire to Receive for food—we are starving and we want a specific food. The lower level of this desire, is when we do not have a strong desire for food—we are just not that hungry and we have desire for a specific food. Nevertheless, even within that lower level of desire, within the realm of Tzimtzum, this Vessel cannot have its ultimate fulfillment because even the lower level of desire, the lower Vessel, has a Malchut and the Malchut, the Fourth Phase, the great desire—even within the lower desires—cannot be filled.

When one is not that involved in the spiritual work, it could be that they have a limited desire. One might think that as long as a person has a limited desire, he can be fulfilled to the level of that limited desire, but as Rav Ashlag reveals, even a limited desire can never completely be fulfilled because there is always a Fourth Phase even in a First Phase. There is an ultimate level of fulfillment even of a limited desire. Even at the lowest levels of desire, complete fulfillment can never be achieved because it is the Fourth Phase of the First Phase. What this teaches us is that there is no way around the process of transformation. Even someone who innately does not have a great Desire to Receive, can never achieve fulfillment without going through the process of transformation.

What Rav Ashlag will now explain is the process by which a Vessel is created. He not only discusses every time a Vessel is created, he also explains about the first time the Vessel was created—the initial Vessel, the Vessel that includes the souls of all humanity, the Vessel of Ein Sof. It is important to realize and remember that as we study the creation of the Vessel, through our consciousness in trying to understand this we are actually, strengthening the Vessel. A Vessel represents desire, the desire of humanity for the Light of the Creator. Therefore, we are not only studying to understand the process but more importantly, we are studying to awaken this Vessel, this desire in the world.

This should be our consciousness as we study. The more we study and understand the process of the creation of the Vessel in the Endless World on a deeper level, the more we strengthen the connection and the Vessel of humanity to this initial Vessel. Therefore, in strengthening humanity's connection to the Vessel, to the desire for the Light of the Creator, we bring the entire world closer to a realization of that Vessel, to the End of the Correction.

# CHAPTER 8

**Chochmah is called Light and the Chasadim, Water.**
**Binah is called Upper Water and the Malchut, Lower Water.**

29. Let us now explain the Four Phases in terms of cause and effect that must apply in order to activate the completion of form of the Desire to Receive, as said earlier in the secret of: "Water conceived and begot darkness." There are two aspects of Light to Atzilut (Emanation): the first aspect is called Light, which is the secret of Chochmah (Wisdom), and the second aspect is called Water, which is the secret of Chasadim (Mercy, Kindness). The first aspect is drawn from Above downward without intervention from the lower part, while the second aspect is drawn with help from the lower part. It is called Water because it is the nature of Light to originate Above and the nature of Water to originate Below. Understand this well. Water itself contains two aspects, namely, Upper Water through the second of the Four Phases, and Lower Water through the fourth of the Four Phases.

An important concept we learn from this is that Pure Light is Light. On the other hand, Light that is affected, created, and drawn by the Vessel is called Water, which is a lower level of Light. Although is a concept that is taught often, we have to be reminding ourselves of it constantly. The moment we have a part in something and have injected ourselves into a process—even a pure thing, even the greatest thing, even something that is only of a spiritual nature, only of a Desire to Share—it is diminished. The only way we can have a pure, complete revelation of Light is when we do not inject ourselves into the process.

To be a pure channel for revelation is something that the Rav spoke about at length. With this explanation we have another understanding of this idea. No matter how pure we are, as long as we are a part of the process, we are Water and not Light. We have diminished the type of Light that can be revealed. It can be perfect, it can be complete but it is already in the Realm of Water, as opposed to Light, it is already a diminished form of the Light of the Creator.

This is the reason that the kabbalists discuss the importance of constantly diminishing our ego and removing ourselves. Moses achieved the highest of levels. He was the Servant of God. In the letters he wrote to the Rav, Rav Brandwein speaks about the constant work to remove ourselves from the equation, the work to remove ourselves even from the process of revealing Light because to whatever degree we put ourselves in the process, even if it is the most perfect process, the most pure of processes, we have already diminished it.

There is the Light of Chochmah, which is called Light. Then there is the Light of Binah, which is, when the Vessel is already involved—the most pure level of involvement. Nonetheless, it is already Water as opposed to Light. It is already a diminished type of Light of the Light of the Creator. Therefore one of the lessons that we receive from this understanding of Water versus Light, is that we should be constantly working, to whatever degrees we can, to diminish our interjection, our involvement, our ego, even in the most perfect, the most pure of processes. There is no way around it. If our ego is involved, to whatever degree, even if we do what we do with the most perfect and pure of desires, we have already diminished it. We have already gone from Chochmah to Binah. We have already involved the Vessel, the desire. And if we have involved the desire, we have diminished the Light.

The only way we can maintain a connection to Chochmah, a revelation of Ohr (Light) and not Mayim (Water), is if we are not involved at all. This is the ultimate level that we want to push ourselves to achieve—to be at the point where we are not involved at all, not for good and not for bad. We want to reach a level where our ego is not involved in the process of revelation. And when we achieve this level of complete removal of the ego, from the process, this is the only time we can reveal Light and not Water. We can reveal a Pure Light and not a diminished form of Light, which is represented by Water.

---

**Explaining the extension of the Endless Light (Ohr Ein Sof)
into the Four Phases in order to reveal the Vessel,
which is the Desire to Receive.**

30. Therefore, there are Ten Sefirot in every Extension of the Endless Light (Ohr Ein Sof), because the Ein Sof, which is the secret of the Root and Emanator is called Keter, and the actual Light that extends is called Chochmah, which is the entire sum of the Extension of Light from Above,

from the Ein Sof. And it is already known that every Extension of Light from Above includes the Desire to Receive, as said, except the form of the Desire to Receive is not actually revealed until the Emanated Being is awakened to wish for and to draw more Light than the measure of its [the Light's] Extension. In such a case, since the Desire to Receive is instantly included in a potential state at the Extending Light, the Light is obligated to turn the potential into actual.

Therefore, the Light awakens to extend additional abundance, more than the amount that extended from the aspect of Ein Sof. Thus the Desire to Receive is actually manifested in that Light and acquires a new small Difference of Form, as said, by becoming dimmer than the Light. The reason is that it is coarser due to this aforementioned newness of form. This coarser part is called Binah and is the meaning behind, "...I am understanding (Binah), I have strength." (Proverbs 8:14) because in reality Binah is part of Chochmah, namely the actual Light of the Extension of Ein Sof, as said, however since [Binah] strengthened Its Desire and drew down more abundance than the amount of the Extension from Ein Sof into it, it acquired a Difference of Form and became a little coarser than the Light and became a Name unto itself: the Sefirah of Binah.

Here, Rav Ashlag adds another wrinkle to our understanding of the formation of a Vessel. We have just learned that there has to be a true and complete desire on this Vessel's part for it to be a true Vessel. Furthermore, as Rav Ashlag makes clear, there has to be a desire to draw more than has been given. This is specifically talking about the Sefirah of Binah—the Second Phase. In the Second Stage, although the Creator gave everything in Chochmah, known as the First Stage, in order for a Vessel to begin emerging there has to be a Vessel that wants to receive something else; something the Creator has not given to the Vessel. This is an important spiritual lesson. The way to know if we are connecting to Light of the Creator is if there is an awakening to something different than what has already been received, than what has already been shared.

In The Wisdom of Truth, Rav Ashlag offers a parable to explain this concept: A wealthy man brings a beggar in from the street and he gives him everything, and after doing so the wealthy man asks the beggar, "Are you completely fulfilled now?" The beggar responds, "No, you have not given me the feeling that I have earned all that I received." The wealthy man answers, "If what you say is true, no person in the world can give you real fulfillment because you will always be lacking the feeling that you have earned what you receive." Nevertheless the Creator can give the feeling of earning to us and it is necessary for us to have it.

Binah says, "I received everything in Chochmah; I received everything the Light of the Creator wants to share but I do not feel I have earned it, let me find a way to start sharing." The consciousness of Binah is where the Vessel, in potential, says, "It is great that I acquired everything from the Light but there is Bread of Shame, so what can I do?" This is not as actualized as it is in Malchut. Therefore the Vessel expresses, "Let me be like the Creator. Let me start sharing."

When the Vessel starts thinking thoughts and doing actions of sharing, this begins a separation. A very important lesson we can draw from this is that to the degree that we represent our ego, to the degree that we are awakening and thinking that we are the ones doing, even thoughts and actions of sharing, we are creating separation from the Light of the Creator.

What we learn from this is that the true culmination of our process is to remove ourselves completely from it because as the Vessel becomes a Vessel it is becoming separate from the Light of the Creator not simply because it has thoughts of selfishness, thoughts of Desire to Receive for the Self Alone but even in the thoughts of Desire to Share, even as the Vessel thinks, "I have received everything in Chochmah—in the First Stage—from the Light of the Creator and now my nature is telling me to share and become a giver as well, which is Binah," this is nonetheless another level of separation because the Vessel is doing. The Vessel is thinking. The Vessel is acting.

Thus, going back to what Rav Ashlag is saying, after Chochmah received everything, all the Light, from the Light of the Creator the Vessel says, "Wait I have a nature, which is the same nature as the Light of the Creator, I have a desire to share." The thought, I would like to find a way to share, makes the Vessel a little more distant than the Light of the Creator. Rav Ashlag says that it becomes darker than the Light of the Creator.

All of this too has a lot of ramifications for our understanding of our ego. When it is important for us that we become recognized, that we have a name, it means that I am now one stage further away from the Light of the

Creator. Of course, we are talking about in the Upper Worlds where all these levels, even the separations between them, that we are learning about, are so minute compared to the unfortunate separations that we make with our ego. However, this is the reality. When my name becomes important, what that means is that there is a separation, one more level of separation. That is what has occurred here. The Second Stage is when Binah says, "I want to do more. I want to share more. I have that innate nature of the Light of the Creator." Now it has become Binah.

> The Essence of the additional abundance it [the Vessel] drew from Ein Sof by means of strengthening its Desire is called the Light of Chasadim or Upper Water, as said. This Light [of Chasadim] is not drawn directly from the Ein Sof like the Light of Chochmah but with the aid of the Emanated that strengthened the Desire, as said. It therefore acquires a Name of its own and is called the Light of Chasadim or Water.

When we discuss the differentiation concerning Keter with Chochmah, Binah, Zeir Anpin and Malchut, none of these are real changes in the Light. They are veils that cover the simple, single Light of the Creator. As we go through life, we make mistakes and we do good things, we go up, and we go down—that we are either connected to different types of Light or we can say of ourselves that our soul becomes more pure or less pure but it is important to know that we can never influence the True Essence. We never, ever—not in the process of Creation, nor in the process of our lives—ever touch or truly make any real change in our soul or in our connection to the Light of the Creator. All we do is add veils or remove veils between us and the Light of the Creator.

Therefore, when we discuss here about what is referred to as the Light of Mercy (the Supernal Waters) being a new type of Light, it is a new aspect of Light that Binah has now awakened but it is not a new Light. It is the Light of the Creator with a different type of veil—the veil of Ohr deChasadim (Light of Mercy). Yet in truth the Light of the Creator always stays the same. It is one simple Light. It is important not to get confused with the fact that there are different types of Light. There is Ohr deChochmah (Light of Wisdom) and there is Ohr deChasadim (Light of Mercy). We relate to them as different types of Light since Binah thinks that It is now awakening a new desire that is a different type of Light, however, in Its Essence it is not different, it is simply a different type of veil.

For instance, we can put a white veil over a light bulb and it will seem like white light is shining from this bulb or we can put a red veil over the light bulb, and the light that shines now will seem like it is red light. Yet the bulb did not change color, there is no white light or red light, it is all the same light, the only difference is in the type of veil used to cover the bulb. This is what is being referred to here. What changed is that Binah, through this awakening of wanting to share has created a different type of veil through which the Light of the Creator is experienced. The new veil and what is felt from that veil is Ohr deChasadim (Light of Mercy), which is called Mayim Elyonim (Supernal Waters).

This is such an important lesson. Is what Binah wants to do a bad thing? Does Binah want to receive for itself alone? Does it want to act with ego? No of course not. What Binah wants is the best thing in the world one could think of—it wants to be a giver. Nevertheless, the lesson is if it is you or me who wants to be a giver, we have already created a separation. We have already become Binah separate from Chochmah. We are already one step further away from the Light of the Creator. If there is a desire to do something, even actions of sharing and it goes back to the ego, to the "I," then this desire creates another level of separation.

Everyone in the world receives from the Light of the Creator. Is there a direct receiving or is it an indirect receiving? The purpose of our lives and of our spiritual work is to become direct receivers of the Light of the Creator. What Binah does here by saying, "I want to be a giver, I want to awaken ways of sharing," is that It receives Light. Ohr deChasadim is Light from the Creator, however, it is an indirect Light. Yet what we want to achieve is to become direct receivers of the Light of the Creator. It is simple. We become a direct receiver of the Light of the Creator when we remove all of our desires—both our Desires to Receive and our Desires to Share.

---

We now find the Sefirah of Binah comprising three kinds of Lights. The first category is the Light of the Essence of Binah, which is part of the Light of Chochmah, as said. The second category is the coarseness and the Difference of Form in it, which it acquired through the strengthening of Desire, as said. The third category is the Light of Chasadim that reaches it through its own drawing from the Ein Sof.

However, this still does not conclude the Vessel of Receiving completely, since Binah comes from the Essence of the Light of Chochmah that is very elevated, which is drawn directly from the Ein Sof. Therefore, what is revealed in Binah is only the Root of the Vessel of Receiving and the aspect of the Activator to the Activation of the Vessel because afterwards this Light of Chasadim that [Binah] drew down with its strength further spread down from it, and an additional illumination came about, less than the Light of Chochmah, and this Extension of the Light of Chasadim is called Zeir Anpin or Chesed, Gevurah, and Tiferet, as will be explained in its place.

Now Binah says, "I want to share, let me draw this new Light that is called the Light of Chasadim (Supernal Waters)." But the Light of Chasadim by itself, meaning, what is awakened by the Vessel, has no standing, it cannot be supported. Therefore, this Light of Chasadim must also include some Light of Chochmah. It also includes some of that Direct Light, some of that Source Light because no matter how great we think we are, no matter how important the Vessel is, nothing can exist without a direct infusion of Light, which is called the Light of Chochmah.

Although the Vessel, Binah, had this great idea of becoming a giver, and it says, "I am going to share, knowing that It has to be a veiled Light called Ohr deChasadim, nonetheless It still knows the truth, which that without Direct Light from the Creator Or deChasadim cannot be sustained. Therefore Binah says to the Creator, "I want to share and I know that I cannot share all by myself, even though I want to, so Creator please make sure to also inject Or deChochmah (Direct Light from the Creator) into this also so that it can be sustained."

Therefore the Third Stage is when the Vessel says, "Okay let me share," but also realizes that It cannot share only Its Or deChasadim, only Its new veiled Light, It also has to have injected in there the Ohr deChochmah—a little bit of the Direct Light, the Direct Essence of Light from the Creator.

Now, the Light of this Extension also strengthened its desire to draw down new abundance, more than the illumination of Chochmah that exists in its Extension from Binah. Therefore, it is considered that this Extension also has two aspects to it: the actual Light of the Extension is called Zeir Anpin or Six Extremities (Lower Six Sefirot) and the aspect of Its strengthening is called Malchut.

Binah can only share its Ohr deChasadim with an injection of the Ohr deChochmah. This new Vessel is called Zeir Anpin. And Zeir Anpin says to Binah "You want to share with Me, so share with Me what you have." What is it that Binah shares with this new Vessel? It shares the Ohr deChasadim with a sliver of Ohr deChochmah—a small taste of the True Essence of connection of the Light of the Creator. Then the Vessel says, "Wow, I really like what You gave Me, Binah, but what I really, really like is that little piece of direct connection that is in this revelation—that little sliver of Ohr deChochmah, the little sliver of complete truth and complete connection to the Light of the Creator. I want that. I want the totality of that."

This is interesting because in this process, Binah has to come to the realization that no matter how important It thought that it was, the Vessel, Zeir Anpin, does not want what Binah has to give. What the Vessel really wants is what it had in Chochmah—the complete revelation of the Light of the Creator.

This has many, many ramifications. When we teach someone, when we share with someone, very often what we are sharing is what we in our own mind understand and every once in a while we inject real truth. Unfortunately for the most part, whatever we think we understand and share with other people, is at best (but probably not) Ohr deChasadim.

Whenever we teach or share, it should be from that place of our own understanding and from what we think they are ready to receive but we have to make sure that we are also always injecting truth. Everyone has processes with their students or with the people they share with and for many people there has to be a logic. There has to be an explanation, an understanding.

This is why I always get excited when I read from Rav Ashlag or I read from the Zohar when I teach because I know this at least is truth. Whatever wisdom we think we are giving, or we think a person is ready to hear, is at best Ohr deChasadim. However, when we inject that sliver of unadulterated real truth from the Zohar or the words of Rav Ashlag, without the adornment of our understanding the student, the Vessel, will say, "I need more of that. All the logic you are giving me is great but I need a connection to the truth."

This is the purpose of true teaching. It is not about giving the understanding or the wisdom that we have, it is about enveloping whatever we think we have, making sure we are always injecting the Essence, the truth. The hope and the reality eventually is that if we are injecting a little sliver of truth, a little sliver of Essence, the person will say, "As much as I love what you are sharing with me, this true connection—this sliver of Ohr deChochmah (Light of Wisdom) is what is most important to me and what I need more of." This is what occurs here with Zeir Anpin.

Binah says, "I want to share." This desire creates a Vessel [Zeir Anpin] that wants to receive what Binah has, which is Ohr deChasadim (Light of Kindness), a veiled Light of the Creator. But Binah cannot give just that because It has no sustainability. Therefore Binah has to give this new Vessel, Zeir Anpin, a sliver of Ohr deChochmah as well.

> This is the secret of the Ten Sefirot: Keter is the secret of Ein Sof, Chochmah is the Light of the Extension from Ein Sof; Binah is the secret of the Light of Chochmah that Strengthened in order to add abundance and thus became coarse, as said; Zeir Anpin—which includes Chesed, Gevurah, Tiferet, Netzach, Hod and Yesod—is the secret of the Light of Chasadim coupled with the illumination of Chochmah Extending forth from Binah, and Malchut is the secret of the second Strengthening to add more illumination of Chochmah than what exists in Zeir Anpin.

There are so many important lessons here. The first is to reawaken and remind ourselves why we study this wisdom. It is not to achieve greater understanding but rather it is to awaken this Light, this Vessel. The gift of the Study of The Ten Luminous Emanations is that as we study the formation of the Vessel, to one degree or another we awaken a Vessel within us, and to the degree we spend the next day and the next week thinking about this, is the degree to which we strengthen and awaken this Vessel in the world and the degree to which it brings us closer to the Final Correction.

The second lesson we learn from this section from Rav Ashlag is the danger of injecting ourselves into the process. Here we are talking about Worlds we cannot even fathom, of changes and thoughts that are completely imperceptible to us, so pure and so perfect. Yet Chochmah had a separation. Binah had a great thought. Zeir Anpin received. And Malchut then had a great thought. All these are separating. As we inject ourselves and our ego into the process, our thought can be the best thought, it can be the best injection, nevertheless, it will have to be a diminishment. It is going to have to be a separation.

The third idea is something that we learn from Binah's sharing to Zeir Anpin and then it is awakening from Malchut. The fact is that when we share, whether we are teaching someone new or we are teaching someone who is not new, we are giving our own wisdom. Whatever we share, whatever we think we are giving over is so veiled and so far away from the Essence that we need to make sure that in our consciousness we are aware to connect the person to the Source. Although it is great that this person loves what we are saying and is feeling and understanding this wisdom we are sharing, we want to make sure that there is a sliver of Truth, whether it is by reading the actual words of the Zohar, the Ari, or Rav Ashlag.

The real hope of Binah is that when the Vessel tastes Ohr deChochmah and the True Essence of the Light of the Creator it will say, "This is what I want. This is what I need. It is Ohr deChochmah. Everything else you have given to me awakened me and gave me some level of understanding but it is not the Essence, the Truth, the direct revelation from the Endless World."

The Light of Binah, which is what most of us receive on many levels is veils upon veils. However, if as we give over wisdom we make sure to think, *"I know that no matter what I give over, it is almost nothing but if I inject, with my consciousness and through my teaching, some slivers of truth, it will awaken them to want to go back to it. However, if I think that I am teaching, that I am giving, then there is no hope because I have severed all ties to Chochmah, I have severed all ties to the True Essence of the Light of the Creator."* If Binah would have given Zeir Anpin only Ohr deChasadim, only of Its own awakening, the Vessel would never have been created and our world would never become perfected.

A student whose teacher gives him only of his own teaching but does not tie him back to the Source, is giving him an end. Binah gives to Zeir Anpin Ohr deChasadim with a sliver of Ohr deChochmah, knowing that once Zeir Anpin tastes that sliver of Ohr deChochmah, It will say, "I need all of the Light of Chochmah back, which is the stage of Malchut, a Real Desire." The Study of Ten Luminous Emanations is important on many levels, yet this essential section concerning the formation of the Vessel is so basic and necessary to our continuous spiritual growth that it is important to not only understand it but really take the time to think these ideas through.

---

**The Four Phases of Desire are the secret of the four letters Yud-Hei-Vav-Hei, which are Keter, Chochmah, Binah, Tiferet (Zeir Anpin), and Malchut.**

31. This is the secret of the four letters of the Tetragrammaton (Yud-Hei-Vav-Hei). The tip of the letter Yud is the secret of Ein Sof, namely, the active Force included in the Thought of Creation "to fulfill His created beings," which is the secret of the Vessel of Keter. Yud is the secret of Chochmah, namely, the First Phase, which is the potential of the Activator, which is immediately included in the Light of the Extension of Ein Sof. The first Hei is the secret of Binah, namely, the Second Phase, which is the actualization (lit. emergence of power) of the Activator, which is the Light that is coarser than Chochmah, as said.

Vav is the secret of Zeir Anpin—Chesed, Gevurah, Tiferet, Netzach, Hod, and Yesod. This is the Extension of the Light of Chasadim extending via Binah, as said, which is the Third Phase, the aspect of the potential to manifest the action, as said. The Lower Hei of Yud-Hei-Vav-Hei is the secret of Malchut, namely, the Fourth Phase, the manifestation of the action with the completion of the Vessel of Receiving that is strengthened to draw more abundance than the amount of its Extension from Binah. This fully established the form of the Desire to Receive, and the Light is clothed in its Vessel, which is the Desire to Receive that is finalized only in this Fourth Phase, not before.

Now you can easily understand that there is no Light in the Upper and Lower Worlds that is not categorized under the order of the four-lettered Name (Yud-Hei-Vav-Hei), which is the secret of the above mentioned Four Phases, without which the Desire to Receive, which is required to be present in any Light, cannot be established. For this Desire is the Place and measurement of that Light, as said.

Rav Ashlag says here that the Yud-Hei-Vav-Hei represents everything. Everything! There is nothing in our world that is not affected by nor completed by It. Even the most physical of objects, like a microphone or the most spiritual of Lights has to go through the process of the Yud-Hei-Vav-Hei.

Hopefully, what this knowledge does is give us an appreciation for the Yud-Hei-Vav-Hei. There is a story about a great kabbalist who was able to be a conduit for tremendous miracles. One of his students had a great desire to discover his secret—the tools his master uses as well as how he was able to create so many miracles. After putting the student through a long process, this great kabbalist finally agreed to reveal his secret to him. The great master lived in a house where he had small room in the back. He took his student to the back room and showed him a beautiful box made out of gold and wood. The teacher opened the box with great care and love and within the box, on parchment was written the letters Yud-Hei-Vav-Hei—the Tetragrammaton. The teacher told his student, this is my secret. It is through the Yud-Hei-Vav-Hei, that all miracles are possible.

The student asked what the big secret was of the Yud-Hei-Vav-Hei. Every single one of us has it in the Siddur (Prayer Book). We all know what the Tetragrammaton is. "The secret," the great master answered, "is the depth of our connection to the Yud-Hei-Vav-Hei." Hopefully, we can strive to truly understand what Rav Ashlag is saying here: that **the totality of existence is the Yud-Hei-Vav-Hei**. The ultimate manifestation of our world, the ultimate removal of pain and suffering, the ultimate removal of death is in the Yud-Hei-Vav-Hei. My hope is that this teaching renews our appreciation for the Yud-Hei-Vav-Hei.

Rav Isaac Luria (the Ari) wrote a song for each of the three meals of Shabbat to connect to the Inner Light of that meal. In one of the verses it says *yegale lan ta'amei devitreisar nahamei* "May He reveal to us the reason of the twelve loaves of bread." And in one of the letters to the Rav, Rav Brandwein, mentions a learned rabbi that sat at Rav Brandwein's table one Shabbat. Rav Brandwein wrote that on this particular Shabbat the rabbi called out to the Creator, "Creator, please reveal to me why it is that we have twelve loaves on Shabbat?"

Rav Brandwein continued writing that this rabbi must not have been a kabbalist because in the Writings of the Ari it is very clear why we use twelve loaves, and explained to the Rav the meaning of the words *yegale lan ta'amei…* "May He reveal to us the *ta'am….*" Rav Brandwein wrote that the

Hebrew word ta'am can be translated as both "reason" and "taste," and that what we are asking for is not to understand the reason why we have twelve loaves because we already know the reason—we can find it in the Gate of Meditations of the Writings of the Ari. Rather, what we are asking for on Shabbat, and this is something we should be asking for all the time, is not to understand but to taste deeper and deeper. Therefore, when we say *yegale lan ta'amei devitreisar nahamei*, we are asking the Creator, "whatever my current connection is, whatever taste I have of the Light of the twelve loaves, make it deeper for me." It is the same request concerning the Yud-Hei-Vav-Hei. With the understanding from Rav Ashlag that the Yud-Hei-Vav-Hei is everything—that the totality within the Yud-Hei-Vav-Hei is the power of the removal of pain, suffering, and death—we have to beg the Creator *yegalei lan ta'amei* "Reveal to us the taste, the Light, the connection to the Yud-Hei-Vav-Hei, the Tetragrammaton."

When we study what Rav Ashlag reveals to us—that the Tetragrammaton is the totality of everything and how the Four Phases are represented in the Yud-Hei-Vav-Hei—hopefully, this knowledge awakens within us the desire for the Creator to reveal to us, not the understanding but an endless sense of taste, as Rav Brandwein tells the Rav in the letter, so that we taste it deeper and deeper and deeper

In the Introduction to the Study of the Ten Luminous Emanations, Rav Ashlag also explains that the ultimate purpose of all our spiritual work is to "Taste and see that the Creator is good…." (Psalms 34:9) We are meant to come to the point where our spiritual work is filled with a physical, sensory taste of the Light of the Creator. This is the purpose of our spiritual work.

Lastly, concerning this revelation from Rav Ashlag regarding the Tetragrammaton, I would like to share that whenever there is the Name Yud-Hei-Vav-Hei in the daily prayers we pronounce this Name as Alef-Dalet-Nun-Yud (Adonai). We never say the Name Yud-Hei-Vav-Hei. The reason is as Rav Ashlag teaches that whatever we cannot comprehend, whatever we cannot get our minds around, we cannot say its name." We do not say—Yud-Hei-Vav-Hei—the Name of the Creator because we are limited in our connection and understanding of the Creator, and instead speak of the Light that flows from the Creator.

As Rav Ashlag explains the Yud-Hei-Vav-Hei is everything. It is the Final Correction. It is the removal of death. We do not pronounce the Name Yud-Hei-Vav-Hei because we do not comprehend it and whatever we do not know, we cannot say. This is the reason why in the prayers we pronounce the Tetragrammaton Name as Alef-Dalet-Nun-Yud, even though it written Yud-Hei-Vav-Hei. Ultimately, God willing, at the Final Correction, when Immortality comes, we will be saying the Name Yud-Hei-Vav-Hei because at that point we will have a true connection to the Yud-Hei-Vav-Hei. This will be the point at which the Final Correction occurs.

---

**The letters Yud and Vav of the Yud-Hei-Vav-Hei are slender because they are solely potential.**

32. One can ask: if the Yud alludes to Chochmah and Hei to Binah, and the entire Essence of the Light in the Ten Sefirot is present in the Sefirah of Chochmah, while Binah, Zeir Anpin, and Malchut are only clothing in relationship to Chochmah, in this case should Chochmah not have obtained the largest letter in the four-lettered Name (Tetragrammaton)? The answer is that the letters of the four-lettered Name do not indicate or allude to the measurement and amount of Light in the Ten Sefirot. Rather they indicate the value of the Vessel's activity, since the white of the parchment of the Torah Scroll alludes to the Light aspect, while the black—the letters in the Torah Scroll—alludes to the quality of the Vessels.

Therefore, because Keter is merely a root for the Vessel's root, it is alluded to only in the tip of Yud. Chochmah is the potential before the manifestation (Activator) is revealed, and therefore it is alluded to in the smallest letter of the alphabet, namely Yud. Binah, in which the potential extended out and became manifested, is alluded to in a wide letter, Hei. Since Zeir Anpin is just the potential to manifest activation, as said, it is alluded to by a slim, long letter, Vav. Slimness is an indication that the essence of the Vessel is hidden within it and unseen. The length of the Line is an indication that at the end of its Extension a complete and finished Vessel manifests through it. However when Chochmah extended, it was not sufficient to manifest a complete Vessel, and Binah is not truly a Vessel but merely the Activator aspect of the Vessel, as said, which is why the leg of the Yud is short: to indicate it is still short, as it did not manifest a complete Vessel by the hidden power in it and by its extension.

---

Now we understand the reason the letter Yud, which is the smallest of the letters, represents Chochmah because physicality limits. And this is not just about the letter but about all physicality. One of Rav's favorite sections of the Zohar (Chayei Sarah 21) "He that is small in this world is great in the Supernal World" is the same idea. The more physicality there is, the less there is of Light. The less there is a connection to the Creator. The Yud is the least physical of all the four letters of the Tetragrammaton, therefore, it represents the greatest Light.

> Like the Sefirah of Binah, Malchut is also alluded to by the letter Hei. This is a large letter, manifested in a whole form. And Binah and Malchut having the same letter should not raise questions, the reason being that in the World of Tikkun (Correction) they are truly similar and lend their Vessels to each other, according to the meaning of the verse, "And the two of them went on…" (Ruth 1:19), as will be explained in its place.

There is a beautiful article in the Prologue to the Zohar titled: "The Mother Lends Its Daughter Its Vessel." In the time of the Correction, the Vessels of Malchut and Binah become unified. Both of their Vessels are represented by the letter Hei. Rav Ashlag explains here how the Yud-Hei-Vav-Hei is a manifestation of the Vessel.

As we mentioned before—and it is important to keep reminding ourselves—that what Rav Ashlag teaches us here is not only about the Yud-Hei-Vav-Hei, it is also about our connection to the Light of the Creator. The more there is of us in any action, the less Light there is. The less physicality there is the more Light. Like the Yud has little physicality and the Vav has little physicality, therefore there is more Light. The more the Vessel, the more we are involved in the revelation. The more we are involved in the process, the less Light that can be revealed.

Hopefully what is ingrained in our mind is the understanding that we have to diminish our ego to whatever degree we can, knowing that to whatever degree our ego is involved in whatever it is that we do, to that degree the Light of the Creator will be missing from there. To the degree that we diminish our ego in whatever it is that we do, to that degree the Light of the Creator will truly be there.

# CHAPTER 9

**Spiritual movement means the newness of a Difference in Form.**

33. We still need to expound upon time and movement, which we come across in almost every word in this wisdom. Know that spiritual movement is not as physical movement from one place to another. Rather, it refers to the Newness of Form. We call every Newness of Form "movement," since that newness—namely the Difference of Form occurring in a spiritual being differs from the preceding general form in it—is considered as if it was divided and separated from that spiritual being, and it became its own name and domain. In that sense it is completely similar to a part of a physical entity that broke off and moves and goes from place to place. This is why Newness of Form is called movement.

Rav Ashlag tells us that words referring to spiritual movement do not represent motion from one point to the other but rather these terms are talking about the formation of a new reality. In the spiritual realm, when a reality becomes different, when a form becomes different it is denoted as movement. Therefore, when studying the Wisdom of Kabbalah, know that all the words that connote movement are referring to change from one frame, one reality, one essence to a new essence.

If we take a drop of water out of a cup and we put it somewhere else, we may think of this as movement; that is, moving a drop of water from here to there. This means that the drop of water has left one form—being in totality with this grouping of water—and it now becomes part of another grouping of water. Even in the physical realm movement refers to the notion of one form disassociating from a previous form and becoming part of a new form.

Therefore, even with regard to the physical world there is an understanding that movement does not simply mean going from one place to the other. Rather what it really means is the idea that material has left a current existence and has gone into another form. For example, a person sitting on a chair changes physicality (moves) to stand over there in the corner. In this way we can understand that in the spiritual realm too, movement is not simply changing location from one place to another, instead there is an element of difference, a differentiation of essences, a new reality existing.

The same is true, and even more so, when we talk about spiritual movement. In the Spiritual Realm matter and space do not exist, so movement cannot be about going from one point to another. Instead, movement refers to a formation of a new essence. When something new happens to a spiritual reality, it is considered a new form; it is considered as if it now separated itself from what was previous, and now becomes new.

This is true about both the individual and the Worlds. For instance, when we say that the Light goes from the World of Atzilut to the World of Briyah or from the World of Chochmah to the World of Binah, of course this does not mean that the Light is moving because Light does not move. What is being discussed is that the Light attains a new essence—a new form—and this new form is referred to, in the words of the kabbalists, as movement.

What this means is that in any matter of a spiritual nature in the Zohar and in the Torah, movement is never about movement from one location to another. Throughout the Zohar the friends travel from one point to another. They go from this city to that city. Rav Ashlag explains that when the Zohar tells us that they are going from one point to the other, it is really discussing elevating from one spiritual level to another spiritual level. So when the Zohar says that one of the friends travelled from the city of Kaputkia to the city of Lod, for instance, there was no physical movement. They did not walk physically from one city to the other, but rather there was a change of essence in them. One city represents a certain type of consciousness, a certain connection and a second city represents a second type of consciousness.

When we understand these rules within the realm of the Study of the Ten Luminous Emanations, it may be easier to see the correlation specifically with regard to the study of the Ari as he discusses the formation of the Physical World and the way the Spiritual Worlds operate.

In studying both the Zohar and the Torah, we have to understand these same rules apply. Rav Shimon stood up, Rav Shimon sat down, Rav Shimon went from one place to the other. All of the words describing movement used in the Zohar are not referring to actions of this physical world. Instead, any reference to movement, as Rav Ashlag says, is discussing going from one level of consciousness to another level of consciousness.

Therefore, the clarity we should have is this: When we read in the Zohar that they traveled from one place to another place, we should not envision them travelling, as we travel today, from one place to another place in the physical realm. Rather we should know that they are going from one level of consciousness to another. That said, if we were looking at them, we would see them sitting in the same room because the Zohar is talking about them going from one level of consciousness to another level, not from one place to another. The same is true, in the Torah. This understanding can open up the gateway to having a better and truer understanding of the Torah.

In the Torah it is written that people travelled from one place to another. Even about Abraham, Isaac, and Jacob it says that they travelled from one place to the other place. Whether their journey physically occurred or not is secondary in importance. The reason the Torah is relating this travelling to us is not to teach us that these people physically travelled from one place to the other, but rather that each one of these places represents a level of consciousness, a level of connection, and that as a result of their spiritual work, they elevated from one level to another, or descended from one level to another.

In saying that the Israelites went to Egypt, the Torah is not referring to travelling from a physical place called the land of Canaan into the physical place known as the land of Egypt. The Bible is discussing spiritual levels. Egypt represents a lower level, a level that is in exile and is concealed. Even in the Torah there is no movement. The perception is that there is movement because unfortunately we have come to understand the Torah in a very physical context. Nevertheless, the essence of the Torah is not that and the movement being discussed is spiritual movement.

It is important we realize that these laws Rav Ashlag reveals to us concerning words and language refer to all true spiritual sources of wisdom, which is the Zohar and the Torah. This is the way we need to open up our eyes to start understanding them.

The second important point about movement in the spiritual realm is where Rav Ashlag discusses the concept that movement represents a formation of a new essence. Any time a change occurs upon an essence and it becomes a new essence, this is referred to as movement from point A to point B. This teaching opens us up to an understanding about how to view our spiritual growth. When we talk about our growth, our own change, we have to realize that we are, literally leaving one form behind and becoming a new form. This is exemplified in the story of the golden calf.

The Negative Side wants us to look back at our past and become sad about our present. The Israelites, led by the erev rav, spiritually fell with the creation of golden calf. When Moses came down from Mount Sinai, the Bible says, "And the people heard this evil thing and they mourned, and none of them put on his adornment." (Exodus 33:4) The Israelites became saddened about building the golden calf, "And the children of Israel divested themselves of their adornment at Mount Chorev." (Exodus 33:6) The Israelites lost that extra Light, the Light that is connected to Immortality, the removal of pain and suffering.

The Chozeh of Lublin (Rabbi Yaacov Yitzchak haLevi Horowitz) says that the order of events in the Torah is not coincidental. There was the golden calf incident, there was the sadness that resulted from the golden calf, and then there was the loss of the Light from Mount Sinai. What the Chozeh explains is that, if not for the sadness that the Israelites felt after the golden calf, they would not have lost the totality of Light that they received at Mount Sinai. Very often what the negative side wants us to believe is that whatever negativity we did yesterday, or a week before, or a month before, should make us feel down today.

The Chozeh of Lublin teaches something amazing: the Negative Side does not want us to sin. It is not as interested in the fall—the action that is not right—as much as he is interested in the sadness that he can inject into us after that fall. It is through this sadness, he can bring us lower. This is an important lesson.

When we realize that spiritual movement is not motion from point A to point B and that it is instead a creation of a whole new form, then we understand that when we change, even if it is a small change, and as long as it is a true change, we become a completely new person. The old person that performed a negative action, or even that negative reality we experienced, does not exist anymore because we are a completely new person. Every morning especially, and certainly throughout the day, when we are growing and we are changing, we can become a completely new person. Therefore, we cannot be brought down or made sad because of what we have done before because now we are a different person. Satan cannot bring us down by saying "Remember what you did yesterday or a week ago or a month ago…" because we are not that person anymore.

This is the Spiritual Realm, as Rav Ashlag describes it here. When we become even slightly different, slightly new, we are completely disassociated in our consciousness from whatever we were before. This means that any negativity that we have created from any negative action performed a day ago, a month ago can no longer bring us down because we are not that person anymore. We are a new essence. We have moved from that point, from that person. We are now a new essence. Even a small change makes us into a new person.

Hopefully this excites us, and motivates us from being brought down by the thoughts that try to tell us, *"Maybe you have changed but do not forget what you have done."* These thoughts are not coming from the Positive Side. When we change, and become a new essence, we leave behind the things we have done.

This leads us to two related lessons: One is from a section in the Talmud that discusses the following: If a marriage is based on a false statement the marriage is null and void. For example, if the groom says, "I am marrying you on the condition that I was born in Los Angeles," and he was not born in Los Angeles, this false statement makes the marriage null and void. Concerning this the Talmud says something very interesting. If a person says to their betrothed, "I am marrying you on the condition that I am a righteous person," it is a good marriage. Yet how can this be if there are a given amount of righteous people in the world? How can anyone getting married say, "I am marrying you now and I am a righteous person."? The Talmud explains that this is not referring to someone who is lying but to someone who actually believes they are a righteous person. This marriage is not void because a person can change—a person can go from being wicked, to being righteous—in one second.

Rabbi Yehuda Hanasi affirms this in the times in the Talmud when he would see a person make a life changing action, and would say "A person can acquire his entire level of consciousness, the entire world in one second." Why? Because through this teaching we now understand that when we change form, change essence, we become a completely new person. Therefore, if we really believe that we are now a righteous person, in this moment we become a righteous person because we are now changed. It can be since in the manner of spiritual essences, movement is when a form changes and is no longer a form with a difference but instead becomes completely different form. It has left the old form behind.

It is not like making a house out of Play-Doh and then squashing the same Play-Doh and making it into a ball—the same Play-Doh that was a house, is now a ball. We are not like Play-Doh. Spiritual essences are not like that. In the Spiritual Realm, if a person is negative yesterday and today is a righteous person—meaning today they are doing the right thing and changing in a positive way—then this person is a completely new form; not the old form with changes. The person is an entirely new form.

This is important to understanding on many levels as we study from the teachings of the Ari, from the teachings of Kabbalah, but also about comprehending our own spiritual process. When we change, we are not that old form with a difference, we are a completely new form. Hopefully knowing this can give us a real appreciation of how connected we can be, even in an instant. When we truly change our essence, even if it is in one second, we are a new person that can be a completely righteous person. On the most basic level, we are no longer brought down by negative actions of the past because we know that right now we are a new form, a new person. We have left that old person behind. We are not a better person we are a totally different reality. This is the meaning of what Rav Ashlag explained concerning the concept of movement in the Spiritual Realm.

---

**Spiritual time means a certain number of novel Differences of Form caused by each other. Before and after means cause and effect.**

34. As for the spiritual definition of time, understand that for us the main concept of time is nothing but sensing movements. The imagining mind in man describes and puts together a certain number of movements that it perceives one after the other and translates it into a certain amount of "time." So if a man is in a state of complete rest with his environment, he would have no concept whatsoever of time. Similarly with spiritual beings, a certain sum of new forms that are considered spiritual movements, as said, enmeshed with each other by way of cause and effect, are named "time" in spirituality. As for the issue of "before and after," it always means the same as cause and effect.

---

One of the many beautiful things about Rav Ashlag, beyond being a tremendous soul, Kabbalist and revealer of this wisdom to our world, is the way Rav Ashlag's mind worked. Rav Ashlag understood not only the Spiritual

Realm but also the Physical Realm. For example, how do we perceive time? We look at a watch and see that five minutes have passed, however in reality, time is not a human sense. As Rav Ashlag says, if we are in a room in complete silence, hearing no noise from the outside, no movement from the outside, and we just sit in that room, we could not tell time because time is perceived by us as things occurring one after another. We are eating dinner: we have the appetizer, the main course, dessert. It probably feels like an hour has passed. We perceive time through physical actions occurring one after the other.

Our mind works in a way that we experience one thing and then another thing, and then another. In this way our mind tells us that time has passed. Time is a construct of our mind. In reality, as the Rav always discussed, there is no such thing as time in a true sense, just as there is no space and no movement.

Rav Ashlag writes about that which is true in the Spiritual Realm as well as the way we perceive things in the Physical Realm. For instance, in the Physical Realm we perceive movement but in the Spiritual Realm there is no movement. In the Spiritual Realm there is no time, yet in the Physical Realm we perceive time. The Spiritual Realm represents the true reality, therefore time is not a true reality, rather it is a construct of the Physical Realm. Our mind creates illusions and thus perceives. Nonetheless, even in the Physical Realm, time is not an essence that really exists, rather it is something we perceive with our mind. Our mind makes up stories and these stories include time.

In the Study of the Ten Luminous Emanations, when we discuss the words that connote time, meaning something happened first, i.e. first there was Tzimtzum (the Constriction of the Creator's Light), and then there was the Line (Kav), our mind seems to think, "At 5:01 am, there was the Tzimtzum and 5:02 pm, there must have been the Kav, and so on." Our mind immediately interprets these as stories or movements of cause and effect to connote time. However, because there is no such thing as time in the truest sense, certainly not in the Spiritual Realm and even not really in the Physical Realm, this is not truth.

Rav Ashlag says that when we discuss this happening and then that happening in the Spiritual Realm, we have to be very careful not to imagine that time is an element of any of this because in the Spiritual Realm there is no such thing as time. Time is an illusionary construct of our Physical Realm. This is also a concept that the Rav spoke about in depth. When we understand that time is an illusion, in the truest essence this means that there is no such thing as time.

Kabbalists were able to travel in both time and space because they had achieved a connection to the Realm that is above the illusion of time and space. When one lives in the Realm that is beyond the illusion of time and space, then one is no longer bound by what has become the physical laws of time and space. Being in one place and another, travelling through time does not restrict a true kabbalist who has achieved a connection to the True Realm. When we understand the true essence of our world, which is the Spiritual Realm, there is no time and space. Therefore, a person who elevates his connection to the truest of worlds, to the spiritual realm, is no longer bound by the realm of time and space.

This is why Rav Ashlag would tell his students who would complain about being far apart from him when he travelled: "If you were really connected to me, you would not feel the distance in space when I am in London and you are in Israel. The reason you feel distance is because you are still within the realm of time and space." We are meant to elevate to a state above time and space and, therefore space and time can no longer influence us.

When we think about this deeper, we realize that almost all of our problems, our fears, our doubts come from the realm of time and space. We are worried that something will or will not happen tomorrow. Almost all, if not all, our concerns are connected to time and space, with the exception of the true concerns like whether or not we are growing spiritually, changing, and becoming a new form. All other worries or thoughts that bring us to unhappiness are related to time and space. Why time and space? Because this is where the Negative Side exists. In the Realm above time and space, the Negative Side does not exist. There is no negativity. There is only Light, which is the true essence of our world.

Pain and suffering can only exist within the Realm of time and space, within the world of physicality, within the world where the Negative Side, darkness, has an existence. In the True World, in the Endless World, the World where time and space, as we understand it in the Physical Realm, do not exist there cannot be pain and suffering, there cannot be worry, there cannot be doubt because, when we think this through—think about the thoughts of doubt and of worry that come, we realize that they all relate to time and space. They are all related to these physical constructs, which are an illusion.

There is a great deal we have learned from this. Firstly, on the most basic level, which is not so basic, Rav Ashlag explains that we should never understand the words of the Ari, the words of the Zohar, or the words of the Torah—words referring to space, or words referring to time—to be a discussion of physical space. Rather when we talk about motion, the words used are about becoming a new form. When we talk about time, we are referring to cause and effect.

# CHAPTER 10

---

**All matter attributed to the Emanated is the Desire to Receive;
anything additional is attributed to the Emanator.**

35. Know that the Desire to Receive aspect in the Emanated, which was
well explained, is the Vessel in it. Know that it is also the entire matter
attributed to the Emanated in such a way that any existence beside it is
attributed to the Emanator.

---

Every person has two parts: the part that is theirs and the part that is not
theirs. There is the part that is the Creation, the Desire to Receive, and there
is everything else, which is the Creator. This very important concept that
Rav Ashlag speaks about in a few places, including in the beginning of the
Introduction of the Ten Luminous Emanations differentiates Kabbalah from
other spiritual paths. What makes us a person, what makes us a creation, is
our Desire to Receive, and whatever is us that is not of the Desire to Receive is
not really us, it is that part of us that is of the Creator. When we comprehend
this then we can understand the importance of actually growing the Desire
to Receive.

Sometimes as people become involved in spirituality, there is a diminishment
of their desire when in reality, true spirituality, having a true connection
to the Light of the Creator needs to awaken a greater and greater desire.
This is something the Rav spoke about often. We can tell if we are growing
and connecting more, if our desire is getting stronger and stronger. If a
person's desire is diminishing, that person diminishes their Vessel, thereby
diminishing how much Light they can receive. When we truly understand this
we can appreciate how important it is to be developing, certainly in the right
way, and growing our Desire to Receive because this Desire to Receive is the
totality of the spiritual material from which we are made.

> **The Desire to Receive is the primordial form of every entity, and we define the primordial form as matter since we have no conception of the entity.**
>
> 36. Even though the Desire to Receive aspect is apparently understood as an occurrence and form in the entity, how can it be grasped as the matter of the entity? This can be so also in entities close to us for it is our way to describe the first form of the entity as the primordial matter of the entity, since we have no concept or grasp whatsoever of any matter because our five senses are not equipped for that. Sight, hearing, smell, taste, and touch offer the conceptual mind merely imaginative forms of whatever happens to the entity, and that take shape in cooperation with our senses.

Every once in a while, Rav Ashlag indicates to us in his writings how vast is his knowledge, not only in the secrets that were revealed to him in Kabbalah but also in the sciences and in philosophy.

Here Rav Ashlag asks a very philosophical question: How can we say that the Desire to Receive is the original matter of humanity? Rav Ashlag states that the Desire to Receive is the essence of humanity, it is the essence of each individual and that this Desire to Receive seems to be an action or a cause that activates something to occur. Right? Meaning "I desire to receive." He uses the example of a gold coin with something stamped on it, like a face on the back and the front. The coin is a manifestation that occurred to the gold. The coin is not the most basic matter, the basic matter of the coin is the gold. The gold was melted and made into the shape of a coin with faces on the front and the back.

We can call it a coin, and we can say that there is a face on the gold, but in reality it is the gold that is the initial matter of the coin, not the coin itself. If we go deeper into the molecules and the atoms that make up the coin, we can at least try to find out what is the original matter of this coin. Rav Ashlag then asks would it not be true to say that although the Desire to Receive is the totality of matter that is humanity and every single one of us this matter, does it not also seem to be a second step, meaning an action upon some other matter; that we have taken this energy and have made it into a Desire to Receive?

If this is true that there was some original matter upon which a Desire to Receive was clothed, then we would have to say that the Desire to Receive is not the first matter, it is not the true essence of humanity or of Creation, but rather is almost a secondary matter, that the essence of humanity, whatever that is, is clothed with the Desire to Receive. Therefore Rav Ashlag asks, "Why do we say that the Desire to Receive is the original matter, the essence of humanity, when it would make more sense that there is some original matter upon which this change of Desire to Receive was made?"

And the answer is that even in the physical world we are incapable of ascertaining, of coming to truly understand original matter. As Rav Ashlag says here, **"...for it is our way to describe the first form of the entity as the primordial matter of the entity."**

A table is called "table" right, although technically first it is wood. Actually, it is a tree. And we can go further back, what is a tree? First it is a seed. We can go further back and further back into all physical matter but the reality of our world is that we call things by the form that they take. So if we call something a "tree" it is because that matter has taken upon itself the form of a tree. Therefore, even in our physical world, we do not really connect to, or speak of, or give names based on original stages or original matter, rather we speak of the form that it takes. In revisiting the example of the gold coin, most of us, if we try to trace things back, we would say gold is the first matter of the coin when, in reality even that is not true. In the physical world we name and associate with the first form that matter takes.

Rav Ashlag says something beautiful, **"...since we have no conception or grasp whatsoever of any matter...."** We think that we come to learn the Study of the Ten Luminous Emanations because we want to understand the spiritual world, yet the reality is, as Rav Ashlag says, we do not even comprehend the physical world. We have a tremendous lack of understanding and depth concerning the physical world, therefore we are not capable yet, for many reasons, to really comprehend and understand the original matter of even the physical objects, which is why we connect it to its first form.

If this energy took its first form in a gold coin, we call it a gold coin. If this energy took its first form in a flower, we call it a flower. The reality, of course, is that it is not a flower, it is not a gold coin. It is a form and probably not the first form that this physical matter has taken.

And with this Rav Ashlag gives us a lesson about the five senses and our physical world. The Rav often used this teaching as a place to start the spiritual work. Some people begin their journey of spiritual matters by understanding how limited their understanding is of the physical matters. What the Rav would do is open our eyes to how limited we are in our understanding of the physical world so that we could begin to grasp that if we are that blind about things that we thought we knew maybe we are also blind about things that we do not think that we know. This is really what Rav Ashlag is talking about here.

This awareness of our blindness is one of the most important spiritual lessons a person can learn. We need to know that we are always blind because when a person thinks they see, thinks they understand, basically, their spiritual growth is over. No matter our level, there will always come a time in our spiritual lives when we are blind.

If we are not constantly aware of the fact that we are always, every moment of our lives, blind to something then when the wake-up call comes, or when a friend shows us where we are blind we are not going to be open to it. Even if we know and we have studied about it, there are going to be times when we are going to be blind to what is around us. The unfortunate reality is that when those real times occur, we are going to be blind to the blindness and being blind to the blindness makes it so that we are completely closed to being awakened.

The most important thing is to constantly know that we are blind, to accept that there is not a moment in our lives when we are not blind. Sometimes we have the merit that someone shows us where we are blind but if right now, today, no one shows us where we are blind, we cannot take this to mean that we are not blind. The consciousness that needs to be developed is that we are constantly blind. We are constantly not understanding the situation. We are constantly not understanding what is around us, and what is occurring to us. And only if we are constantly in that awareness can we have the merit for someone to open up our eyes and show us where we are blind. If we do not have this awareness of constant blindness, then we will never have the merit and the opportunity of others showing us where we are blind.

The five senses do not give us a true reading of what is in front of us. They give us the current form that the matter has taken. Therefore, when we look at the reality, even the physical reality that is around us, our five senses give us a very limited sense of what is true. This is such a key understanding because physicality is something upon which we base so much of our awareness and consciousness. When we truly open up our awareness and consciousness to how limited our five senses are, to what we think we already know, to what we think that we already see, then and only then can we truly open ourselves up to levels beyond in the spiritual Worlds that we do not see and do not connect to.

When we look around a room, we see walls, we see tables, we see chairs, so we think, subconsciously at least, our mind, our ego tells us we see everything around us. Even in the physical sense. Therefore Rav Ashlag is saying that if we do not see the essence of what is around us then we are not seeing reality.

Once we understand that what we are seeing is a tremendously limited aspect of what truly is occurring around, and when we know (even those who have a little more understanding even in the most physical senses of the sciences) how little we comprehend and see and feel about what is around us on the purely physical level, it should open up our eyes, consciousness, and awareness to the fact that there is so much about us and the spiritual realms that we do not understand, think, or see.

For example, take even the smallest, microscopic atoms in the primordial elements of any entity, which can be separated through the science of chemistry, these too are merely imaginative forms that take shape before our eyes or, to be more specific, they are distinguishable and recognizable through the ways of the Desire to Receive and be Received that we find in them, such that according to these actions, these atoms can be distinguished and separated according to types, all the way to the primordial matter of that entity. Even then, they are merely the forces in that entity and not matter. We thus find that even in physicality we have no other course to understand primordial matter but the hypothesis that the first form is the primordial matter that carries the rest of the occurrences and forms it will assume later. And needless to say [this is true] in the Supernal Worlds, where perception and imagination does not apply.

Those who have had the merit (or will have the merit) to study from the Rav's Ten Luminous Emanations know this is a concept that the Rav spoke about again, and again. Within physics and in theoretical physics there is the idea that even on the atomic level there is a great deal of uncertainty in the understanding of the most basic of physical structures.

Rav Ashlag tells us that this is because of the nature of humankind. As long as we are within this Physical Realm, as long as we are within the Realm of the Desire to Receive for the Self Alone we are incapable of experiencing the true source of anything—even physical matter. We are incapable of experiencing the true source of ourselves, the true essence of ourselves, and the true essence of our world.

Therefore Rav Ashlag says that even as we delve into the atomic level—into physics—studying these aspects, we will realize that we can never come to the first point. This is why when there is exploration and theorizing about the Big-Bang and the creation of our world there has never been an understanding that goes back to almost the beginning. There has never been the totality of the picture—what science calls the grand unified theory. Rav Ashlag tells us here that this will not happen until humanity achieves a critical mass that begins to truly connect to the essence of who we are and what this world is. It is impossible to ascertain and identify the true essence of anything—physical reality, humanity, every single person—while still living in this physical world, living within a consciousness of the Realm of the Desire to Receive for the Self Alone. Regardless of when each one of us individually will get to the point when we can truly delve and grasp the true essence of things, we should know that until this point of critical mass, we will never see the whole picture, the true essence.

Rav Ashlag explains that no matter how deeply we delve into, even the sciences we can never come to the essence. We can dissect further and further and find other aspects and parts but the true essence, we cannot yet achieve. Therefore, even in the physical world we have no way to understand the initial matter.

Assuming that the first form that we see, in this case, the form is the Desire to Receive for Oneself Alone, we make the assumption that the first form that we see is the essence, but in reality it is probably not the essence but the first form. It is the first level that we can connect to.

Concerning the matters of the Spiritual World that we are able to connect to our understanding of humanity, the first matter of humanity, the first form of humanity, is the Desire to Receive. However the truth of the depths and the true connection to the essence of humanity, and therefore the true connection to the initial form that was at the Source of the creation of our world is something that we cannot yet understand. Therefore, although we talk about the Desire to Receive as being the first form of Creation, the first form of humanity, Rav Ashlag gives us the warning: "Do not think that you understand it completely because you cannot understand it completely."

There is a beautiful quote from the Ramchal (Rabbi Moshe Chaim Luzzato, the great Italian Kabbalist) who says: "After one has studied all of the secrets, he comes to understand that he does not know." The Rachmal was asked, "If at the end of all the study one comes to the understanding that he does not know, then what is the purpose of the study?" The Rachmal replied "Although both in the beginning of the study and after all the study, one does not know, the not knowing at the end of the study is full of Light. And then it is all worth it."

This understanding of our innate blindness is the most important spiritual lesson. As long as we are still not perfected and completely transformed of our Desire to Receive, we constantly have a blind spot. When driving in a car there is always a blind spot, we always have to turn and look over our shoulder. When we understand that in our spiritual lives there is constantly a blind spot, we act differently, we are more careful. We are more open because we know that we are blind.

There is a story in the Talmud (Berachot 28b) about Rabbi Yochanan ben Zakai, one of the greatest souls to ever come down into our world. As he was about to leave this world he said: "I know that after I leave this world there will be two paths for me, one that leads to Light and one that leads to darkness, and I don't know which path they are going tell me to go on."

Think about it, how can one of the greatest souls that ever came down to our world—living his life in a way that most of us could not even hope to aspire to live—make such a statement? He knew and understood that he had to be of the constant awareness that he was always blind. And although we, looking externally know that this was not true, for him it had to be true. He had to be in the constant awareness that it could be that the totality of the way he saw things right now was completely wrong. And because he lived his life this way, he became who he became.

For us the lesson is that we have to constantly be living with the awareness that we are blind. We need to say to ourselves: "There is no question that right now there is a big part of my life to which I am blind and I hope and I beg that I have the merit that someone will be kind enough to show me."

If we constantly ask and if we are constantly of this consciousness that we are blind then we will merit for people to show us. If we go a day or a week, or a month, or any length of time without being aware of our blindness right now then we can lose the merit that people will show us our blindness. This is a key and important understanding. Rav Ashlag teaches us how this is true both in the Physical World and certainly in the Spiritual World. This important teaching is something that we have to take with us every day of our lives in our spiritual work.

# TABLES OF
# QUESTIONS AND ANSWERS

# TERMINOLOGY QUESTIONS

1. What is Light?
2. What are Light and Vessel?
3. What is Circular Light?
4. What is Simple Light?
5. What is the Light of Chochmah?
6. What is the Light of Chasadim?
7. What is Empty Air?
8. What is After?
9. What is Middle?
10. What is One?
11. What does "Creates" mean?
12. What is Cleaving?
13. What is Equality?
14. What is Extension?
15. What is Pure?
16. What is Time?
17. What is Darkness?
18. What is Chochmah?
19. What is Space?
20. What are Before and After?
21. What are Singular and Unified?
22. What is Yichud (Unification)?
23. What are Right and Left?
24. What does "Forms" mean?
25. What is a Vessel?
26. What is Up?
27. What is Emanator?
28. What is the Quarry of the Soul?
29. What is Down?

30.  What is Unified?

31.  What is Malchut of Ein Sof?

32.  What is the meaning of "from Above Downward"?

33.  What is Filled?

34.  What is Above, Below?

35.  What is Place?

36.  What is a Square?

37.  What is a Triangle?

38.  What is Touching?

39.  What is the Middle Point?

40.  What is End?

41.  What is a Circle, Circles?

42.  What is Supernal, Higher?

43.  What is Separation?

44.  What is Vacant?

45.  What is Simple?

46.  What is Tzimtzum?

47.  What is a Line (Kav)?

48.  What is Close?

49.  What is Head?

50.  What is Ruach (Spirit or wind)?

51.  What is Simple Desire?

52.  What is a Name?

53.  What is Inside?

54.  What is Movement?

Note: Forgetting the meaning of one term of any subject is worse than erasing that word from the related subject, since the wrong understanding will distort the whole issue. Become familiar with the index of questions and answers until you can effortlessly repeat them.

# SUBJECT QUESTIONS

55. What are the concepts that are negated in the Wisdom of Kabbalah?

56. What is the language commonly used in the Wisdom of Kabbalah?

57. What separates and divides in spirituality?

58. What is the origin of the Desire to Receive?

59. How does the Light depart from being part of the Emanator to become Emanated?

60. What is the primordial matter of every emanated being?

61. From what point is an Emanated Being so called?

62. A spiritual entity underwent within it a Difference of Form. As a result that part separated from it and became a different aspect, as is known. Does the original spiritual entity lose anything on account of this?

63. In what manner, and with whom, can the multitudes of forms and changes in the Worlds be distinguished?

64. How are newness and movement depicted in the Light?

65. How can all the multitudes of forms and opposites that are drawn from the Creator throughout the Worlds be included in His simple unity?

66. By whom and by what is the Line drawn forth from the Ein Sof?

67. Did anything change also in the Ein Sof after the Tzimtzum?

68. When was the coarseness of the Fourth Phase revealed?

69. What are the Four Phases of the Desire to Receive?

70. What are the four letters of the Tetragrammaton (Yud-Hei-Vav-Hei)?

71. What is the uppermost Head of the Line that touches the Ein Sof?

72. What is the sole Thought that includes all the kinds of forms and opposites in the entire Reality?

73. In which place do kabbalists begin to delve?

74. What are the two principles that comprise everything?

75. What is the meaning of "He and His Name are One"?

76. What is the name "Ein Sof"?

77. What is drawn forth from the Desire to Receive included in Ein Sof?

78. What is the reason for the Contraction (Tzimtzum) of the Light?

79. What type of Receiving is considered as Sharing?

80. What is the purpose of the Tzimtzum?

81. Why did the Light depart from the Middle Point, never to return?

82. Why was no finiteness formed by the Tzimtzum?

83. Why was the Light absent during the Tzimtzum, from all Four Phases?

84. Before the Line came into being, why were the Four Phases not distinguishable as levels one below the other during the Tzimtzum?

85. Why did the Fourth Phase not automatically become coarser once the Contraction of the Light occurred but rather all Four Phases remained equally even?

86. Which Phase remained empty of Light?

87. When will the Fourth Phase also be filled with Supernal Light?

88. What is the Cause for the creation of the Worlds?

89. What is the desired objective from the Torah and from performing good deeds?

90. What is the benefit caused by revealing Holy Names?

91. How are the Holy Names revealed?

92. What is the Final Correction?

93. What is the root of all damages and corruptions?

94. Why can a Vessel of receiving be transformed into a Vessel of Sharing only in this World rather than in the Supernal Worlds?

95. What are the two aspects of Light?

96. What is comprised in the Extension of Light from the Emanator?

97. Which Light is revealed with the strengthening of the Desire to Share?

98. What are the two Lights comprised in each Emanated Being?

99. Why is the Light of Chasadim lower than the Light of Chochmah?

100. When is the Vessel of Receiving completed?

101. What is the difference between something that receives within itself and something that receives outside itself, like in the Ein Sof?

102. What are Circular Sefirot?

103. Why are the Phases not distinguishable in the Circles as one below the other before the coming of the Line into being?

104. Is there inherent evil in the Desire to Receive?

105. What is the meaning of "drawn indirectly from the Emanator"?

# TERMINOLOGY ANSWERS

1.  **Light** (Volume 1, Inner Observation, Section 18)
    All that is received throughout the Worlds as Something out of Something, which includes everything except the matter of the Vessels. Study sections 2 and 24 [of the Answers Index].

2.  **Light and Vessel** (Volume 1, Inner Light, 6)
    The Desire to Receive in the Emanated Being is called Vessel, while the abundance it receives is called Light.

3.  **Circular Light** (Volume 1, Inner Light, Chapter 1, 19)
    Light that does not cause distinction between the Phases.

4.  **Simple Light** (Volume 1, Inner Light, Chapter 1, 12)
    Light that includes within it the Vessel, to the point that the Light and Vessel are indistinguishable.

5.  **The Light of Chochmah** (Volume 1, Inner Light, Chapter 1, 14)
    Light that is drawn unto the Emanated Being during the First Extension, and it is the entire vitality and essence of the emanated.

6.  **The Light of Chasadim** (Volume 1, Inner Light, Chapter 1, 5)
    The Light that clothes the Light of Chochmah and is drawn unto the Emanated Being due to the First Strengthening.

7.  **Empty Air** (Volume 1, Inner Light, Chapter 1, 5)
    The Light of Chasadim before it clothes the Light of Chochmah.

8.  **After** (Volume 1, Inner Observation 34)
    That which is the effect from a preceding Phase. See section 20 [of the Answers Index].

9.  **Middle** (Volume 1, Chapter 1, Inner Light 14)
    See section 39 [of the Answers Index].

10. **One** (Volume 1, Chapter 2, Inner Light 1)
    The Supernal Light that extends from the Essence of the Creator is **one** and simple, like His Essence. Just as it is in the Ein Sof, so it is even in the World of Asiyah, without any change or any additional form, Heaven forbid. It is therefore called **"One."**

11.  **Creates** (Volume 1, Inner Observation 18)
     The word "creates" is only used in relation to newness, namely, the production of Something out of Nothing, which is the material aspect of the Vessels alone. This Vessel is defined as the aspect of the Desire to Receive in every entity that of necessity did not exist in the His Essence before the Creation.

12.  **Cleaving** (Volume 1, Chapter 1, Inner Light 12)
     The Similarity of Form that brings spiritual entities together and makes them cleave to each other. Difference of Form, on the other hand, separates them from each other.

13.  **Equality** (Volume 1, Chapter 1, Inner Light 18)
     If the Four Levels of the Desire to Receive are non-recognizable and indistinguishable, it is said that they are equally even.

14.  **Extension** (Volume 1, Chapter 1, Inner Light 1)
     Light that comes out of the category of Emanator and enters the category of an Emanated Being is called the "Extension" of Light. In actuality, the Supernal Light is not affected because of this, just like lighting from candle to candle, where a candle that lights another candle does not lack in anything because of it. Yet it is so named because of the Emanated receiving it.

15.  **Pure** (Volume 1, Chapter 1, Inner Light 18)
     The First Phase of the Desire to Receive is considered the purest in relation to the following Three Phases.

16.  **Time** (Volume 1, Inner Observation 34)
     The sum of Phases evolving one from the other and interconnected by way of cause and effect, such as days, months, and years.

17.  **Darkness** (Volume 1, Inner Observation 24)
     The Fourth Phase of Desire that does not receive the Supernal Light within itself due to the force of the Tzimtzum is considered the root of darkness.

18.  **Chochmah** (Volume 1, Chapter 1, Inner Light 14)
     The Light of the essence of the vitality of the Emanated. See section 5 [of the Answers Index].

19.  **Space** (Volume 1, Chapter 1, Inner Light 6)
     The Fourth Phase of Desire that was emptied of Light is considered as darkness in relation to Light. And in relation to the Vessel it is regarded as "space," since the Fourth Phase in essence is not missing from the Emanated due to the Tzimtzum but remains in it in the form of empty space with no Light.

20. **Before and after** (Volume 1, Inner Observation 34)
When we discuss cause and effect of emanated beings: to express 'cause' we use the word **before**, and the word **later** to express 'effect.' See section 16 [of the Answers Index].

21. **Singular and Unified** (Volume 1, Inner Observation 1)
**Singular** indicates the Supernal Light that shines and governs over the multitude of different levels to the point of transforming them and making them equal to His Single Form.
**Unified** indicates the conclusion of this governance, that is, when He has already realigned and reverted their forms into a single form, like His own. See section 10 [of the Answers Index].

22. *Yichud* **(Unification/Oneness)** (Volume 1, Chapter 1, Inner Light 12)
Two different aspects that make their forms equal are unified into one aspect. See section 12 [of the Answers Index].

23. **Right and Left**
A lower level sometimes rises to a stature equal to a higher one when the higher one needs [the lower one] for its own perfection. Then the Lower one is considered as **Left** while the Upper one is considered as **Right**.

24. **Forms** (Volume 1, Inner Observation 18)
The word "forms" is used only in relation to the pouring forth of Light into the Worlds. This includes the entire existence except the matter of the Vessels. See above sections 11 and 1 [of the Answers Index].

25. **Vessel** (Volume 1, Chapter 1, Inner Light 6)
The Desire to Receive in an Emanated Being is its Vessel.

26. **Up** (Volume 1, Chapter 2, Inner Light 4)
The aligning of form of the Lower to the Upper is considered an elevation upward.

27. **Emanator**
Every cause is called "Emanator" in relation to the level that is its effect. The name Emanator also includes both the flow of the Light as well as the Vessel that receives it.

28. **The Quarry of the Soul** (Volume 1, Inner Observation 15)
The aspect of Desire to Receive that is imprinted upon the souls differentiates them and "quarries" them from the Supernal Light, since it is the Difference of Form that separates between spiritual entities (as mentioned in Section 12 [of the Answers Index]). The matter of the Quarry of the Soul is that it is a transition phase between the World of Atzilut and the World of Briyah, which will be explained in its place.

29. **Down** (Volume 1, Chapter 2, Inner Light 4)
    That which is lesser in quality than the other is considered lower than the other.

30. **Unified**
    See the word **singular** above.

31. **Malchut of Ein Sof** (Volume 1, Inner Observation 14)
    The aspect of the Desire to Receive that of necessity is there.

32. **From Above Downward** (Volume 1, Chapter 2, Inner Light 4)
    From the First Phase to the Fourth Phase, since the Fourth Phase that was left without Light is considered the lowest of all Phases. Also, whatever has a slighter Desire to Receive is considered Supernal. Thus, the First Phase is considered to be above the rest.

33. **Filled** (Volume 1, Chapter 1, Inner Light 7)
    This is when there is no lack whatsoever, and nothing can possibly be added to its completion.

34. **Above and Below** (Volume 1, Chapter 2, Inner Light 4)
    That which is more important is considered **Above**, and the least is considered **Below**.

35. **Place** (Volume 1, Inner Observation 11)
    The Desire to Receive in the Emanated Being is the **Place** for all the abundance and Light in it.

36. **A square** (Volume 1, Chapter 1, Inner Light 21)
    A Phase including within it all Four Phases of Desire

37. **A triangle** (Volume 1, Chapter 1, Inner Light 22)
    A Phase containing only the first Three Phases of Desire

38. **Touching** (Volume 1, Chapter 2, Inner Light 6)
    If a Difference of Form of a certain level relative to the root is not recognizable to the point of being separated from the root, the level is considered to be "touching" the root. The same applies for one level to another.

39. **Middle Point** (Volume 1, Chapter 1, Inner Light 14)
    The Fourth Phase in the Ein Sof is so named after its unity with the Light of Ein Sof.

40. **End** (Volume 1, Chapter 1, Inner Light 11)
    The end and conclusion of every Emanated Being is established by the Force of Obstruction that is in the Fourth Phase, since the Supernal Light ceases from illuminating there as the Fourth Phase does not receive the Light.

41. **Circle** (Volume 1, Chapter 1, Inner Light 19)
If there is no distinction between high and low among the Four Phases of the Desire to Receive, it is considered a **Circle** (that is, like a physical round shape where there is no up and down). Due to this, the Four Phases are called four ball-like Circles one within the other, and thus there is no higher and lower to be found among them.

42. **Supernal, Higher** (Volume 1, Chapter 2, Inner Light 4)
That is, the one in higher regard.

43. **Separation** (Volume 1, Inner Observation 4)
Two Phases without Similarity of Form between them in any way are considered to be completely separate from each other.

44. **Vacant** (Volume 1, Chapter 1, Inner Light 4)
A place ready to receive corrections and perfection.

45. **Simple** (Volume 1, Chapter 1, Inner Light 9)
Something in which there is no distinction between Phases and sides.

46. **Tzimtzum (Contraction or Restriction)** (Volume 1, Chapter 1, Inner Light 13)
He who conquers his desire, in other words, delays himself from receiving even though he very much craves to receive, is considered as restricting or contracting himself.

47. **Line** (Volume 1, Chapter 2, Inner Light 1)
This indicates a distinction between Up and Down, something that did not exist before. It also indicates that its illumination is very scant compared to what was before.

48. **Close** (Volume 1, Chapter 2, Inner Light 4)
Whatever has its form closer and more similar to the other is considered closest to it.

49. **Head** (Volume 1, Chapter 2, Inner Light 5)
That part in the Emanated Being that is most similar to the form of its Root is called the Head.

50. **Ruach (Spirit or wind)** (Volume 1, Chapter 1, Inner Light 5)
The Light of Chasadim is called Ruach.

51. **Desire**
See section 25 [of the Answers Index].

52. **Name** (Volume 1, Inner Observation 5)
The Holy Names are explanations of how the Lights alluded to in them can be conceived, i.e. the name of the level explains the ways of conception within that level.

53. **Inside** (Volume 1, Chapter 1, Inner Light 14)
When one receives within oneself, it is considered that the Light is measured and limited within a Vessel. When one receives outside oneself, it is considered that one creates no limitations upon the Light one receives.

54. **Movement** (Volume 1, Inner Observation 33)
Every newness of form is considered as spiritual movement because it is differentiated from the previous form and acquires its own name. This resembles a part separated from a physical object, moving and leaving its former position.

# SUBJECT ANSWERS

55. Throughout this wisdom, from beginning to end, there is not even one word that contains an imaginary perception or sensory concept, such as place, time or motion, and so on. Lack, too, does not apply to spiritual matters. Any Change of Form does not mean that something is absent from the first form. Rather, the first form remained in place without any change, while the acquired Change of Form is added to the first form. (Inner Light at the beginning)

56. This language is the "Language of the Branches" that point to their Supernal Roots: there is no blade of grass below that does not have its root above. Hence the sages of Kabbalah found a readymade language wherein the Branches allude and teach about their Supernal Roots. (Inner Light at the beginning, and Inner Observation first paragraph)

57. A Difference of Form separates and creates differences between spiritual entities. (Inner Light 12)

58. The Desire to Share within the Supernal Light stipulates the Desire to Receive within the Emanated Beings. (Inner Observation, Section 11 first paragraph)

59. Due to the Desire to Receive that comes anew with the Desire of the Supernal Light to Share, this new part left off being part of the Emanator and became part of the Emanated. (Inner Observation, Section 11, first paragraph; Section 15, first paragraph)

60. The new form that emerged as Something out of Nothing, namely the Desire to Receive that exists in every entity, is "the primordial matter" in any Emanation and any entity. Moreover, whatever is in the Emanated or in the entity beyond that matter is considered Light and abundance drawn from the Supernal Light as Something out of Something and is not part of the Emanated or Created Beings. There is no need to wonder how a form turns into matter because this is the case even in physicality. We tend to establish the original form of the entity as the original matter because we cannot conceive any matter throughout reality, since our senses can only grasp what happens to matter, meaning the forms that transpire and appear in the original matter. (Inner Observation, section 36)

61. In the very beginning of the formation of the Desire to Receive within the Emanated, namely the First Phase of Desire, it immediately no longer became part of the Emanator but of the Emanated. (Volume 1, Chapter 2, Inner Light 2)

62. No lack or loss applies to spiritual entities. Moreover, the part withdrawing due to Change of Form does not cause any lack or loss in the Supernal Light, just like when one uses a candle to light another candle, the former does not diminish. Hence, every Change of Form is an addition to the first Form. (Volume 2, Inner Observation, Chapter 9)

63. All the multiplicities and changes are only a result of the Vessel's reaction to and receiving of the Light of the Creator. But the Supernal Light in Itself is in a state of complete rest, meaning, without any change or newness. (Volume 1, Chapter 2, Inner Light 1)

64. There is no movement, namely newness in the Supernal Light. Rather, only that part that is accepted by the Emanated from the Supernal Light (in the way of lighting from candle to candle, where the first candle does not diminish) becomes "renewed and multiplies according to the various new forms in the Vessels." Each one receives according to the level of its Desire to Receive, and their Phases differ from each other and evolve down from each other immeasurably and to no end. (Volume 1, Chapter 2, Inner Light 1)

65. See Inner Observation, sections 1, 2, 11 and 22.

66. The Curtain, which was made after the Tzimtzum, is the power of obstruction over the Fourth Phase so that it would not receive more within it. It was the Curtain that caused the emergence of the Line from the Ein Sof, since the Supernal Light does not ever go through changes, and It shines after the Tzimtzum as it did before. But this Curtain now makes it so that the Supernal Light is received only by the Three Phases of Desire, whose measure is much smaller in relation to the [Desire to] Receive of the Fourth Phase in the Ein Sof. Thus it received merely a thin Line of Light in relation to the amount of Light in the Ein Sof. (Volume 1, Chapter 2, Inner Light 1)

67. Even though the Fourth Phase of the Ein Sof contracted itself, this is still not a matter of divesting a shape and then taking on another after the first one is gone, for this is the custom of physical entities. Rather, this is a matter of adding a new form to the first form while the first form does not move whatsoever since there is no case of lack or disappearance in anything spiritual. Thus this new change of the Light disappearing and the Force of Obstruction being placed upon the Fourth Phase so that it cannot receive within it, is considered as another, new, and unique World unto itself that is now added to the Light of the Ein Sof that remained in Its original state without any change whatsoever. Apply this understanding to all newness of Form made in spiritual entities. (Volume 1, Chapter 2, Inner Light 1)

68. Once the Line flows from the Ein Sof, and the Curtain obstructs it from shining upon the Fourth Phase, the coarseness of the Fourth Phase becomes apparent because it remains without Light. (Volume 1, Chapter 2, Inner Light 4)

69. At first, the Light extended and emerged from the Emanator as Light of Chochmah, which is the entire vitality belonging to that Emanated Being. It contains the first aspect of the Desire to Receive and is called the First Extension or the First Phase. Then the Desire to Share strengthens in that Light. This strengthening of Desire causes the Light of Chasadim to flow from the Emanator, and this is called the First Strengthening or the Second Phase. Then the Light of Chasadim extends greatly, namely with the illumination of Chochmah. This is called the Second Extension or the Third Phase. Then the Desire to Receive included in the Light of the First Extension again strengthens in that Light. Thus the Desire to Receive is completed to its greatest magnitude and perfection. This is called the Second Strengthening or the Fourth Phase. (Volume 1, Chapter 1, Inner Light 14)

70. The Yud of Yud-Hei-Vav-Hei stands for the First Extension of the Light that is called the First Phase (see entry 69). The first Hei of Yud-Hei-Vav-Hei stands for the First Strengthening in the Light called the Second Phase. The Vav of Yud-Hei-Vav-Hei stands for the Second Extension of the Light called the Third Phase. The last Hei of Yud-Hei-Vav-Hei stands for the Second Strengthening in the Light called the Fourth Phase. (Inner Observation, section 31, first paragraph)

71. See Section 49 [of the Answers Index] above.

72. The intention "to give fulfillment to His creatures." (Inner Observation, Section 22, first paragraph)

73. Everything spoken of throughout the Wisdom of Kabbalah relates solely to the extension of Light from His Essence. Of the actual Essence of the Creator, we have neither utterance nor word. (Volume 1, Chapter 1, Inner Light 2)

74. The first principle is that the entirety of existence in front of us was already set and present in the Ein Sof in its full and ultimate perfection. This is called the Light of Ein Sof. The second principle is the Five Worlds called Adam Kadmon, Atzilut, Briyah, Yetzirah and Asiyah, which evolve down from Malchut of Ein Sof after the Contraction. Whatever is in the second principle derives from the first principle. (Inner Light, Volume 1, Chapter 1, 3; and Inner Observation, Section 5)

75. "He" indicates the Light in the Ein Sof; "His Name" indicates the Desire to Receive within the Ein Sof, which is called Malchut of Ein Sof; "One" indicates that there is no Difference of Form whatsoever registered there between the Light that is represented by "He" and the Vessel that is represented by "His Name." Rather it is all Light. (Volume 1, Chapter 1, Inner Light, 12; and Inner Observation, Section 13)

76. [Reality] before the Tzimtzum is called "Endless," to indicate that no end nor finiteness can be depicted there at all, since even the Fourth Phase receives the Light. Thus there is no reason there to bring the Light to a halt and for end and finiteness to be formed. (Volume 1, Chapter 1, Inner Light 11)

77. The creation of the Worlds and their entirety: He contracted Himself in the Fourth Phase in order to reveal these Worlds until this World, since here it is possible to transform the Form of Receiving into the Form of Sharing. (Volume 1, Chapter 1, Inner Light, 18; and Inner Observation, Section 17)

78. The subject of the adornment that the Malchut of Ein Sof felt in order to achieve Similarity of Form with her Maker, which would be made possible only by the creation of the Worlds, is the reason why She [Malchut] contracted herself. (Volume 1, Chapter 1, Inner Light 13 and 18)

79. That which receives only through the Desire to give Pleasure to the giver. (Volume 1, Chapter 1, Inner Light 18)

80. To transform the Form of Receiving to the Form of Sharing. (Volume 1, Chapter 1, Inner Light 18)

81. See Volume 1, Chapter 1, Inner Light, 13; and Inner Observation, section 22.

82. Since the Tzimtzum did not happen due to a Difference of Form detected in the Desire to Receive that needed fixing, it took place only for the sake of adornment that was neither needed nor stipulated. (Volume 1, Chapter 1, Inner Light 13 and 18)

83. Since no notion of "a little bit" applies to spirituality. (Volume 1, Chapter 1, Inner Light 16)

84. Before the illumination of the Line, the Fourth Phase in Itself was not considered coarse and lowly, as said in Section 83. Therefore, there was nothing that would mark the levels. (Volume 1, Chapter 1, Inner Light 18)

85. Since the Tzimtzum did not take place due to a Difference of Form. (Volume 1, Chapter 1, Inner Light 18)

86. Only the Fourth Phase. (Volume 1, Chapter 2, Inner Light 4)

87. When the Vessels of Receiving will acquire the Form of Sharing. (Volume 1, Chapter 1, Inner Light 13)

88. The Desire to Receive that is necessarily there wanted to adorn itself and completely resemble the Form of the Light. This became the Cause for the creation of the Worlds. (Volume 1, Chapter 1, Inner Light 18)

89. To transform the Vessels of Receiving so they will be For the Sake of Sharing. (Inner Observation, section 22)

90. Their beneficial effect is mostly transforming the Form of Receiving into that of Sharing. (Volume 1, Chapter 1, Inner Light 18)

91. Through putting an effort in the Torah and in performing good deeds. (Volume 1, Chapter 1, Inner Light 13)

92. When the Vessels of Receiving will revert into the Form of Sharing. (Volume 1, Chapter 1, Inner Light 13)

93. The Difference of Form from the Emanator present in the Desire to Receive. (Inner Observation, Section 18)

94. Damaging and correcting a single subject applies only to this World. (Inner Observation, section 11)

95. The Light of Chochmah and the Light of Chasadim. (Volume 1, Chapter 1, Inner Light 14)

96. The Desire to Share and the Desire to Receive. (Volume 1, Chapter 1, Inner Light 14)

97. The Light of Chasadim. (Volume 1, Chapter 1, Inner Light 14)

98. The Light of Chochmah and the Light of Chasadim. (Volume 1, Chapter 1, Inner Light 14)

99. Since it is drawn by the strengthening of the Emanated Being's Desire. (Volume 1, Chapter 1, Inner Light 14)

100. After the Fourth Phase of Desire is revealed, which is the magnitude of the Desire to Receive. (Volume 1, Chapter 1, Inner Light 14)

101. Whatever receives into itself, the Vessel limits the Light it can hold by its measure. Whatever receives outside itself, the Vessel does not limit the Light it holds, and the Light is immeasurable. (Volume 1, Chapter 1 14)

102. When there is no distinction between Up and Down among the Four Phases in the Desire, they are considered as Four Circles within each other like onion peels. (Volume 1, Chapter 1, Inner Light 19)

103. Since the Tzimtzum did not take place due to the lowliness of the Difference of Form. (Volume 1, Chapter 1, Inner Light 19)

104. There is no lowliness inherent in it; neither would any lowliness have appeared in it were it not for the Tzimtzum upon it. (Inner Observation, Section 19)

105. See Inner Observation, Section 19.

# RAV ISAAC LURIA

Born in Jerusalem in 1543, Rav Isaac Luria, known as the Ari, is regarded as the most influential kabbalist in history. Before his birth, his father was visited by Elijah the Prophet, who foretold, "Through him shall be revealed the teaching of the Kabbalah to the world." A brilliant scholar from a young age, by eight, he was recognized as a prodigy and became known as the Ari, the "Holy Lion."

After his father's death shortly after his eighth birthday, the Ari and his mother moved to Cairo, Egypt, to live with a wealthy uncle. There, he studied under Rav David ben Zimra and Rav Betzalel Ashkenazi. Married at 15, the Ari discovered the Zohar at 17 and obtained his own copy. He often meditated on a single verse of the Zohar for months until its hidden meaning was revealed. His years in Egypt were dedicated to purifying his consciousness and transcending physicality.

In 1570, the Ari moved to Safed, Israel, where he fulfilled his life's purpose by teaching the secrets of Kabbalah to his most cherished student, Rav Chaim Vital, who arrived in Safed in February 1571. The Ari told Rav Chaim that his sole reason for coming into this world was to impart the secrets of Kabbalah to him and future generations. After completing this task, the Ari passed away on July 15, 1572 (5 Av 5332), at the age of 38.

The Ari did not document his teachings, reportedly saying, "I can hardly open my mouth to speak without feeling as though the sea had burst its dams and overflowed. How then shall I express what my soul has received, and how can I put it down in a book?" Rav Chaim Vital and his son Rav Shmuel Vital took on the task of recording the Ari's teachings.

The Ari's greatest legacy is his kabbalistic compositions, forming the spiritual system known as Lurianic Kabbalah. This system, when fully understood, provides humanity with a road map and guide for body and soul to relieve chaos, fear, pain, and suffering. Lurianic Kabbalah has profoundly impacted the world, and the wisdom disseminated by the Kabbalah Centre is rooted in Lurianic Kabbalah.

The main works of the Kitvei Ha'Ari ("Writings of the Ari") are the Etz Chaim ("Tree of Life"), Pri Etz Chaim ("Fruit of the Tree of Life"), and the Shemoneh She'arim ("Eight Gates"), including Sha'ar HaGilgulim ("The Gate of Reincarnations").

# RAV YEHUDA ASHLAG

Rav Yehuda Ashlag was born in Warsaw, Poland, in 1884. From early childhood, he demonstrated remarkable ability, originality, and dedication in the study of the Talmud, the Zohar, and other sacred texts.

In his 30s, Rav Ashlag met a Warsaw merchant, a great kabbalist who became his teacher. Their relationship ended when, as Rav Ashlag admitted, "My arrogance caused a separation between us," and the teacher disappeared. They later reunited, and after much pleading, the teacher revealed an important kabbalistic secret to Rav Ashlag, then died the next day. The teacher's identity and the secret have remained unknown.

After his teacher's death, Rav Ashlag moved to what is now Israel, where he transformed Kabbalah from a secret wisdom into a widely accessible body of teachings aimed at revolutionizing the world. Drawing on the Zohar, he predicted that 1995 would mark a turning point toward a mass movement for Kabbalah and spiritual transformation.

Rav Ashlag wrote and published two major works: "Talmud Eser Sefirot" ("Study of the Ten Luminous Emanations") and his "Sulam Commentary on the Zohar," completed over ten years (1943-1953). This monumental work earned him the title Ba'al HaSulam (Master of the Ladder). The Sulam includes a translation of the Zohar from Aramaic to Hebrew, with detailed commentary and interpretation.

In addition to his writings, Rav Ashlag founded The Kabbalah Centre in Israel in 1922. He was the teacher and spiritual master of Rav Yehuda Brandwein, who succeeded him as leader of The Kabbalah Centre upon Rav Ashlag's passing in 1956. In 1969, Rav Brandwein passed the leadership to his student Rav Berg. Rav Ashlag had foretold that one of his students would bring Kabbalah to the world. Under Rav Berg and Karen Berg, The Kabbalah Centre became an international spiritual movement with millions of publications sold and tens of thousands of students worldwide.

Rav Ashlag was the first kabbalist to make the Zohar and the wisdom of Kabbalah accessible to everyone. His legacy continues to guide us toward personal and global transformation.

# RAV MICHAEL BERG

Rav Michael Berg is co-director of the Kabbalah Centre International and a distinguished kabbalistic scholar and teacher. He was born into a kabbalistic tradition as the son of the Rav and Karen Berg, the founders of The Kabbalah Centre. Raised within a lineage that dates back more than 100 years, Rav Michael Berg steeped himself in the wisdom of the Zohar from a young age. He became adept at combing through ancient materials and distilling complex information into elegant thought and language. He was the first person to translate the entire 23-volume Zohar and commentary from ancient Aramaic into English, beginning this monumental task when he was only 18 years old and completing it ten years later. He also completed the translation of the Tikunei HaZohar ("Corrections of the Zohar") Volume III from Aramaic into Modern Hebrew. Under his supervision, the Kabbalah Centre has increased the distribution of Zohars to millions of people in need across the globe.

His compendium of works includes the translation and editing of some of Rav Ashlag's fundamental texts: The Wisdom of Truth, And You Shall Choose Life, On World Peace, and The Thought of Creation. Rav Ashlag is the founder Yeshivat Kol Yehuda, the forerunner of The Kabbalah Centre, and the author of the Sulam ("The Ladder") and Talmud Eser Sefirot ("Ten Luminous Emanations,") both central texts in the study of Kabbalah.

Rav Michael Berg penned the first book under the Kabbalah Centre Publishing imprint: The Secret, in addition to, Becoming Like God, Secrets of the Zohar, and Secrets of the Bible. His book The Way (Wiley) became a national bestseller.

Born in Israel, he studied at The Rabbinical Seminary of America in New York City, and at Yeshiva Shaar HaTorah, following which he earned his rabbinical ordination.

Along with his wife, Monica, he co-hosts the Spiritually Hungry podcast, exploring life's big questions offering spiritual guidance in contemporary terms. He also directs Kabbalah.com, the Kabbalah Centre's online learning platform, which provides kabbalistic wisdom through written and video content in multiple languages.

His teachings bring new insights to this ancient wisdom, reaching thousands weekly on Kabbalah.com. He resides in New York with his wife Monica and their four children, David, Joshua, Miriam, and Abigail.

www.ingramcontent.com/pod-product-compliance
Ingram Content Group UK Ltd.
Pitfield, Milton Keynes, MK11 3LW, UK
UKHW050651100225
4517UKWH00011B/53